Letters to Lee

*From Pearl Harbor to the
War's Final Mission*

LT. GENERAL
JAMES V. EDMUNDSON

. . . .

EDITED BY DR. CELIA EDMUNDSON

*For Terri and Dave
My dear friends!
with happy memories
of Lee and Nute
Love, Celia*

FORDHAM UNIVERSITY PRESS

New York : 2010

Library of Congress Cataloging-in-Publication Data
Edmundson, James V. (James Valentine), 1915–2001.
Letters to Lee : from Pearl Harbor to the war's final mission /
Lt. General James V. Edmundson, edited by Dr. Celia
Edmundson.
p.   cm.— (World War II—the global, human, and ethical
dimension)
ISBN 978-0-8232-3096-9 (cloth : alk. paper)
1. Edmundson, James V. (James Valentine),
1915–2001—Correspondence.   2. World War,
1939–1945—Personal narratives, American.   3. World War,
1939–1945—Aerial operations, American.   4. Soldiers—United
States—Correspondence.   I. Edmundson, Celia.   II. Title.
D811.E3224A3   2010
940.54'4973092—dc22
2009036161

Printed in the United States of America
12   11   10   5   4   3   2   1
First edition

To Those Who Serve

CONTENTS

After my mother's death on January 24, 1999, my dad began writing a series of vignettes about their life together. They had been married for 58 years. He said then:

> I saw ahead of me an empty, barren, and lonesome existence. The one real activity that I could think of that had meaning was to recall the wonderful life I had shared with my Lee. As I sat and remembered, little bits and pieces of our life began to stand out like cameos, little spots of special joy that were engraved in my mind. I began writing myself notes of these special times, and there were many of them.
>
> I decided that it would be fun, as well as therapeutic, for me to keep a file, and whenever time hung heavy on my hands and it seemed pointless for me to go on alone, I could think about the wonder of being married to Lee, relive one of the highlights of our life together, and get it on paper. This gave me a chance to remember the special charm of the past while continuing to make the most of what was left of the rest of my life without her.

He would share each new story with me at the close of the day. I would often read it aloud, and we would talk about that time. The stories begin in the Territory of Hawaii when my parents first met and are filled with the adventures and the enduring love they shared. His writings are amazing in their detail and give background to both family legends and world events that my brother and I had grown up hearing. He titled the collection *Life with Lee* and kept it in a binder with treasured pictures.

Two years after my dad's death in 2001, I discovered a very old trunk in the storage room. It was partly hidden by two large, mounted rifles. One was inscribed near the bottom: "From the Irregular Forces of South Laos." A crude crossbow lay over them both. These mementos, from the Vietnam War, were given to Dad by his troops when he was the Vice Commander of Pacific Air Forces and was flying combat missions in Vietnam.

The top layer of the trunk held photos, albums, newspaper clippings, and playbills from the motion picture industry of 1911, when Dad's mother and father were acting in silent movies and plays around Hollywood, California. The bottom part of the trunk contained letters—hundreds of letters—written by my dad, beginning in 1937, as an Army Air Corps Cadet, and continuing to 1964, as a Maj. General commanding the 17th Air Force in Europe during the Cold War. The early ones were written to his parents from flight school, before he was married. The majority were written to my mother, Lee, and began in earnest when she was evacuated to the States after the December 1941 Japanese attack on Pearl Harbor.

At first, I read letters at random, excitedly and quickly, uncertain of what I had found. Then, I sorted each letter by year and then by date. Even the envelopes had stories to tell. The return addresses told of rapid promotions and changes in location. The front and back of most of the envelopes from the early 1940s were stamped by censors and signed by inspectors.

This book began to unfold then. The chronological vignettes provide the structure and the big-picture view. The letters are interwoven and provide incredible descriptions and detail of the conditions in the Territory of Hawaii, both before and after the United States' entry into World War II; of the early fighting in the South Pacific; of the highly secret development and implementation of the Superfortress, which ultimately brought an end to Japan's war against the United States; and of the China-Burma-India Theater, as the war accelerated and the last mission is flown. The writings of correspondents from the United Press and *Newsweek* who accompanied my dad on combat missions enrich the story. Their stories gave an anxious nation a first-hand account of the war effort and of the men who were fighting.

For the sake of authenticity, I made changes to the letters and vignettes only where necessary for clarity and context. Where an explanation of something was required I inserted it in brackets, but if the explanation was lengthy, I included the information in a footnote so as not to interrupt the flow of the narrative.

Letters to Lee is a first-person account of two of the heroes of World War II and of the love they shared across the years and miles. They lived their lives with integrity and courage, but they were not the exception for this time and generation. They are, however, one example of this great generation and this incredible period in time.

Our love was entwined with our love of our country and all the things about America that were good and clean. We were a part of it all, Lee and I. Our love and the life that we shared, even at that great distance, were a part of America and its glorious history. That brought pride to both of us and made our very private and very wonderful love even closer.

Celia Edmundson
Florida, 2009
www.letterstolee.com

Letters to Lee

part one

RANDOLPH AND MARCH FIELDS, 1936–39

chapter one

HOW TO WIN
WHILE LOSING, I

There wasn't a military tradition in our family. When I came home and told the folks I was going down to Randolph Field to train to be an aviator, it was almost beyond their comprehension.

My interest in flying really took over my life in 1936. At that time, I was a 21-year-old kid, working as a timekeeper on the graveyard shift at the Douglas Aircraft plant in Santa Monica, California. Watching the large numbers of military airplanes rolling off the production line set me thinking. It appeared to me that with so many military airplanes being turned out, there must be a pretty good demand for somebody to drive them. This induced me to write a letter to the Secretary of the Army and another to the Secretary of the Navy, asking each a simple question, "How do you get to be a pilot?" Each responded by sending me application forms to fill out for the Flying Cadet program in the Army and for the Aviation Cadet program in the Navy. I filled them out and mailed them in, and the Army answered first.

I was sent out to the Army Air Corps March Field in California for a physical examination. They had more kids coming down the pipeline than they could use, and so they were very generous in weeding them out. When I took the physical, we started with about 50 candidates; when we broke for lunch, I was the only one left.

The doctor called me in, and said, "All right, your tonsils are enlarged and have to come out. I left that line blank because I wanted to wait until this afternoon and see how your eyes checked out. Your eyes are fine. I can leave this blank, and you can go back and get somebody to pull your tonsils. If you can get here before noon tomorrow, open your mouth, and show me you don't have any tonsils, I'll fill this in as though you never had any, and we will file your papers. If you can't do that, then I am going to write 'enlarged tonsils,' and you will have to start all over again. You may miss two or three classes of Flying School."

So, I went home and worked that night at Douglas on the graveyard shift, found a doctor who would take my tonsils out for $50 on credit the next morning, drove on out to March, and opened my mouth.

After being accepted, I was shipped off to Randolph Field near San Antonio, Texas, as a Flying Cadet. I was deep into the Army's flight instruction at Randolph when the Navy's answer came through, telling me to report to the Naval Station in San Diego for a physical. Thus, only by the random inefficiency of some clerk in a Navy office in Washington, I was spared from becoming a Navy aviator and having to do my flying off the decks of aircraft carriers. That method of making a living does not appeal to me, and I don't really believe I'd have been very good at it.

As a new cadet, I was as green as hell. I was saluting all the sergeants with lots of stripes on their sleeves. I didn't know anything about these people with the little doohickeys on their shoulders. The airlines were after us, and many of my classmates quit and went to fly for the airlines, but I wanted no part of being a flying bus driver. It wasn't a way of life that appealed to me.

I took my primary training in Boeing PT-13s. These were biplanes made of wood and fabric and painted bright blue and yellow. The first time they strapped me into one of those beautiful little machines, I knew what I wanted to do for the rest of my life. Of course, I got airsick and burped all over myself and the rear cockpit when my instructor decided to demonstrate his aerobatic skills, but as was the Army's custom, when we were back on the ground, the crew chief provided me with a bucket of water and a rag to clean things up. This disgraceful conduct on my part didn't bother my love of flying, and I was never again sick in the air.

Much of our primary flying training was accomplished at outlying fields, little grass fields with a shack in the middle and a "T" laid out on the ground to tell us the direction of the landing pattern. After I accumulated about seven hours of dual time with my instructor, we were practicing landings at Cade Field, one of the outlying landing fields. When taxiing after a landing, my instructor suddenly shook my hands off of the controls, taxied over to the staging shack in the middle of the field, climbed out, and said, "Okay, kid, take it around."

Golly, that front cockpit sure did look empty. What an experience! I taxied to the downwind side of the field, turned the PT-13 into the wind, and gave her the gun. The take-off went fine, and I set up a box pattern to come around and shoot a landing. It seemed pretty lonesome up there, but I was working so hard to do all the things my instructor had drummed into me that I didn't have time to be scared. I checked the "T" to make sure that the landing pattern hadn't been changed since I took off and began my final approach. There was a little bit of a crosswind, and I held a bit of a slip, as I had been taught to do. As I neared the ground, I brought up the nose, bled off the airspeed, kicked her around, and had myself a very tidy three-point landing. On the landing roll, I remember hoping my instructor had been watching that one.

Suddenly, it seemed like all hell broke loose when another student shooting a landing had been unable to correct for the crosswind. He came sliding in on an angle over me, and his wheels seemed to straddle my head while his propeller chopped through the front cockpit where my instructor usually sat. As this plane slid by me to the left, it tore off my upper-left wing, and then hit the ground and flipped over on its back. I saw the pilot hanging there upside-down from his seat belt, and I tried to get out of my airplane as fast as I could so I could go over and help him. I unsnapped my safety belt but didn't remove my parachute. And worst of all, I forgot to take off my cloth helmet, which was connected to the Gosport tube through which my instructor had been able to yell instructions to me from the front cockpit. As I dropped out of the cockpit and then went down the side of the airplane, the Gosport tube jerked me up short about two feet before my feet hit the ground and nearly tore my head off. The tube broke seconds later and left me flailing around on the ground, all fouled up with my parachute. The other guy, hanging upside-down from his cockpit, saw the mess he made of my plane. Not realizing that the front cockpit had been empty, he wanted to get there in a hurry and help. He unsnapped his safety belt, fell out on his head, and nearly broke his neck.

About that time, the instructors came running over from the stage house* to see if anyone had been hurt. I felt kind of sheepish as I finally got untangled from my parachute and stood up rubbing my neck. My instructor looked at me, and then he looked at what was left of the front cockpit and said, "You know, kid, I think I let you solo at just about the right time."

---

* The operations center for the flight instructors.

After that memorable day, the remainder of my Flying Cadet year was relatively uneventful. Most of the trouble I got into was in town on Saturday night, rather than in the air. I'm sure that I was a mediocre, run-of-the-mill student, and I'm also sure that my skill in tearing up that PT-13 convinced them that I was ready to pin on my wings, be commissioned as a second lieutenant, and sent out to March Field to fly A-17As in the 95th Squadron.

I enjoyed flying the A-17As. As a very junior officer in the 17th Attack Group, I was eligible for all the routine and tedious ground jobs. Most of my time in the air was spent flying on someone else's wing and letting them lead me around the sky. It was fun, but I was a junior birdman, and I knew it.

By the spring of 1939, more second lieutenants had reported in to the squadron for duty, and I'd built up enough seniority to serve occasionally as a flight leader. One day, I was scheduled to take another second lieutenant and a Philippines Air Force third lieutenant out to do some tactical flying over the desert, land at Bakersfield, have lunch, and bring them back to March Field in the afternoon. All went well until our take-off from Bakersfield. I took off first and began a slow turn to the left so that my wingmen could join formation. The second lieutenant slid into formation on my left wing in good shape, but the third lieutenant had problems. He made a wide turn to get on my right side, and then he came sliding in too fast. Before he was able to slow down, he had jammed his left wingtip into the trailing edge of my right wing. It hardly scratched his airplane, but it tore off about three quarters of my aileron,* and the rest of it was hanging by one hinge at a funny angle.

My airplane was sluggish in the roll axis and tried to fly with the right wing down. I was sure we'd make it back to March okay, but my third lieutenant was scared to death and refused to close into a nice, tight formation. He trailed us back to March at what he considered a safe distance. When I talked to him on the radio and tried to get him to close in, he answered in some language that must have been Tagalog, refusing to speak English or to close in.

When we got back to March, I sent the two wingmen in to land, and the group engineering officer was in the control tower to tell me what to

---

* A movable flap on the trailing edge of the wings that controls the plane's rolling and banking movements.

do. He told me to make a fast approach and not to reduce power until I was only a foot or so off of the ground, explaining, "You can't fall far from there." He was right, of course. The fire trucks and ambulance were standing by along the runway and followed me in a parade as I taxied back to the ramp. It was quite a return to my squadron.

My skill at breaking airplanes and walking away from them must have impressed somebody because soon thereafter, they shipped me to Hawaii and promoted me to first lieutenant.

Letter to Dad, April 5, 1937

I hope this won't be too much of a shock to your nerves, but it is just part of the life here. You will note from my post card that I soloed today. I wound up my fourth landing by having a West Point student officer, Lt. Meany, land his airplane on top of me. For the sake of your nerves, I will leave out the details as neither one of us was even scratched, although both planes were chewed into kindling, and his turned completely over. Mine had the wings torn off and was chewed up by his propeller. They were sure a mess.

They had me climb right out and into another plane and fly back to Randolph. It seems to be part of their policy to get a student into the air as soon after a crackup as possible to see if it has affected his nerves. I made my best landing at Randolph—better than I have ever made. I wasn't even shaky.

I hesitated to write this but I hate to feel I'm holding anything back. I like it better now than ever. I am about the third or fourth man in a class of 125 to solo. Write soon and don't worry. Planes are still twice as safe as autos.

part two

TERRITORY OF HAWAII, 1940–42

chapter two

I MEET MY QUEEN

Letter to Mom while at sea, January 28, 1940

Gosh, I've been busy. I was Officer of the Day the first day out, as you know, and they also made me commanding officer of the 1st Company of soldiers down below. I've 91 men, and for the first two days, they were all too seasick to move. By now, half of them are able to laugh at the other half, so things aren't so bad.

My steward says this has been the roughest crossing he's ever seen, and it really has been rough. Ever since we left Frisco, the boat has been pitching and banging around like a feather in the wind. I haven't even had a tinge of seasickness. I'm sure lucky because over half of the first class passengers have been in bed ever since we left. The food aboard is sure swell. I haven't missed a meal.

I spend most of my time just watching the water. It is beautiful. There is a nice young Ensign in the Naval Air Service going over to duty at Pearl Harbor and two swell Army nurses aboard, and we've been playing quite a bit of bridge and some shuffleboard when it isn't too rough.

They have a movie every night, and the men put on boxing and wrestling matches every evening down on the after well deck where we watched them load baggage. It sure is funny to watch them because the boat bangs around so much they can hardly stand on their feet anyway, let alone when they get hit.

After the entertainment is all over and everyone has gone to bed, the nurse I met and I set out on the stern balcony on the boat deck and watch the moon and the water until the moon goes out of sight. It's really beautiful. I've never seen anything like it. I'm even glad it's so rough because those of us who aren't sick are so much better friends than we would be if it was all smooth sailing. I actually like this weather.

I got a radiogram yesterday with my orders in it. I am going to Hickam Field, so I guess I'll fly bombers whether I like it or not. Oh, well! I'll get used to it if I have to. Anyway, Hickam is a much nicer post, and it's only two miles outside of Honolulu, so it won't be too bad.

I stepped off the Army transport in January 1940, onto the dock at Honolulu Harbor and into a new world. It had been a rough crossing. The ship was loaded with troops, most of them Air Corps troops on their way to the Philippines. The war in Spain had been boiling for several years; Hitler was biting off pieces of his neighbor's property and bunching his muscles for even bigger things. And Japan, having declared its Greater East Asia Co-Prosperity Sphere, was beating up its neighbors in places like Nanking and Manchuria. It was an angry and dangerous world, and America was pretending that it wasn't happening. The United States had declared its noncombatant status and hoped it would all go away. Finally, long-overdue action was being taken to strengthen places like the Philippines. Dropping a few of us off at Hawaii was incidental, but it got me to Hawaii in the midst of a rumbling and dangerous world.

But to a 25-year-old bachelor, second lieutenant, arriving in the fabled and beautiful Hawaiian Islands, the rumbling over the horizon was hardly noticed. I was glad to get off the boat. My new squadron commander was there to meet me as I stepped off the gangplank. So was my friend Ercell Hart.

When I was a teenager growing up in Santa Monica, California, I belonged to Sea Scout Ship 16. There were about 20 of us. We were all Eagle Scouts; we did things together and were very close. We sailed together; we were patrol leaders at Emerald Bay, the Scout Camp on Catalina Island, in the summers; and we all went to high school together. We were a group of Depression kids with a special feeling for each other. One of the members of Ship 16 was Ercell Hart.

I found myself assigned to the 31st Bomb Squadron of the 5th Bomb Group, on Hickam Field, flying B-18s. Hickam was a new field, still under construction with no bachelor's quarters on the base. I was invited to move in with five other bachelors into a beautiful home they had rented in Manoa Valley. A Japanese couple, John and Massawa, came with the house. They did the cooking, serving, cleaning, and everything else. John even washed all our cars once a week. It was Hawaii at its best.

Letter to Dad, February 9, 1940

I've moved into a big house up in one of the canyons behind Honolulu with five other young officers, and it is really swell. We have a Japanese couple to cook and wait tables and do everything from taking out our laundry to shining our shoes. It sure is a beautiful house and a nice part of town. It's a little cooler here than down in the city proper and much cleaner. It rains up here at least once every day, usually in the afternoon or evening. It only rains lightly for a minute or two at a time, and nobody pays any attention to it, but it sure keeps everything green. The lawns never need watering, and as there really are no seasons over here, the trees never lose their leaves, and so the leaves never need raking. What a place!

I spent two and a half hours this morning flying all over the island of Oahu and looking it over in an A-12. I haven't flown an A-12 since I left Texas, and I sure did enjoy it. The island is beautiful all right, and even flying bombers is enjoyable when you can go out in a little ship and relax whenever you wish, as I did this morning.

I do think I'm going to like it here. There really is a swell bunch of guys I moved in with, and my squadron has a great group of officers in it, too. It's hard to imagine a nicer arrangement than I have here. I sure do have better than my share of good luck. Ercell has a place right down in Waikiki Beach where I can go to swim, and the Army also maintains several nice beaches for officers.

I had only been in Hawaii a few days when Ercell had a party for me to meet a few people. He was established with three other Navy ensigns in a lovely cottage on the beach, right behind the Royal Hawaiian Hotel on Waikiki. Ercell got me a date with a nurse who worked at Queen's Hospital, and there were half a dozen of Ercell's Navy buddies there with their dates. The moon was full, the waves were lapping on the beach, and the wind was in the palm trees. What a night!

Introductions were casual. It was a nice group of young people, and the men were all Navy pilots, which gave us much in common. My blind date was a pleasant gal who already knew most of the people, and I felt right at home. I met everyone in due course, and I found myself repeatedly zeroing in on a beautiful little lady who was the date of one of Ercell's Navy buddies. My nurse would drift off on her own with friends, and whenever I could, I would join the cluster around the little beauty who had caught my eye and seemed to have me hypnotized. I found out that her name was Lee. She had been in Hawaii about a year. She lived in Waikiki, just off the Ala Wai, with two other girls, and she was head of a ladies-wear department at Liberty House, the biggest department store in Honolulu.

I didn't learn much else. She was always busy and surrounded by guys; her date was beginning to get suspicious of me. She was pleasant enough to me but totally without interest, and I had my own date to be politely attentive to. I did ask Lee if I could drive her home from work some time if I happened to be in Liberty House around 5 o'clock some evening. She didn't say yes, but she didn't say no, either. She kind of shrugged her shoulders and said, "We'll see."

That was enough. The door was open just a crack, and I intended to make the most of it. The party wound on to a finish. I took my nurse back to where I had found her and never did see her again. To this day, I can't remember what her name was or what she looked like. But I had been harpooned. I couldn't get Lee out of my mind. The next day, I asked Ercell about her. He didn't know her well, but said she was quite popular and seemed to date this guy she was with at the party fairly regularly. Ercell told me that this guy was the great operator in his squadron. He rode a motorcycle and had a lot of wahinis, but Lee seemed to be his favorite. It wasn't an awful lot to go on, but it was enough. I was fascinated by Lee. Now, of course, I realize that I had already fallen head over heels in love with her and wasn't smart enough to know it at the time.

chapter three

HOW ABOUT A MARTINI?

Hawaii was a wonderful place for a young bachelor, second lieutenant pilot. There were a bunch of nice guys in the 31st Squadron. It was a casual life in the military then. Every Wednesday was a half holiday, and work stopped at noon. About one Saturday each month, there was a big parade, review, and inspection in the morning. Otherwise, we had two-day weekends. And of course, the last day of every month was payday and a holiday. On payday, the eagle screamed, the troops were paid, and the rest of the day was off.

It is also well to remember that in those days, the Hawaiian Islands were a far-away place. Now, you can fly there in a few hours, Hawaii is a state, and Honolulu is no more distant or romantic than Los Angeles or New York. Back then, though, the Pan American flights were pretty iffy. They flew once a week if the winds were favorable, they carried very few passengers, and they were extremely expensive. The only real way to get to Hawaii was by boat. Matson had a liner going back and forth from San Francisco once a week and there was an Army transport once a month that stopped in on its way to and from the Philippines. The military tour of duty in Hawaii was three years, and there was no commuting. When you joined the "Pineapple Army," you were a "Pineapple Soldier" for three years. It was a way of life, and a good one for young bucks like me.

Within a week after Ercell's party, I just happened to be in downtown Honolulu, in the Liberty House about closing time. After much hunting up and down the aisles, I finally located Lee's department. I lurked until she was free and then, putting on my biggest smile, I pounced. At first, she didn't remember who I was, but I was persistent. She finally agreed that she would let me drive her home if one of her roommates could ride with us. Who was I to say no?

I found a handy place to park where I could keep my eye on the working girls as they filed out after closing time. Sure enough, here came Lee with another girl, who turned out to be Jane. I escorted them to the car with a flourish and began wending my way through traffic towards Waikiki. As we wound our way down Kalakawa Avenue, I asked the girls if they had time to stop for a short nip at one of the many spots along the way. After consulting, they agreed that they had time for a very short stop, and we located an appropriate cocktail lounge.

I was a "beer after work" kind of guy and was slightly taken aback when Lee ordered a martini. I had never had such an exotic libation, but I joined her and enjoyed the experiment. After the martinis, I took the girls to their apartment and met their other roommate, Jean. Lee insisted that she was busy that evening. Both Jean and Jane seemed fairly receptive, but I wasn't about to fall into that trap. I left quickly because Lee seemed anxious to get on with other things, and I kept hearing the ominous roar of a motorcycle patrolling up and down the street, waiting for my car to disappear. My options were few, and I left with the hope that Lee had found a ride home with a martini stop infinitely more attractive than a bus ride.

This story about my first one-on-one encounter with my future bride may sound like a casual event in a young man's life, but it has grown in importance over the years. Martinis became a part of our life together. I acquired the knowledge about the proper way to make a martini and some of the nuances of icing the glasses and using fresh lemon peel on the rims. Throughout the years, Lee and I have enjoyed a quiet martini together before dinner and serving them to our friends. I came to consider myself an expert at the construction and treatment of fine martinis. But every time I would tell the story about Lee introducing me to my first martini, her instant comment was, "Oh I did not! You introduced *me* to martinis." Nineteen-forty was a long time ago. Perhaps my memory is faulty, but for the many wonderful years we have shared martinis, I have never been able to convince her that she brought this enlightenment into my life. She might have been correct. Perhaps plying her with martinis was just part of my evil plan to lead her astray. We never did decide, and now I might never know. It's probably just as well. Our first martini together gave us something to kid about for 58 years. I leave you with the choice of believing my story or Lee's.

chapter four

KISS AN ANGEL IN
THE MOONLIGHT

I had always been a guy to play the field. I enjoyed the freedom of bachelor-hood, as much as I enjoyed the freedom of flying like a bird. I had made it a habit not to see the same girl too often and to avoid establishing any kind of a pattern that might lead to a loss of my freedom, either on the ground or in the air.

And then I met Lee. Strangely, I found little interest in seeing any other girls and spent my time trying to insert myself into her life so that being together would seem as normal and proper to her as it did to me. But I was very careful not to push it. It seemed that at least three or four times a week, I would find myself in the Liberty House about closing time and, of course, I would check with Lee to see if she could use a ride home. Sometimes she could, and sometimes she couldn't. Sometimes Jane would be with her, but every so often, Jane would have other plans, and I'd have Lee to myself. Sometimes, she'd have time to stop for a martini, but not very often. This was pretty good for weekdays, but it left me with long, empty weekends. And I saw that damned motorcycle lurking in the neighborhood too many times when I left her at her apartment. Something had to be done.

The first time Lee agreed to go out with me on a Saturday night was a major event in my life, and I planned carefully. In Hawaii, rather than bringing a corsage for your date, the standard practice was to bring a lei. Leis were easy to come by. Lei ladies lined Kalakawa Avenue with their little push carts selling gardenia and plumeria leis for a dollar or two. But we flyboys had a jump on the rest of the guys.

At the airport at Hilo, on the Big Island, there were lei ladies selling orchid leis. Orchids grew like weeds along the rain-swept valleys of the Hamakua Coast of the Big Island, and they made the most beautiful leis in the world. Every Saturday morning, a B-18 would be scheduled on a lei flight to Hilo, and the pilot who had lei duty that Saturday morning would take orders from the rest of us who had dates that Saturday night. I made sure that for our first date, Lee would be wearing the biggest and most beautiful lei she had ever seen.

In and around Honolulu, there were myriad Army posts. Each had its own Officers Club, and if you belonged to one, you had reciprocal privileges in all of them. Fort DeRussy was right in the middle of Waikiki Beach. It was a small coast artillery post with a battery of big guns, with the mission of providing protection to Honolulu Harbor. The DeRussy Officers Club was on pilings out over the water. There was a canopy in case of a rain shower, and the water around the pilings was lighted at night so that you could look over the railing and see hundreds of brightly colored fish swimming around. It was a beautiful spot. For our first date, I invited Lee to go to the DeRussy Officers Club with me for dinner and dancing.

I put on my white tux, got the orchid lei out of the icebox, and went to pick her up. She couldn't have been sweeter or more beautiful, and I had her all to myself. She was impressed with the orchid lei, it was a gorgeous night, and we had a nice dinner. There was a full moon, the fish were darting around in all their colored glory, and the band played some wonderful music. There was one problem, of course: I am a lousy dancer. I hear the music, and my body wants to respond properly, but somewhere around my knees, my sense of rhythm gets lost, and my feet get in each other's way. Lee, on the other hand, is a beautiful dancer, and she flowed so smoothly with the music that it seemed contagious. Even I managed to dance my way through the evening without falling down.

I was a *malihini* (newcomer), but Lee was a *kaamaina* (old timer). She had been in Hawaii over a year and enjoyed sharing her lore of the islands with me. When the band quit around midnight, we both agreed that it was too early to go home. It was a beautiful night, and she asked me if I had ever been to the Pali. I told her I hadn't. She explained that at the head of Nuuanu Valley, you came to a cliff that fell off about a thousand feet to windward Oahu. According to Hawaiian legend, she told me, this is where King Kamehameha I defeated the enemy forces to become the first king of all the Hawaiian Islands. He backed them up the Nuuanu Valley and pushed them over the Pali. Lee suggested that we go see this historic spot. It lived up to all the advertisements. You could look out to the north and see Kaneohe Bay shimmering. You could smell ginger in the air. As we stood at the railing looking out over this exquisite panorama, I pulled her toward me, and she gave me a kiss. It was just a simple little kiss, soft and gentle and rather short, but it was my first of a kind, and I know my ears lit up and glowed in the dark. From that moment, I was a young man with a single purpose. I wanted this little lady beside me for the rest of my life.

We drove home without doing much talking. I guess we both had a lot to think about. I didn't even try to kiss Lee when I walked her up to her door. Suddenly, I no longer enjoyed the freedom of bachelorhood. My world had changed dramatically, and for the better.

Letter to Mom, February 27, 1940

There's a boat leaving for the coast tonight, so I'll whip off a letter this afternoon and then run down town with it and make sure it gets on this boat.

I have met a fine new girl. She's the manager of the women's accessories department in the biggest department store in town. Her name is Lee Turner. Dad may know her father who is a realtor in Long Beach. She lives with two other very nice girls down Waikiki way.

Letter to Dad, March 4, 1940

Things are settling down over here. I'm Squadron Adjutant, and it's quite a job. I'm the Squadron Commander's right hand man and take care of all personnel matters as well as supervise the running of the mess and other things. I'm learning a lot. I have an office of my own with a big desk and three clerks. Some stuff!

I'm getting in quite a bit of flying time, too. Tomorrow I'm flying to Hilo, which is a city on the island of Hawaii. It is the second largest city in the islands. Sunday, Lee and I, Jasper, my roommate, and Jean, her roommate went out to Waialua Beach near Lualualei and had a nice day. Then the four of us went out to dinner and for a drive up around Punchbowl, an extinct volcano crater behind Honolulu, in the evening. A most enjoyable day.

We had a little excitement today. General Marshal flew in on the Clipper this morning, and we all got up at 4:00 a.m. and flew out to meet him and escort the Clipper in. There were 30 bombers and 30 pursuit planes. It was quite a sight around sunup. As we were circling over the Pan American Base, two peashooters flew together in the P-26 formation. They both bailed out and rode their chutes down into shallow water and waded ashore. They just got their feet wet. Their two ships fell apart and both crashed, one into the ocean and one on the beach. It was quite a sight from the air.

I'm going over to Lee's to a party tonight, and her two roommates are having their boyfriends over. It should be nice. She's quite some girl. She's much too pretty and has far too much on the ball for me to hang on to for long, but it's a lot of fun.

Letter to Dad, March 14, 1940

I was very interested in your observations of Margaret; they coincide closely with mine. She is a very nice girl down inside, a "diamond in the rough" as you might say, and I'm sure with time and energy expended, she would turn into an alright article, but I'm sure I can find one tailor made and save myself lots of trouble.

I've been going down to pick Lee up after work every afternoon, and it makes a nice break in the day. I have also seen her every evening since the first date. There are so many guys here to every girl that you can't use kid glove methods. You have to dive in and hang on with both hands and feet or somebody else will be beating your time.

Letter to Mom and Dad, April 9, 1940

Saturday was Army Day, and there were big doings at the field in the morning. Lots of taxpayers were out seeing how their money is being spent. We had an hour and a half formation flight over the city with 33 bombers. I took Ercell along with me in my ship, and he seemed to enjoy it. Afterwards, he took Jasper and me over to Pearl Harbor, and we looked over the Navy's new four-motored Sikorsky. It had just arrived that morning on a long flight from San Diego. It's quite a ship.

Sunday night, Mauna Loa started erupting, and so Monday morning, I took a ship and flew down to Hawaii to look it over. It was a sight I will always remember. Mauna Loa is about 14,000 feet, and the activity was in Mokua-weoweo, which is the name of the crater in the very top. There was a column of sulfurous smoke that went up to about 25,000 feet that could be seen from a long way off. As we got up close enough to look into the crater, we could see it was about three quarters full of molten lava, and there were fountains along the fault throwing fire and lava 200 or 250 feet into the air. It was the most startling cherry-red color you can imagine. We could see the lava flowing down the Kai [ocean] side of the mountain where it had broken through the crater. In one place, it was dropping off a 50-foot cliff and looked like a red-hot Niagara Falls.

The air was so rough around close that it was really hard to fly, and we could feel the heat up where we were in the ship. About the most remarkable thing about it all was to see snow all over the top of the mountain and even a few patches in the crater itself where the lava hadn't gotten to it yet. It was sure something you see once in a lifetime. I was really lucky to get to see it as well as I did. It's inconceivable that this whole group of islands is sitting on the tip of a red-hot seething mess like that, and the only place it breaks out any more is down there at that one little spot.

Today we had a 6:00 a.m. alert, and we were supposed to go way out to sea and drop some simulated bombs on the aircraft carriers that are moving in to supposedly attack the islands in these maneuvers we are having.

Lee and I are going out to play bridge again tonight. She sure is a swell girl, prettier than any I've gone with and very clever. How I've been able to hang on to her so long I'll never understand, but it's fine while it lasts.

Letter to Mom and Dad, April 16, 1940

Lee and I came to the parting of the ways a little over a week ago. It's kind of too bad, but I've seen it coming from the beginning, and the sooner it came, the easier it would have been. She sure was a fine girl but way over my head.

Thursday night, we took a big formation down to look over the volcano after dark, and it was a wonderful sight. Much more impressive at night than in the daytime.

Friday night, I had a date with a Portages Hawaiian girl I met, and we had a nice time. Saturday I had a date with Lyn, the nurse I met on the boat coming over, and she and I and Jasper and his date had a house-warming party down here at our new place, and afterwards we went to the Royal Hawaiian Hotel to dance.

Major Bertholf has invited me to a cocktail party a week from Saturday, and I accepted. I don't know him very well and couldn't quite figure out why he asked me. On enquiring, I find he has a daughter, which, I suppose, is the answer.

Today we flew a five and a half hour interception mission way out to sea. Kind of miss seeing Lee, but if I stay busy, it will wear off. It always does. At least I had the satisfaction of nipping it short myself rather than letting it taper off and get left holding the bag. I could probably iron it out yet, but I honestly feel it's better this way, so I'll just let it ride. Something else will show up.

Letter to Mom and Dad, April 24, 1940

Things here are about the same. Last Friday night, I had a date with Martha Scott. Ben Norris and an English professor and their dates went with us to the Young Hotel to dance. Last Saturday night, Jasper and I double-dated to the Pavilion Club at Fort DeRussy to dance. I was with a very nice Island girl named Dee Schoafsma.

We've been doing lots of flying, as usual, but it's all very much the same over here, especially in bombardment. I never will like bombers no matter how they fly, and if I don't get out of bombardment pretty soon, I'm going to blow a fuse.

Saturday evening is Major Bertholf's party, and Sunday, six of us are having a picnic and steak-fry over at Waimanalo Beach on the other side of the Island. I'm taking an Army brat from Schoffield Barracks who is a little above the average run of Army brats, but she's still a brat.

I haven't found anyone to compare with Lee, yet, but I suppose I will in time. I haven't seen or heard from her for over two weeks, and I don't expect to. That's the way it goes.

Letter to Mom and Dad, May 16, 1940

We are having maneuvers here, and they have us flying all hours of the day and night. I flew from 2:00 a.m. until 5:00 a.m. this morning. I'll fly from 3:00 to 5:30 this afternoon and have another mission from 3:30 until 7:30 tomorrow morning. Things are really mixed up, and it's hard to keep night and day separated.

Besides all the flying, I've been keeping a very ambitious social schedule as well. I haven't missed a night in weeks. Lee and I have been going out a lot and have really been having a swell time. I don't know just what the magic words were, but anyhow, I have the situation well under control now.

Everything considered, I believe I'm much happier now and am enjoying myself more than I ever have before in my life. My work at the field keeps me busy, and yet it is interesting and pleasant, and I've made more real friends here than I ever would have thought possible. I'm sure glad I have the ability to enjoy myself and to realize how extremely lucky I am. Having a fine time is useless unless you can realize you are having one at the time.

chapter five

ARE AIRPLANES
HERE TO STAY?

After that night on the Pali, my world revolved around Lee. All my waking moments were either with her or planning how I could be with her. From that time on, other girls were friends or acquaintances, period! Things were a little different with her, though. She continued to date other guys although not quite as often as she once had, and I began to see less and less of that damn motorcycle when I came to pick her up. While my acceptance by Lee was lukewarm, I did manage to win over both Jean and Jane. I tried my best to convince them that I was the only guy for their roommate, and I brazenly solicited their help.

Lee did seem to enjoy being with me. She tolerated my clumsiness on the dance floor, but it was clear that I had two strikes against me. First, she wanted no part of the military service, particularly the Army. And second, she didn't particularly care for airplanes. She felt that they were the invention of the Devil. She considered them loud, dangerous, and useless. People who flew them were not to be taken seriously. Other than that, she seemed to figure I was okay, but she made it clear that she had no intention of letting me become a serious factor in her life. There was no question that I had a couple of pretty high hurdles to get over.

Lee and I continued to see each other, and we had fun together. We went to the beach, drove around the island. We had Sunday brunches, and our Saturday night dates became so regular that she came to expect orchid leis as a matter of course. I had a civilian pilot's license; time after time, I invited her to go out to John Rodgers Airport and go for a flight with me in a little airplane. I told her that she could see for herself how much fun airplanes were and how beautiful Oahu was from the air. She was tempted a few times, but she always came up with an excuse at the last moment.

All my efforts seemed to be useless. Lee was sure that I might have been acceptable in some ways, but airplanes were no darn good, and anyone whose life was built around them was someone to be avoided.

chapter six

DOWN WITH UNIFORMS

Lee had an inherent dislike for the military services. She grew up in Long Beach, California, which was a Navy town, and the Army's Fort MacArthur wasn't very far away. Her only contact with either the Navy or the Army was to watch the soldiers and sailors on the streets of the town on Saturday nights. Then again, in her job at Liberty House, she came into contact with military wives, and she had become convinced that they were dowdy, snooty, bossy, and generally unpleasant. Lee was sure that military people were not as nice as ordinary people. And of course, those military people who had anything to do with airplanes were the worst.

Lee and I hadn't been dating very long when I asked her to go to the Hickam Field Officers Club for a formal dance. The idea seemed to Lee like being thrown into a room with a lot of half-baked aviators and their dowdy, pushy wives, and she wasn't keen on it. She finally agreed to go, but reluctantly.

I will admit that this was probably not the best way to change Lee's opinion of the military. Hickam Field was still under construction. The Officers Club was yet to be built. The rear part of the Base Operations building was being used as a temporary club, and this, at best, was pretty makeshift.

Lee was dressed in a gorgeous long gown when I came to get her, and she couldn't have been any prettier. I had on my dress white uniform and was on my best behavior, but even the orchid lei did little to make Lee happy about where we were going. It went from bad to worse. The temporary club was small and crowded, and it lacked air conditioning. The band was not the best. It was loud and hot and crowded. I tried to introduce Lee to a few of the people I knew, but I didn't know many. It was so noisy that she couldn't hear the names of the people she was meeting and so hot that you couldn't dance without suffocating. My feet picked that night to be particularly clumsy. I was in a disaster area.

Then the band played a ruffle, and it was announced that there was going to be a receiving line for the *malahinis* who had arrived on the last boat to go through the line and meet the senior commanders on the base. It was a "get acquainted" affair. I asked Lee if she would go through the line with me, and she declined. She wasn't interested in meeting any of those stuffy old people. She had no intention of seeing any of them again, and she really didn't care whether they knew who she was. I explained that I would have to go through the line and that we could find someone she knew to talk to while I was going through the line. She said, "Don't worry about me. I can take care of myself. You just run along and do your chores."

The line seemed to take forever, and by the time I was finished, I found Lee standing by herself near a door. She wasn't very happy. I was afraid that she would ask me to take her home, so I said, "Let's get out of this hot place and get some fresh air." I took her arm and hustled her out before she could object, and we strolled in the cool night air down to the flight line.

It is hard to believe now, but in those pre-war days, there was no flight line security. We wandered around the airplanes parked on the ramp, not saying very much, and I asked her if she had ever been inside of an airplane. She told me that she hadn't, so I tried the door on a C-33 Gooney Bird parked in front of base operations. It was open. The step was inside the door, and I set it on the ramp and helped Lee into the plane. We climbed forward through the passenger cabin to the cockpit. I opened the windows so the breeze could blow through and then sat Lee down in the co-pilot's seat. I sat in the pilot's seat. Her eyes were as big as saucers. She asked about what things were, and I told her which instruments would tell her how high she was and how fast she was going and which handles to push or pull to make the airplane do various things. We talked about airplanes for quite a while. Then we talked about people. I told her that I knew the crowd we had just left seemed like a howling mob of idiots, but if she met them in bunches of twos and threes, she'd find that they were pretty nice people.

We must have sat there for about an hour, and then we climbed back down through the cabin, went out, closed the door, and went back to the dance. Things had thinned out quite a bit by then, and the band members must have had a few drinks because the music sounded a lot better. We had a couple of dances, and then I took her home. She was quiet on the way, and when I went up to the door with her, she said, "I wish I had gone through the line with you." I gave her a quick hug and told her, "I do too, but I know I was crowding you, and we have lots of time."

After that night, which I have always referred to as the Night of the Gooney Bird, there was a warmer and closer feeling between us. She was beginning to accept airplanes and uniforms into her life, and they seemed to be okay—if kept in their place. As time went on, I assured her that I loved airplanes and that I was proud of my uniform, but she would always come first. She didn't insist on it. It just seemed to work out that way.

chapter seven

PAPAYA TREES FOR SALE

The very southernmost tip of Hawaii, the Big Island, is called Ka Lae, meaning "South Cape" in Hawaiian. Hickam Field maintained a bombing range at South Cape, with a target so that we could drop our practice bombs, known as "Blue Whistlers," and measure the accuracy of our bombing. There was a dirt runway for use in emergencies and where we could land to get people to the target and maintain the range. There was a detachment of about 30 men kept at South Cape, with an infirmary, a mess hall, and tents to live in. The 5th Bomb Group rotated bachelor Second Lieutenants to serve a month's tour at South Cape, commanding the detachment. My turn was coming up.

This meant that Lee and I would be separated for a month, and as you might guess, I felt that it was totally unfair that only bachelors got this duty. I decided to leave my car with Lee so that at least she would not have to ride the bus back and forth to work. Lee hadn't driven very much and didn't have a driver's license, but she practiced in my car and got her license, and I took off for my tour at South Cape knowing that it was only for a month.

South Cape was pretty isolated. Sleeping in tents wasn't all bad, but the place was loaded with tarantulas that had the unpleasant habit of climbing into your shoes at night when you weren't wearing them. I soon learned that most of the men assigned to the South Cape detachment had gotten into some kind of trouble and had volunteered for this isolated duty rather than receiving more serious punishment. The only civilian living within miles was Gibby, the South Cape lighthouse keeper. Gibby had problems, too, which was why he had this desolate assignment. Gibby liked his liquor, and he liked company. He was also a pretty good cook, and I had many dinners at the lighthouse listening to Gibby's stories about tending lighthouses around the world. I actually enjoyed my duty at South Cape, and if it hadn't kept me apart from Lee, it wouldn't have been half bad. As it was, that month seemed like the longest month of my life.

When my month was up, they picked me up in a Gooney Bird, and I could hardly wait to see Lee. She, however, seemed quite distant and reserved. I had a sinking feeling that in my absence, that damn motorcycle had crept back into her life. It was a real relief to learn that Lee's problem was something else. When parking the car the night before I came home, she had gotten too close to a papaya tree that grew next to the curb beside her apartment and knocked it down. The dent in the fender was minuscule, but she hadn't had time to get it fixed before I came home. I quickly set her mind at rest, and we were both relieved. The crowning blow came a few minutes later when a couple of little Hawaiian boys came by, dragging the remains of the offending papaya tree, calling at the top of their voices, "Papaya trees for sale."

Letter to Mom and Dad, June 10, 1940

Here I am down at South Cape, and this is really the jumping-off place of the world. I have a camp here with an emergency landing field and a construction gang of 150 soldiers, and we are building a permanent camp. We are putting up some mighty fine buildings, and while I'm no construction engineer, I'm learning fast. All our materials and supplies are flown in from Hickam Field.

I am the only officer here and am in charge of the construction and the administration as well. I have bull gangs, a crew of carpenters, plumbers, electricians, surveyors, as well as a truck, a tractor, a cement mixer, a rock crusher, and a station wagon for myself. It's quite a job keeping everything going, as it should besides running the mess, supervising the Post Exchange store, and the hospital and maintaining discipline. It's 17 miles to the nearest road, so I really have the place to myself.

It's hard work, but I'm enjoying it, and it is good experience as well as being good for me physically. We go to bed at 8:00 and get up at 5:00 and work like the dickens all day. Twice in the evening I've gone fishing and have caught quite a few wus. This is a red fish that can only be caught at night by the light of a lantern and makes very good eating.

I guess about the worst part of this place is the eternal wind and dust. The wind blows about 20 miles an hour always, day and night, driving this red volcanic dust into everything. We breathe it, eat it, and live in it. We never do get really clean, but I'm even used to that by this time.

The nicest part of this place is the extra $5 a day I get for staying here, which kicks my monthly wage up to about $400. When you consider I get room and board here, too, and can't spend a cent, it isn't so bad.

Gosh! I wish you and Dad could meet Lee. She is really something. Head and shoulders above anyone else I've ever gone with, including Clara, and even nicer than she is pretty, which is saying a lot.

We have one good feature here—a radio that reaches around the world. We get England and France and Germany, and we heard Mussolini declare war this morning on Britain and France. What a mess that is. I wish we could build a fence around our half of the world and forget about them.

Letter to Mom and Dad, June 21, 1940

It's great to be back at Hickam. I went shopping this afternoon and picked up $297.50 worth of ring for $175. Through the Army, I got a 40 percent reduction and went right down to the wholesale house where they had a large selection. I picked out the mountings I liked and got the biggest rock I could afford to go in it.

They are rather pretty although nothing fancy. The stone is .42 Carats. It's not very big but a perfect stone and perfectly cut. It should do the job, and maybe when I get to be a General, I can replace it with a big one.

chapter eight

B-18 IN A SUGAR CANE FIELD

In the fall of 1940, Lee was scheduled to make a business trip back to the States to buy merchandise for her department at Liberty House. She had a busy program of meetings in San Francisco and Los Angeles, and planned to take a few days off to visit her folks in Long Beach. She had been in the Islands a long time and was looking forward to the break on the mainland.

I, of course, had an entirely different feeling about her trip. I even envisioned the awful possibility that she might decide not to come back. To protect myself, I went out and made a major purchase. I bought an engagement and a wedding ring. I kept the latter to myself, but the night before she was to sail on the *Lurline*, I gave her the engagement ring and asked her to marry me. I didn't do it all very well. She was utterly surprised, and after looking the ring over, she gave it back to me and told me that she was not ready to tie herself down. She wanted to relax and enjoy her visit to the States, and if and when she came back to the Islands, she would think about it. I made an ass of myself, of course. I took the ring back and casually tossed it behind the sofa and told her that if I was lucky, I could sell the ring and get enough money to buy a motorcycle. I saw her off on the boat the next day, but the atmosphere between us was not the best. I was kind of ashamed of myself, and she was looking forward to her trip.

As soon as the *Lurline* had cast off, I waved to her from the dock and then dashed back to Hickam Field and took off in a B-18 to go out and buzz the boat. It was just going around Diamond Head when I got there with my airplane. I made several low passes along side of the ship and had no trouble spotting her at the rail waving. On one pass, I saw her drop something red overboard, and I thought she had lost her purse. Later, I learned that she had thrown a red lei I had given her into the water. Hawaiian custom said that if you threw your lei overboard when you left and it floated ashore, it meant that you would return to the Islands.

The next few weeks, I felt deserted. These were difficult days for our under-sized and under-armed military. War clouds were gathering around the world. The British had been pushed off the Continent at Dunkirk, and things were pretty bad in the far Pacific, too. The British had been kicked out of Singapore, and the Japanese were taking over everything they could get their hands on. The American position in the Philippines didn't look too secure, either. The 19th Bomb Group in Clark Field, near Manila, was in worse shape than we were in Hawaii. The military forces in Hawaii conducted practice alerts continually, and I spent about half of my nights on alert at Hickam. There were earthshaking events going on all around me, but my biggest concern was whether Lee would ever return to the Islands.

One afternoon, on a routine training flight, I took off in a B-18 toward the mountains. Just as I lifted off the runway, my number-two engine quit on me and started to burn. I immediately had a problem because B-18s were notorious for not flying very well on one engine. I couldn't get back to the field and land because the ground on my left was high, and I couldn't turn into the dead engine. The dead engine was beginning to show a lot of flames around the cowl flaps. The Koolau Mountains ahead of me were getting closer, and the sugar cane field under me was sloping up to meet them faster than I was able to climb on one engine. I had no choice but to chop power on my good engine and belly into the cane field. It was a smooth landing. The B-18 cut a swath through the sugar cane and came to a stop. My crew and I got out of there as fast as we could. We had seen sugar cane fields burn before, and we didn't want to be around if our burning engine set this field afire.

My adventure was big news in Honolulu. The radio was full of the story about how Lieutenant Edmundson had safely landed a crippled bomber in a sugar cane field. I didn't know about it, but there must not have been much going on in the mainland that evening because stateside radio picked up the story. That night I received a wonderful phone call. Lee got through on the trans-Pacific cable and wanted to know if I was okay. I assured her that everything was all right. Then she told me that she was going to cut her trip short and would be returning to Honolulu on the first available boat. She also said that she hoped that I hadn't bought a motorcycle because she wanted her ring back.

When the *Lurline* came around Diamond Head the next week, I went out to meet it on the pilot boat. I climbed the rope ladder and surprised my little sweetheart. I had the ring with me and a dozen leis to put around her neck. As was the Hawaiian custom, I got a kiss for each one. I was, without question, about the happiest First Lieutenant (I had been promoted while Lee was gone) in Uncle Sam's Army Air Corps.

I had had airplane accidents before and have had a few since, but this was the luckiest one I ever had. It was an event to remember. It brought my sweetheart back to me.

Letter to Mom and Dad, June 21, 1940

Got a nice letter from Dad telling about meeting Lee's mother and dad. Lee received a letter from her mother on the same day. They were very happy about the whole thing. I'm glad you feel the way you do about it. It's nice to know you both are behind me, and I assure you, you won't be disappointed. She just couldn't possibly be improved upon.

We are all on 24-hour alert and have to sleep in the hangars at night, when we sleep at all. Nobody seems to know just how long this will go on, but we hope to see it over by the end of this month.

chapter nine

GUNNERY CAMP

After Lee's return from the mainland, I was walking on air. Lee left her job at Liberty House so she could concentrate on getting ready for the new life that faced her. We selected "Franksgiving Day"—the 21st of November—as our wedding day. For those of you who might not remember, President Franklin D. Roosevelt, in order to make the Christmas shopping season longer and boost the economy, had declared that Thanksgiving Day would be celebrated on the third Thursday of November rather than the fourth, and it became known as Franksgiving Day.

In the meantime, I had put in for a 30-day leave for our honeymoon. My leave was approved, but my squadron, the 31st, was scheduled for a week at gunnery camp. This was not a big deal. The squadron going to gunnery camp moved, with all its airplanes, across the island to Bellows Field. Bellows wasn't far away, only a 45-minute drive to Honolulu. We slept in tents and ate in a field mess hall and flew a full schedule, towing targets and qualifying all our gunners in aerial gunnery. Most pilots also took their turn and qualified as aerial gunners. Friday, our last day at Bellows, was also my last day of duty prior to going on leave. The squadron had a big party and barbecue around a bonfire that last night. I drove into Honolulu to get Lee that night to share the party with us. Most of the squadron wives and girlfriends were there. It was a beautiful, balmy night. We had a great little Hawaiian band to play for us, and everybody danced in the sand in their bare feet. Hilo Hattie was there to put on her show for us, and the squadron gave us a big silver pitcher engraved FROM THE OFFICERS AND NON-COMS, 31ST BOMB SQUADRON. We called it our Martini Jug, and over the next 58 years, it had many a martini stirred in it.

It was quite a night. It was my last night on duty before I took a long leave and a big step into a new life. Lee enjoyed it, too. Before the evening was over, I had danced with Hilo Hattie, and Lee had danced with just about every member of the 31st Bomb Squadron.

Letter to Mom and Dad, June 4, 1940

Lee and I are going to be married some time this fall, probably around October. It's sure the best thing that's ever happened to me in my life. I've done quite a bit of shopping around in my time and have had a lot of silly ideas, but I always had sense enough to keep out from under, but this is so absolutely different than anything else has been that there is no comparison.

She is just absolutely perfect. You'll just have to take my word for it until you meet her, but you can't help but think so, too.

This is all very strange to me as I had no intention in the world of getting married before, but I'm absolutely sure that what I'm doing is the smartest thing I've ever done. I've never known anyone I've enjoyed being with so much. We have many of the same interests and look at things in the same way. She is clever and pretty and sweet, and I'll be proud to take her anyplace with me.

Letter to Mom and Dad, October 31, 1940

Sure have been busy these days. I've gotten just about all the clothes I need—a light brown gabardine suit, shirts, shoes, ties, and all the rest to go with it. I've ordered calling cards for us. The "Lt. and Mrs." kind so we can make our calls when we come back to work without too much bother. I've been making arrangements with Mrs. White concerning the actual ceremony and am now awaiting an appointment to go up and have a talk with the minister.

I'm going to have the car completely worked over so it will have a fresh start, too. Completely straightened out, tightened, painted, washed, and polished. I'm still working on finding a house.

I'm living about three weeks in the future—so much of what goes on about me goes way over my head.

Letter to Mom and Dad, November 16, 1940

Lee and I are both so happy it's hard to concentrate on anything including writing letters, so you'll have to make allowances for this one.

We found a house last week over in Kailua on the beach, and yesterday we took a carload of stuff over. We are very pleased with it, and while it is nothing fancy, it is just about what we wanted. We are both busy writing letters this morning, and this afternoon we are going to take another load of stuff over to our house. We'll be all ready to move in by Thursday night.

Friday night, the last night in camp, we had a big chicken dinner and then some entertainment for the soldiers. We had a Hawaiian band and hula girls and Hilo Hattie to put on a show for us. The setting was perfect with the breeze and the palm trees and the soldiers all sitting around. We had a platform set up outdoors with a public address system, and Hilo Hattie put on a swell show. All the officers had their wives and friends out, and I wish you could have been there. You certainly would have enjoyed it. Lee seemed to enjoy it immensely.

Col. Farthing was at the party and informed me that on my return from leave, I am going to be the Group Engineering Officer. That was quite a surprise because they have nothing below a Captain on the Group staff now, but it will sure be good experience for me if I can handle the job. He was very nice, telling Capt. McCaffery that he was sorry to take me out of the 31st Squadron, but that I was the best qualified man in the Group for the job. All this conversation went on where Lee could hear it and she was quite thrilled about it.

My leave starts tomorrow, so I have the next few days for last minute running around, and there sure is a lot that needs to be done. We applied for the license Wednesday afternoon, and I'll pick it up tomorrow. All our plans are coming along in fine style, and the wedding itself promises to be a very nice affair.

Everything is all I could wish for, and I've never been so happy in my life. If you were only here to share it with me, I couldn't ask for anything more.

chapter ten

WEDDING BELLS
AND TIN CANS

Our wedding was a dream affair. Lee had decided to be married in the beautiful home of a friend of hers, Mary White, which was in Nuuanu Valley. Mary's sister, Katharine, gave the bride away. The Reverend Henry Judd performed the ceremony. He was a very nice man. He was a friend of the Whites', and it wasn't important just what church he belonged to. If I ever found out, I don't remember. He did a good job. After the ceremony, he told me that he had performed a lot of weddings, and he knew that this one was going to last. How right he was!

I had bought myself a new double-breasted suit for the occasion, and Lee had a beautiful gold-colored gown. Instead of a bridal bouquet, I got her a gigantic, ten-strand *pikaki* lei, which hung down to her waist. The *pikaki* is the sweetheart flower in Hawaii. All our friends were there, including Lee's two roommates and my roommate, Jasper. Lee had a lot of civilian friends, and I had a few. And, of course, just about all the 31st Bomb Squadron was there. It took place in the late afternoon, outdoors. The ceremony was followed by a reception in the same home and a turkey buffet. It was Hawaiian hospitality at its best.

I had rented a little cottage on the beach at Kahaluu, on Kaneohe Bay, on windward Oahu, for a month. It was a perfect spot for a Hawaiian honeymoon. At the appointed time, Lee and I went out to our car, which was parked in the driveway. After a shower of rice, we were on our way. We had gotten about ten yards down the driveway when we heard a strange, loud clattering, and it became apparent that that some of the pranksters in the squadron had tied an assortment of tin cans to our bumper and they made quite a racket. I told Lee that we could get out of the driveway and around the corner, and then I would stop and get out and untie the cans, but she would have none of it. She insisted that she was not going clattering around the island making all that din and that I had better get out of the car and remove the cans before we moved another inch. I got out in the driveway and untied the cans while all the guys in the squadron gathered around and laughed and hooted.

We finally got on our way, and Lee had a satisfied smile on her pretty little face. She had made her point, and I had gotten the message. One gay blade of a carefree, bachelor aviator had found out in a matter of minutes where his orders were now coming from, and it didn't bother him a bit.

Letter to Mom and Dad from Mrs. Hart [Ercell's mother], November 22, 1940

The wedding was lovely in every way. Lee and Duke faced the front lanai. We were all in a circle close up in back of them. The lawn was beautiful, surrounded by lovely trees. The Mango trees were in blossom (white blossoms), a fall of mountain water running into the lily pond with lilies in bloom.

Lee and Duke were a very attractive couple, and were at ease through it all. When I kissed the groom, I gave him the second one and told him that was from his mom. Then I drank King Kalakaua punch for his dad. So, you see I had you both in my thoughts and in my heart.

Duke read the telegrams from you and Lee's folks while we were eating. We were served refreshments and didn't stop there. There was a full course dinner with turkey, baked ham, and everything that went with it.

Mrs. White's sister, Mrs. Caldwell, gave the bride away. She is a grand person. Jasper was best man, and he did a good job. Of course, he and Ercell put the finishing touch on by wiring the tin cans to front and back bumpers of the car.

Dr. Judd performed the ceremony. Speeches were given while we were eating. Ercell and Jasper both said a word or two. Mrs. Caldwell made a cute little speech about giving the bride away. Then, Dr. Judd said his speech in Hawaiian. Yes, he translated it into English for us. He spoke very nicely of the groom and bride, also said we firmly expect happiness for them.

chapter eleven

UNEXPECTED GUESTS

As we drove away from the wedding in our can-free car, we drove up Nuuanu Valley, over the Kamehameha Pali that had so many happy memories for both of us and down the windward side of the Waianae Mountains toward Kaneohe Bay. We were a couple of happy kids. The world was our oyster. We had 30 days to loaf on the beach and swim and surf and get to know each other.

Lee was properly delighted with the little cottage, which she hadn't seen before. I had stocked it with the basics, so we could eat for a day or two without having to go shopping. And of course, there were the makings of martinis and flowers all over the place. We sat on the beach for a while and listened to the lapping of the waves in the moonlight. Then we went inside and had a drink together and both agreed we were tired.

Lee had first shot at the little bathroom. When she was showered and tucked into bed, she let me know, and I followed her in my brand-new pajamas, purchased for the occasion. It took only a minute or two for us to realize that we were not alone. The bedroom was full of mosquitoes; they were big, and they were hungry. They went after us like a pack of wolves. There was nothing we could do but go on a mosquito hunt. I found the screen that had been left unfastened. Without spray, it took a long time to swat all those mosquitoes. For some reason, it seemed like forever to me.

For the rest of our married life, whenever we would hear the buzzing of hungry mosquitoes in the night—and that was fairly frequently when we first moved to Florida—we'd ask each other if that strange noise reminded us of anything. It was our own private joke. The wonder of the wedding bed is an American tradition, but to Lee and me, the memory was always laced with a touch of humor. The ability to find something to laugh about during disasters was a special trait of my wonderful Lee, and it was a gift that she never lost throughout her long and busy life.

Letter to Mom and Dad, November 27, 1940

Everything went off as per schedule, and the wedding was as nice as it could be.

We received and appreciated your radiogram. We are now very comfortably and happily established in a beach house over in Kailua and are having the time of our lives.

Today is kind of a rainy cold day, so after a breakfast of waffles on our new iron, we have settled down to a couple hours of concentrated letter writing. I wish you could see our place. We sure do like it, and as it is on the beach, we have gone swimming every day so far. It really seems like home already, and we will be sorry to leave it when our month is up.

The wedding was awfully nice, and we were thinking of you and wishing you could have been here. It was a beautiful day, and so the ceremony was held out of doors in the Whites' yard that was very pretty and green. Mrs. Hart and Ercell were there. Lee looked beautiful. You saw her dress, and I got her a big pikaki lei with an orchid.

chapter twelve

LUMPY GRAVY

Our month in our little cottage on the windward side of Oahu was idyllic—endless days of sunning and strolling on the beach and reading aloud to each other in the evenings. We had eggs and bacon for breakfast and sandwich makings for lunch. In the evenings, we usually went out to one of the many little spots on the windward coast and listened to Hawaiian music, danced, and had quiet dinners.

But after a couple of weeks, we decided that we'd better touch base with the real world. We decided that we could have Lee's former roommates (Jean and Jane) and my former roommate (Jasper) over for dinner. Lee said that she would have no problem whipping up a simple dinner, and if I mixed up a few martinis in our silver pitcher, our guests wouldn't know what they were eating, anyway. We went out and did the necessary shopping and were ready to take our first stab at being hosts. It didn't look too complicated.

When the big day arrived, we were all set. Jean, Jane, and Jasper showed up at the appointed hour and welcomed us back into civilization. We decanted martinis from our silver pitcher, and the party was under way. Eventually, Lee excused herself and retired to the kitchen to do her thing. All seemed to be going the way it should, but funny noises started coming out of the kitchen. I went out to check, and Lee was in a snit. I have forgotten just what we had planned for dinner, but it included mashed potatoes and gravy, and the gravy was giving Lee fits. It was full of lumps, and Lee's solution was to throw it all out and go out for dinner. I suggested that she go out in the other room and have a martini with our guests and leave the gravy to me. She left reluctantly. In about 15 minutes, she was back out in the kitchen to check up on things. When she saw the lumpless gravy, she shouted, "Hallelujah!" and served up a delicious dinner like an experienced hostess.

After our guests were gone, Lee couldn't wait to ask me what I did to the gravy. I told her that all I did was keep on beating it, and after a while, all the lumps would disappear. She asked how I knew that, and I told her that my mother taught me that when I was a little boy. I didn't have any sisters, so my brother and I learned a lot about what went on in the kitchen when we were growing up. Lee never forgot the incident. When she met my mother much later, she told her that in my upbringing, there were several rough spots that hadn't been knocked out of me, but she was eternally grateful that my mother had taught me to de-lump the gravy.

Every now and then, throughout the years, I would stick my head in the kitchen and ask, "How's the gravy?" It was always good for a laugh. During our 35 years in the Air Force, Lee was an accomplished and charming hostess, but I never let her forget our honeymoon gravy.

Letter to Mom and Dad, December 13, 1940

We plan on buying furniture and moving out to Hickam in about a month. The places out there are as nice as they can be, and it will be much nearer and handier all around than living in town.

Lee is very sold on the Army by now. We went out to the field Wednesday night to a party and both had a wonderful time. Lee was the belle of the ball. She was so completely surrounded by Majors and Colonels, I could hardly fight my way in to her myself.

Lee's letter to Mom and Dad, December 19, 1940

So many times I have thought of you and have wanted to write, but this past month has been a full one—then there have been thank-you notes, and too, it seems to keep me busy planning and preparing the simplest of meals. But we haven't starved; on the contrary, I think we've both added a pound or two.

I hardly know where to begin—there is so much to tell. First, I'll start with our brand new apartment. We are just in love with it. We had looked and looked for a place to live in town and couldn't fine anything for love nor money. When we'd about given up hope, we found this. It is a one-bedroom apartment—all new—it even smells of fresh paint. The walls are of a very light grey with lahala mats on the floor and rattan furniture upholstered in turquoise blue. The drapes are multi-colored. On a little white end table we have a beautiful red poinsettia plant with five double blossoms. That was a surprise Duke brought home one afternoon. He is full of them—surprises, I mean. The other day, it was a card table with end coasters all complete.

Now, the kitchen is a young bride's dream. It's all white woodwork with precious red Venetian blinds—a new electric stove and Frigidaire, shiny new pots and pans, and a gay yellow pottery set. The bedroom is in yellow and green, and the bath in green. So much for our dollhouse.

Your gifts are so beautifully wrapped and so Christmassy—and the tree!! It is precious and is now mounted on top of the radio—just as perky and pretty as can be. You are so thoughtful and always seem to do and to say just the right thing at just the right time.

I didn't know one person could be so happy. I thought I was in love with Duke when I married him—but how wrong I was—that was nothing as compared to the way I feel now. It just grows and grows. In my wildest dreams, I didn't know there was anyone as grand as Duke in every way. We are both sitting on top of the world.

Merry, Merry Christmas to you—one full to the brim and bubbling over with all the best!

Lee's letter to Mom, January 7, 1941

Nora, I want you to know I made your "ham loaf" the other night for dinner, and Duke was duly impressed—it was dee-licious! And, surprise, so easy to make. So far, cooking has been a success. Duke is a wonderful person to cook for. He always likes everything—anyway, he had me convinced that he does. There are two things we can put on the reserve shelf and leave there—jellied consommé and broiled grapefruit. He didn't say so in so many words—he ate them to the last drop and then suggested I serve them sometime with boiled ice cream!!

chapter thirteen

LOVELY HULA HANDS

When our month-long honeymoon at Kahaluu was over, construction at Hickam Field was still underway, so there were no quarters ready to move into on the field. We found a nice little apartment in Kaimuki, up behind Diamond Head, where we lived until we could move on base. I carpooled with some other guys out to the base so that Lee could have the car three or four days a week, and we settled into married life. It was a cute little place. Lee had a chance to study up on her cooking, and we began to learn a little about each other. There is much about our months in Kaimuki that is still vivid in my mind.

We had our first Christmas together, and we trimmed a tree and exchanged presents. Johnny Paterson, one of my Sea Scout buddies from Ship 16, was in port in Honolulu. Johnny had gone to the Merchant Marine Academy and was serving as an officer on a freighter. We picked him up and brought him home to spend Christmas Eve with us. We entertained a little, but mostly, we strolled around the neighborhood in the evenings. After dinner and the dishes were done, we'd walk together down to the Kaimuki business district, buy a couple of ice cream cones, sit on a wall, and watch a bunch of Hawaiian youngsters play basketball.

I have mentioned that Lee was an extremely good dancer. She was graceful, and she enjoyed dancing. When she first came to Hawaii, she had joined a group of girls that met at the Royal Hawaiian Hotel where Hilo Hattie taught them to hula. Lee was a natural for the hula because her hands were so mobile and flexible. As I have said, dancing was not one of my graces. My feet are not connected, somehow, to the rhythm that I feel in the rest of my body; they refuse to do what I want them to, but it was a delight to dance with Lee. I particularly enjoyed watching her hands when she danced the hula.

The one overwhelming memory I have of our stay in Kaimuki was strolling with her, hand in hand, in the evenings and learning how incredibly small her hands were, tucked into mine. Her delicate little hands were a delight to me then, and one that I never outgrew. I can still feel her hand in mine when I'm alone at night. We had hand signals that we used to exchange secretly when we were in a crowd, and the beauty of feeling her precious little hand squeezing mine is something she left with me when she was taken from me.

Letter to Mom and Dad, January 30, 1941

Just a year ago today, I arrived in Honolulu and now I'm starting into my second year. A lot has certainly happened in just one year.

All Air Corps Officers have to study Spanish now, in view of the fact that so many Air Corps missions are being sent to South America. We spend three hours a week listening to Spanish phonograph records, but it's a vain effort as far as I'm concerned. I still don't like it any better than when I flunked it in college.

I've been busy as the very dickens at the field these days. My new job takes an awful lot of time and work, and as I am flying every day as well, I don't have much time to spare.

Lee is really a swell little cook. Everything she tries comes out just as it should. We are still living in Kaimuki and like it very much, but it will be nice to live on the post. No telling when it will be.

We start drawing First Lieutenant's pay in another two weeks, which will sure help when it comes to buying furniture.

chapter fourteen

HOW TO ROAD-TEST A TANK

In March of 1941, quarters became available at Hickam Field, and we left our apartment in Kaimuki and moved on base. It was a nice little two-bedroom duplex, quite close to Pearl Harbor channel. When the huge Navy vessels went to and from Pearl Harbor, they seemed to tower over our house. The government provided a couple of dressers, dining room furniture, and Army cots. That was it. Lee immediately used her initiative in many ways. Between us, we owned a lot of books, so we got some boards and some bricks and improvised some bookshelves. She devised a *hikiea* (day bed and couch combination) in the living room out of bricks, Army cot frames, and GI pillows and mattresses. We bought a bed for ourselves, a *lahala* mat for the floor, and some curtains, and we were in business.

Letter to Mom and Dad, March 22, 1941

We are all moved in now, and while there is still lots to do, we have a little more time. Our place on the post is perfect. We are in a duplex, and we have Les and Helene Bratton on the other side of the house so it is a wonderful arrangement. The house is swell, and we have more room than we have ever had before. A big kitchen for Lee, and we've turned the second bedroom into a combination spare room with a cot and a den. I have a desk in there and all the things that won't fit anywhere else, like my bookcase and books and my pipes. It will be the nicest room in the house before we are through with it.

The quartermaster furnished us with some furniture, but we are getting quite a bit of our own as we can afford it. We got lahala *mats for the front room and dining room and a swell inner spring bed and cover, and Lee is making curtains. In about two months, we will have it just the way we want. I sure wish you could come over and visit us now. How's about it?*

Lee's Letter to Mom and Dad, March 28, 1941

The days aren't long enough. We are so eager to get our drapes up that we work night and day on them. Duke cuts, and I sew. They are all being done by hand and take just so much time, but it is such fun! Tomorrow we are going into town and select our living room furniture. We do wish you were here to see and enjoy it with us. We think it is about the most beautiful apartment we've ever seen.

Here comes Duke to gather the mail for the boat. . . .

Soon after moving on base, I got a new job. The Army Air Corps was expanding. The 5th Bomb Group was split in half, and one half became the 11th Bomb Group. Then the 18th Wing was activated to control the two groups, and Brig. General Jacob H. Rudolph came to Hawaii to command the 18th Wing. For reasons unknown, I was assigned as the general's aide-de-camp. I didn't know doodly about how to be an aide, and without Lee's help, I would never have made it. She got along famously with the general's wife and the general; his wife learned to tolerate me. Lee and I had a lot to learn about the protocol of living on an Army base as well as being a general's aide. We had fun learning it all together. When we were to go to a reception at a consulate in town or somewhere else, the general would send his car and driver around to pick us up first. When the general's car came by to pick us up and we'd go out and get in, all dressed up, the entire neighborhood would turn out to watch the launching. The general's driver, Private First Class Sanford, retired in Clovis, New Mexico, and we kept in touch for many years.

General Rudolph was a very understanding gentleman. He told me that being his aide was not going to be a full-time job and that he didn't want me sitting at my desk outside his office all day long, every day. He wanted me to stay current with my flying and had me assigned back to the 31st Squadron for transition training in B-17s. He also made me commander of the Wing Headquarters Squadron and assigned me as an assistant in the Wing Intelligence Office.

The Wing Headquarters Squadron was a little outfit to which all Wing staff personnel were assigned. It had about 200 men and 5 officers in it as well as a variety of airplanes, including two B-18s, an OA-3 Douglas Dolphin, and a P-26, which was a vintage pursuit plane. It wasn't much of a command, but it was my first one, and I made the most of it. I was real proud of myself, flying the P-26. One day I asked Lee to drive the car down to the line and watch me take off in my little beauty. I could hardly wait to get home that night to find out if she had seen me soar into the air in all my glory. She told me that she thought she had. She said she had seen several beautiful B-17s take off, and then that funny looking little plane came putt-putting along—and was that me? I was crushed. But the command of the little Headquarters Squadron did have a bright spot for us. Our five officers got together and threw a party for us at the Officers Club (one had finally been built) on 21 November 1941. We had been married one year, and this was our paper anniversary. We both always remembered that evening. It marked the first of many milestones we were going to pass in the next 58 years.

My job in the Wing Intelligence Office, however, got me into trouble. One of the functions of the office was to put out the weekly base newspaper. On the newspaper staff was a corporal named Bill Brimm, who was a fairly talented cartoonist. One day, he had what he thought was a good idea—entitled "Sunday Driver"—but he didn't know just whose name to use without getting himself in trouble. I told him to go ahead and use mine. It kept him out of trouble, all right, but it got me into trouble up to my ears. Lee didn't think it was a bit funny.

Letter to Mom and Dad, March 22, 1941

We are getting all our B-18s ready to ship to the Philippines within the next couple of weeks and are getting B-17s, the four-motored ships, sometime next month. I sure am ready to begin flying the big ones. Last month I crossed my 1,500-hour of flying time, so I'll be all ready for them when they get here.

Col. Farthing called me in this morning and told me he was very pleased with my work as group Materiel Officer and that I had been selected to be General Rudolph's aide. He is the wing commander, and it is really a step up in the world. Col. Farthing said he didn't suggest me for the job, but after my name came up, he recommended me highly for it although he hated to lose me in the Group.

The job will consist of mainly being the General's Man Friday. I'll have an office right outside his and take care of all I can for him. He's only a restricted pilot and can only fly as a co-pilot, so I'll fly him around everyplace he goes. It will also mean that Lee and I will have to go to all the parties and functions that the General goes to, so it will be a really tough job, but if I can make a go of it, it will sure help my record with the Army, and I'll learn a lot, too. This has been my second big step up in the last few months, so I sure have been lucky. It is all very much on the quiet yet, but it should take place within the next two weeks.

Letter to Mom and Dad, April 30, 1941

Tomorrow is May 1st or "Lei Day." They make quite a fuss about it over here, with a lei exhibit in the afternoon at the city hall and a pageant in the evening with a Lei Queen and all the trimmings.

Lee and I have received special invitations from the Mayor of Honolulu with reserved seats and all that. The General and his wife and Lee and I will go, and it should be quite interesting.

Baseball season is getting under way here, and Lee and I have gone to several games. As it is getting quite warm again, we have spent a couple of afternoons on the beach in the last few days.

Last Thursday evening, we went out on the battleship Tennessee *and had dinner and saw the movies. Lee rode up in front of the motor launch on the way home and seemed to get quite a kick out of it. The boys in the Navy really lead a life apart from the rest of the world. Much more so than the Army.*

Saturday night, six of us went in to town to dinner and a show to celebrate Les Bratton's birthday. We saw The Thief of Baghdad. *It was rather interesting, and the color photography was beautiful, but it seemed to drag in places. I can still remember Doug Fairbanks and all the stunts he pulled in his version of the story, and this one seemed rather flat. Lee is going to begin hula lessons this week, so she's liable to be quite a shark at it by the time we get home.*

Lee's Letter to Mom and Dad, May 15, 1941

Yesterday was an exciting day for all of us on the post. Twenty-one new B-17 Bombers arrived, and we think these new four-motor, sleek-looking planes are about the prettiest yet.

Duke knew several of the officers who flew them over, so yesterday afternoon was "old home day" at our house. It was interesting, though, and I know the boys enjoyed getting together.

Mr. and Mrs. Abel sent us a darling set of wee sterling salt and peppers. I should say four sets—and they are wee. I think them the prettiest I've ever seen and certainly a gift to delight the eye of any hostess.

I do wish we were a bit closer so you could share some of our prettys and our good times with us. We both miss you and often speak of it. It won't be long before we're back if our plans work out as we hope—that is, if we don't have to extend our stay.

Letter to Mom and Dad, May 19, 1941

Our B-17s got here the other day, and I'll start checking off in them right away. Twenty-one of them came in, and they were all flown over by March Field officers. I met a bunch of the boys again that I had known before. We are having a couple of them over to dinner tonight.

Sure was nice to hear that you will probably come and visit us if we extend. There is nothing either of us would enjoy more than a chance to show you our house and things. We are having so much fun with it.

We are trying to coax a lawn to grow around the place, and I spend nearly all of my spare time watering and pulling weeds. I really enjoy it.

We've gotten a squadron of Douglas A-20s at the field now, and they are beautiful, two-motors and a single pilot ship and fast as the very dickens. The export version is the DB-7. I've pulled strings until I've gotten myself attached to this squadron for flying in addition to my other duties, so within the next couple of days, I'll get my first hop in one of these. I like this much better than the prospect of flying the four-motored jobs because I still prefer flying smaller ships. It's quite a relief to get some new ships in to fly.

The Abels sent us a set of little individual salt and peppers that are certainly cute. They hardly seem practical to me, but I've learned by now that I'm not an authority on such matters. Lee likes them so they must be okay.

Letter to Mom and Dad, May 26, 1941

I've spent this morning flying the A-20s around for the first time. Golly, what an airplane! It's the first time I've ever flown anything with quite that much dynamite. After flying the B-18s for two years, I sure had my hands full for a while. They cruise at about 250 MPH indicated and dive up to 412 MPH indicated, which is nearly 500 actual. It's almost like flying a pursuit ship except for the two motors, and it will walk away from the P-40s over here. I got myself attached to the A-20 outfit for flying, so I'll fly the General around in the B-17s and do the rest of my time in the little fellows.

You were asking about what happened to the guy who had this job before. He was kind of a loud-mouthed yokel and got so many people mad at him that the General finally did away with him.

I might get myself in bad, too, but so far, all has gone well. I sure have to meet all the rank in the Army, but its kind of fun in a way. All the big shots treat me like a buddy so they can stay on the inside track with General Rudolph, and I sure get in on the inside of everything that happens.

Last week Mayor Petrie, the mayor of Honolulu, was out with some friends to look the field over, and the General sent me around with them to show them the airplanes and buy them a drink at the club. It's really working into a fine job.

Letter to Mom and Dad, June 3, 1941

Lee and I really enjoyed that stereoscope you sent her for her Birthday. It is really a wonderful little instrument. It is such an improvement over the old type like Al and I had when we were little. It will be something nice to keep, and we are going to send for some more reels of pictures for it.

Orders came out this week automatically extending everyone's tour of duty here from two to three years, so it will be a year from February, at least, before we return to the States. At any rate, it's nice to know, and now you can definitely plan on coming over next year.

We are sure happy with our house. Lee has fixed it up beautifully inside, and I am working like the dickens in the yard with pretty fair results. I got the man at the nursery to plant some extra shrubs today, so it will really be pretty by the time you get here. We have several Gardenia bushes and a great many hibiscus bushes of assorted colors. The lawn, too, is coming along.

I'm getting more time off to fly these days and am getting time in every type of ship here. These A-20s are the hottest ships I've ever flown, and I sure do enjoy them. Besides the A-20s (Douglas), I am also flying the old A-12s (Curtis), the B-18s (Douglas), the B-17s (Boeing), and the little 047 (North American). Prospects also look bright for our getting a couple of little Pursuit ships down here for the staff to fly. That would make things perfect. It's much more interesting to switch around than to fly only one type of ship, but it really keeps me on my toes because they are all so different in size, flying characteristics, and performance. I've had the A-20 up to 400 MPH in a dive that is as fast as I've ever been in anything. The General likes me to keep up on my flying, so I have wires out to half a dozen different organizations so I can fly almost every day in some type of ship.

Letter to Mom and Dad, June 20, 1941

Lee gave me three swell books for my birthday. One of them is The Honorable Enemy, which is an account of the Japanese and their way of thinking and method of living. It's an interestingly written psychological study of them as a nation and as individuals. Quite interesting to me both professionally and otherwise.

My job is going on about the same except that I'm taking more time to fly. We have a little Boeing P-26 here now, and I got my first acrobatics in years the other day. I still do most of my flying in A-20s, and they are without a doubt the sweetest ship I've ever flown.

Our yard is coming along in fine style. We will have a real lawn in another month or so.

Johnnie Vogt, a Navy ensign who flies off the Enterprise, came over and had dinner with us last week, and last Tuesday I went and took a ride with him. We made a dive-bombing attack that was quite something and a carrier landing and take-off. It was my first. I got to watch them operate at their busiest. It was really interesting, and I enjoyed it very much.

We had a chance to move into a much bigger house last week, but after thinking it over, we decided that our place is as big as we want it. Besides, we have gotten so attached to the little place and hate to think of leaving it.

Letter to Mom and Dad, July 15, 1941

I'll have been here one and a half years this month, and that leaves me with one and a half years to go. "Over the hump" they call it.

The islands of Melanesia, Micronesia, and Polynesia have always fascinated me. We had a guy here the other day who lectured on the history and physical aspects of all the islands. Also, the English Captain Cook was the first white man to get to Hawaii, and he was killed here by the natives. I saw his grave down at Honaunau Bay on the Big Island.

We've covered the wall of our den with a huge map of the Pacific Ocean and all the accompanying islands, and Lee and I have been coloring them in and writing down who they belong to. It really makes quite a colorful and interesting wall design.

Our yard and house are keeping us busy. The lawn doesn't really amount to anything as there is only a couple of inches of soil over the bare coral, and it was improperly sown in the first place, but we water it and mow down the weeds as they grow in, so at least it's sort of green.

The house is more encouraging, however. We bought a new bed frame last week, and now about all we want is a nice bookcase for the front room to hold all the new books we are buying, and a nice radio phonograph combination with an automatic record changer so we can play our records with a minimum of bother.

Letter to Mom and Dad, August 8, 1941

We've been so darn busy over here the last couple of weeks we haven't had much time for anything. The latest turn of events in the Japanese situation has really put us on our toes.

I spent yesterday morning shooting water landings in our Douglas Dolphin. My first water operation, and I really enjoyed it. I'm now a rated 1st Pilot in our Amphibian and okayed for water landings. Today I started checking off in the B-17s. I've steered clear of them up until now because I really don't care for flying the big ships, but it looks now as though we are going to get a little action, and the B-17s will be the only ones that will get into it, and I want my share of the fun.

Our yard is improving gradually. We don't work on it too hard, but whenever the notion hits us, we go out and pull weeds for a while.

Letter to Mom and Dad, September 3, 1941

I'm now Squadron Commander of the Wing Headquarters Squadron, and that sure is a big job. I have about 200 men in my squadron and only two other officers at the present time, although I'm getting three more on the next boat. I have four airplanes, one of which is my own personal little P-26. I sure am enjoying the job, but it takes a lot of time handling the administrative papers of an organization of that size. It's a lot of responsibility too, as I have complete charge of the men. I decide who to promote and who to give what jobs to, who gets paid how much, and who to punish for what reasons. I am in complete charge of the Squadron. Some fun!

I'm also General Rudolph's Aide, and my duties in that capacity are still going strong. Besides, I'm always on some extra duty. For instance, I'm a member of the Courts Martial Board, and we try cases about two afternoons every week; I'm a member of the Accident Classification Board or "Crash Board," as it is called, and we fix the responsibility for all airplane accidents. I've also been on the Flying Cadet Board, deciding which Cadets to commission and which ones to pass over. I've been on three other investigating boards in the last month. I'm responsible for training my two officers in Bombardment flying and so am running a regular Flying School as they must learn weather, bombing, navigation, gunnery, and a number of other things as well as how to fly a B-18. Besides this, I have to keep up my own flying proficiency in half a dozen types of airplanes, so I don't have much spare time. Lee is a good sport about it, however, and she never expects me home until she sees me coming.

We've had time to have fun in our spare time, such as it is, however. Last Monday was Labor Day, and we went to the beach for the day. The Sunday before, we went out to Stell and Ted Locey's ranch and looked at their menagerie. They have a baby elephant named Bickel, a baby camel named Sheba, and a chimpanzee named Mary Jane.

Baseball season is winding up now, and Hickam has a team in the final playoff for the Island Championship, and as Lee and I have followed the teams quite closely, we are very interested. Mrs. Rudolph doesn't care for baseball, but the General, Lee, and I are taking in the games from choice seats the General reserves for us. Col. and Mrs. Hegenberger are also in our baseball party as it is his team that is playing. You may remember Hegenberger and Maitland who made the first flight to Hawaii from the States many years ago. He is the one.

Nobody has a tougher job these days than a regular Army Officer. The entire weight of all this expansion is on our shoulders. The Army moral has dropped because we have draftees instead of enlistees, which the Navy and Marine Corps don't have to worry about. Some of the reserve officers now on active duty are fine officers, the majority are inexperienced and green, and many are of distinctly low caliber. The regular officers have many times their normal work to do with poor materiel, as far as drafted soldiers go, and we are still short of vital equipment. We are getting promotions, but these promotions carry no increase in pay, and our paychecks buy less and less each month while prices go up. Civilians can strike for higher pay, and they seem to be getting it, but in the Army, that old stuff doesn't go.

We are all open to criticism from all sides, and we can't answer back at those who crack at us because the War Department won't let us and because so much of what we know is of a highly secret nature and can't be used in arguments, even if we could argue.

Americans are funny people. They've been whittling down the Army for years in order to economize. As recently as two years ago, when anyone with any brains could see all this coming, there were orders out restricting the number of hours per year a pilot could fly in order to save gasoline. Now, things are breaking around our ears, and the handful of regular officers, from General Marshall right on down to me, have to build a first class fighting machine out of nothing overnight.

I'm prouder of being in the Army now than I ever have been before to see the way the few regular officers pitch in and work long hours at jobs way over their heads and greatly underpaid, taking criticism from all sides without grumbling. If the civilian population only had an inkling of what is going on, most of them would be heartily ashamed of themselves.

I believe that the Army will get the job done in spite of the people, and by the time public opinion catches up with the actual trend of events, they'll scream their heads off about the good old Army. Americans are funny people.

I guess this sounds like a lot of flag waving to you, and yet it's actually the way I feel. You can see what the spirit of the old, pre-draft Army is when they can instill, in such a small cog in the machine as I am, a feeling of the importance of his little job.

When people criticize the Army for inefficiency and waste, they would do well to remember that you can't save time and money at the same time. They are paying now for their false economies over the past few years when all this could readily be seen approaching, and a very few regular Army officers are carrying the entire weight of the taxpayers' worries. When inefficiencies occur and money is wasted on Army contracts, you can be sure the Army men haven't gotten any of the money. It's gone to crooked civilian contractors, and it's been wasted in fulfilling requests made by lobbying politicians. Enough of this. . . .

Lee's Letter to Mom and Dad, September 3, 1941

Duke has been very busy and now has five officers in his squadron. Five young boys just out of Flying School. Duke is responsible for the welfare of his men (some 200), and they all come to him with their problems and troubles. Parents write Duke wanting to know why their sons aren't writing home, how they are working out in the Army, if they've had their teeth taken care of, etc., etc. Then, if any one of the boys gets into trouble in town, it is up to Duke to discipline or excuse. The other day, a sergeant's wife came to Duke with her problem. It seems her husband wants a divorce. and she does not . . . and so it goes.

chapter fifteen

GATHERING WAR CLOUDS

Things on Hickam Field were pretty tense as 1941 wound its way through the summer. We completed the conversion from B-18s to B-17s, which made a tremendous improvement in our combat capability, but the world was at war, and it seemed like only a matter of time until we were involved. Admiral Lord Louis Mountbatten put into Pearl Harbor with a battle-damaged British aircraft carrier that the Japanese had beat up in the South China Sea. He spoke to a gathering of American officers and told us, "This is your war, just as much as it is ours. While you fiddle around about making up your mind as to what you are going to do, we are buying you time with British blood." None of us could argue with him.

The 14th Squadron of the 11th Group received orders late in the summer to be transferred to the Philippines. General Rosie O'Donnell,* then a major, loaded up his flight crews in their 12 B-17s and headed west. His ground echelon went by boat. It was a PCS (Permanent Change of Station), so the wives that were left behind were shipped back to the mainland. Our neighbor Colin Kelly went with the squadron, and Lee and I helped his wife get packed up for her return to the States.

While all that was going on around us, Lee managed to turn our little two-bedroom duplex into a warm, snug home, with little in the way of add-ons to pretty up the harsh and sparse GI furniture. Lee was interested in the world way out there, and she shared my fondness for maps. I brought home a set of charts of the Pacific, and we papered one wall of the spare bedroom with a big map of the Pacific Ocean. It was full of little islands like Canton, Palmyra, Christmas Island, French Frigate Shoals, Midway, Wake, Truk, Eniwetok, Kwajalein, Bikini, and Tarawa that were just dots on the map with exotic names, but were to be such critical factors in our lives in the next few years.

---

* General Emmett "Rosie" O'Donnell Jr.

Whenever the lieutenants and captains got together at a party, the talk was constantly about the war that was coming. We expected Hawaii to get hit on a Sunday morning at first light by airplanes from a Japanese carrier task force. That's just about the way it finally came, but we had expected that the air strike would be quickly followed up by a beachhead landing by ground forces. We were wrong about that.

But there was little question in our minds about what was coming, and our wives heard our talk. Lee and I talked it over. There were continuing alerts and maneuvers to keep things stirred up. But we were newlyweds, and while we recognized the gathering war clouds, we were too busy enjoying the beauty of our Hawaiian life to really understand that the coming world upheaval would steal away some of the precious, golden years of our married life. Lee was a spunky little girl. She said many times that she knew we could come through anything, just as long as we did it together.

Lee's letter to Mom and Dad, October 9, 1941

It has been raining these last three days and how we have loved it . . . such a relief from the hot Kona weather. In fact, it has helped put us in the Christmas spirit and one we need to get early this year. We are both like a couple of kids—talking and planning Christmas already and getting as excited about it as I used to when I was a wee girl at home. Duke wants a six- to seven-foot tree, and we've already planned where it is to go. The bookcase is to be removed for the duration of the holidays. This is a new one. It is made with six boards of various lengths—the longest six feet and the shortest two feet. They are stacked together with bricks. It is really quite effective and causes comment from all who see it. It beautifully answers our need for our fast growing library.

Baseball season is over, and we came out with all the honors. Now, basketball is under way, and there are three games a night. Duke's squadron has a very promising team, and, of course, we are there at every game giving our moral support. Duke's squadron plays only one night a week, but we feel we must see the other team, too. Before this season is over, I expect to be quite a basketball expert or watcher anyway.

Lee's letter to Mom and Dad, October 22, 1941

What a yummy afternoon! The rain is coming down in real tropical style, which makes being indoors a cozy treat. Duke is curled up with navigation books.

These have been such busy days for us. We woke up last Saturday morning to find a small army of B-17s had arrived here. One of the pilots, a friend of Duke's, stayed with us here. Yesterday another bunch of B-17s arrived, and this morning, some of them took off for parts unknown. Our little post is fast becoming a stomping or over-night place for B-17s on their way from and to ???

Seems our house is the meeting place for so many of the boys. It does keep me running, planning and getting meals. And I never know just how many are going to be in for breakfast, lunch, or dinner—so meals are the kind that can be stretched. I do enjoy doing it, though, and am so happy Duke wants to bring his friends to his home. So many of the boys have left wives and families not knowing when they will see them again. It is certainly little I can do to make their stop over as pleasant as possible. I only wish now that we had a larger house so we could take in more.

Then in the midst of all these planes taking off and landing, Ercell announced he was taking a bride home with him!! Everything happens at once. So, the bride to be, Tillie, and Ercell and Mrs. Hart were here for dinner, and Duke was asked to be best man. The wedding was Sunday afternoon. How handsome they were—Ercell in his Navy Whites and Duke in his Army Whites. Plus, he had the gold braid on his shoulder (as General Rudolph's aide), which dazzled all the girls. One of the pretty young things met me as I arrived at the church and cooed, "Oh, I just saw your husband. Oh, he is so handsome." Then she paused and said, "I didn't know whether you would be here or not." I kidded Duke about it afterward. The wedding was very lovely—very simple, and the reception was held in Mrs. Hart's home.

Lee's letter to Mom and Dad, October 30, 1941

This note is to tell you about our new interest, "Eight Ball," a wee black kitten given to us yesterday. Duke has him all fixed up on the service porch: his bed, his food, and his ball of newspaper hanging from the door knob via a piece of string. The service porch is to be Eight Ball's room!! While we were rinsing the dinner dishes last night, Duke was telling me that for the first night or two, Eight Ball was to be shut in on the porch—he probably wouldn't like it all first, but after a few nights, he would know that that was where he was to sleep, and then the door into the house could be left open.

Last night when we were playing bridge with the Coddingtons, Duke tucked Eight Ball away for the night on the porch and closed the door. It wasn't long before the kitty started to cry, and in less time than it takes to tell it, Duke had the door open, and Eight Ball was free to roam at his heart's content! He is a beautifully mannered little beastie, and we do enjoy him so much—cute, little, and so cuddlesome.

Letter to Mom and Dad, October 31, 1941

Last Wednesday, a boatload of Australian Cadets came through on their way to Canada for further training and then on to England. I took three of them in tow and showed them around the field, had them to the house for lunch, and then went down to their ship with them. They were fine kids, and we had quite a day talking and swapping insignia.

A couple of weeks ago, a flight of B-17s came through here traveling from East to West. I had several friends on the hop including a kid named Sig Young who used to live next door to me at the March Field BOQ [Bachelor Officer Quarters]. He spent about four days with us and stayed in the guest room.

A big Consolidated B-24 was through last week going the other way. It had been around the world, stopping at England, Norway, Russia, India, China, Dutch East Indies, the Philippines, and Australia. Quite a trip.

I guess Lee told you we have a cat. He is a solid black kitten. We named him Eight Ball, and he is a fine little cat and has taken over the running of the house already. Lee is quite sold on him. She has never had much to do with cats before, and she can't get over how cute and smart he is.

We are already busy getting ready for Christmas. We have room for a full-sized tree this year, and as we already have lots of ornaments from last year, we will be off to a flying start. We have finished most of our shopping for things that will be mailed away.

Letter to Mom and Dad, November 15, 1941

My Squadron is sure growing. I have eight officers in it now and will get about four more next month. They are a fine bunch of boys, but just kids, and they take a lot of working with.

I had a swell flight all planned in a B-17. I'd have gone back to the coast for a couple of weeks and also hit Australia, the Philippines, and China, but the General wouldn't let me go, so somebody else went. I'll be glad to get out of this Aides' job so I can do a little traveling around, but he hangs on to me pretty tight. Something is liable to break pretty soon. Anything can happen now.

We are certainly building up a fine library. Our one big extravagance is books, and we are getting some fine ones. A lot of these books on the foreign situation are professional reading, as far as I'm concerned, but they are darned interesting, too.

Lee's Letter to Mom and Dad, December 2, 1941

Let me tell you about the wonderful thing that happened to us this last Saturday night. We had been asked to dinner by one of the young officers in Duke's squadron—dinner and dancing at the club. When we arrived, we were both decorated with lovely leis from Hilo, and gathered together were all the boys from the squadron and their dates. So it was decided that we would all have dinner together.

The first inkling we had that the whole affair had already been planned was when I found a package at my place and opened it to find a little sugar bride and groom. So it was an anniversary dinner given to us by the boys in the squadron! They all think so much of Duke, and they are all of them grand fellows, and they seem to stick together more so than most officers in other squadrons. After dinner, we were presented with a large bundle of packages. The boys had gone through Kress [dime store] and picked out paper straws, shelf paper, paper doll cut-outs, stationery—and on top of all of that was a beautiful print of a yellow hibiscus. A really lovely one and one we want to frame right away and hang in our living room. We were so pleased and so surprised.

One of the chaps fell asleep driving home and ran into a telephone pole and ended up in the hospital. I took him some books yesterday afternoon. He is doing fine, and we expect he will be out in a few days. Two of the fellows came to dinner last night . . . and so it goes. Duke and I thought it would be fun to have the boys here for "Tom & Jerrys"* the Saturday before Christmas—the boys and their dates. The club will roast a turkey for me, so we have planned a hot buffet dinner.

By then, our tree will be up in all its glory, and we thought it would be fun to have some little package under the tree for each guest.

I'm all curled up in a big comfy chair with wool slacks on and a sweater and a lightweight wool slack coat. It is cold and has been. Duke even closed most of the windows, and when Duke starts closing windows, it is really getting chilly!

Your son has been the busy one—flying night and day, and he loves it. He is now a B-17 pilot—and, I understand, one of only two officers on the post who have checked off to fly. Sunday, we sandwiched in a bit of domesticity. We rearranged our furniture getting ready for our expected guest—The Christmas

---

* A holiday cocktail made with rum, brandy, and eggnog.

Tree. He is to be a big one this year and is to hold forth in all his glory in the front of the living room windows.

After much heaving and hauling of furniture (by Duke) and much changing of mind (by me), the room is finished and quite nicely done, we think. So, bring on the Christmas tree!

Our Christmas box to you should arrive on time. It seemed odd at first shopping so early, but the boats are so uncertain these days it seemed the best. Last week, the government took over the Matsonia; that leaves only the Lurline to shuttle back and forth. Of course, there are the Navy transports, but their sailings and arrivings are so secret.

Letter to Mom and Dad, December 5, 1941

There is a slight lull in activities this morning, so I'll write a letter right away quick before something springs up.

I've just had another change in jobs. I'm still General Rudolph's Aide, but I've been relieved of duty with the Wing Headquarters Squadron and am now Assistant Wing Operations Officer. It will be good experience and will give me more time to fly although I can't complain about flying time lately, either.

I have sad news about the fate of our little cat. He had a touch of mange, so we took him to a cat hospital to be cured quickly before it got bad. When we got him back, the mange was apparently under control, but they had fed him something that had poisoned him, and we had to have him put down. We sure do miss the little rascal.

I've recently checked off as a B-17 first Pilot, and I'm getting in lots of B-17 time. Last night, I was out until midnight on a celestial navigation mission, and I'll fly again tonight and tomorrow morning. I like the B-17s much better than the B-18s, but I still prefer flying the little A-20 to either of them.

There has recently been a change in Army Regulations regarding taking wives, mothers, etc. for rides. We are no longer restricted to half an hour, but can make the hop as long as we like just as long as we don't land away from our home station. Lee is due for another ride, so next week she's going to spend the morning out flying around and looking all the islands over. It will really be a treat for her.

This time next year we should be making plans for a return to the States.

chapter sixteen

SPECULATION AMONG

LIEUTENANTS

Did we know what was coming? At the lieutenant level, we had a pretty good idea. There were a lot of signs.

Early in 1941, Colonel Claire Chennault had come through Hickam on his way from Washington back out to China. He was recruiting Flying Tigers and painted a bright picture of all the money to be made and all the fun to be had flying shark-nosed P-40s out of Kunming. The pay was roughly ten times what a lieutenant made, including those who drew flying pay, and there was a $1,000 bonus paid for every confirmed Japanese plane shot down. To us, it all sounded very lucrative and like something we should be getting in on. And it was a clear indication of America's involvement in a coming Pacific war. Colonel Chennault picked up about a half-dozen recruits at Hickam who resigned their reserve commissions and followed him out to China. In those days, less than ten percent of the officers in the Army Air Corps were regulars. The rest were reservists on extended active duty. I had received a regular commission in 1939, and the Army wasn't releasing any regulars. I don't recall that any of my friends who flew with the Flying Tigers made a lot of money, but they picked up much valuable experience.

Another indicator of things to come. I remember Captain Hugh McCaffery, commander of the 31st Squadron, getting us all together one day and predicting that America would soon get into the war that was already under way in Europe, and that when that happened, America would need an Air Corps hundreds of times larger than the one we now had. He said, "Every enlisted man in this squadron will make Master Sergeant during this war. They haven't even enlisted all the Master Sergeants they are going to need." This was exciting talk in an Air Corps where it took an enlisted man a minimum of six years to make corporal. He went on, "Every officer will make colonel before it's over. I'm holding out for a star, myself." This sounded like a pipe dream to lieutenants who hoped to make major before they retired. Captain Mac was conservative. He was a colonel when he was killed in an aircraft accident less than a year later. Had he lived to the end of the war, he would have been wearing several stars. Actually, most of the lieutenants who heard him and who lived through the war came out colonels. As for the enlisted men, many were selected to return to the States for pilot training or to attend Officer Candidate School, and many ended the war as field grade officers.* Captain Mac hadn't foreseen that development, but he wasn't far off in his prediction of what was in store for us. This was a pretty clear look at future events.

In June of 1941, Admiral Lord Louis Mountbatten put into Pearl Harbor in command of a Royal Navy aircraft carrier that was knocked around in the Singapore area by Japanese dive bombers. While his ship was being repaired and refitted under Lend-Lease,† the Hawaiian Department held an Officers Call in the theater at Fort Shafter so Lord Louis could talk to us. He had a magnificent presence and was tall, handsome, articulate, self-possessed, and every inch a proud fighting Englishman with royal blood. I got to know him better when I served under him later in the war, but to a lieutenant in Hawaii in 1941, he was pretty overwhelming. He told us about having a destroyer sunk under him during the evacuation of the British Army from Crete, and about some of his experiences as a commander of an aircraft carrier in Asiatic waters. He expressed the thanks of the British people for all America was doing under Lend-Lease while at the same time letting us know that we weren't doing nearly enough. The gist of his presentation was that we had a lot more to thank the British people for than they had to thank us for—and he was right, of course.

In August of 1941, Major Rosie O'Donnell, who went on to become a general and one of the outstanding air leaders of both World War II and Korea, took the 14th Squadron of the 11th Group from Hickam out to the Philippines to augment the 19th Group, which was already there. We, in the Army Air Corps, knew that this move was a clear sign of things to come. The move was a permanent change of station, and the wives left behind were returned to the mainland. For them, America's participation in the war had begun.

---

* Major, lieutenant colonel, and colonel.
† Under the 1941 Lend-Lease Act, war materiel and support were granted principally to Great Britain and the Soviet Union.

The 14th Squadron, in their B-17s, took the same route that the Pan Am Clippers had flown: Hawaii, Midway, Wake, Guam, and the Philippines. There was great concern about the security of this route. Wake and Midway were obvious weak links, very vulnerable to interdiction, and if one base were lost, the entire route would be knocked out. Hurried efforts were being made to develop a new route across the South Pacific that would be easier to protect. The new route was called the Southern Cross Route and went from the west coast of the mainland to Hawaii: Christmas Island, Canton Island, the Fiji Islands, Australia, New Guinea, and the Philippines.

Yes, I think we all knew with considerable precision what we could expect. When lieutenants would gather in the evening over a couple of drinks, we were pretty much in agreement. We expected a carrier attack on the Oahu military complex. It was the one place where the Japanese had a good chance of knocking out a large portion of the Pacific fleet if their timing was right. And, of course, if they could get Oahu, they would neutralize the one base common to both air routes to the Far East. Without Hawaii, the only way to get aircraft to the Far East was to send them eastward from the United States—around the world. We looked for the attack to come from the northwest, with a first-light take-off and a target time about an hour later, and for the strike to come on a Sunday morning when the Army stood down and the Navy was in port for a weekend of shore leave.

In one respect, we were in error. We all expected a quick follow-up with troop landings because the garrison strength on Oahu was light and without mobility, and the coastal defense batteries of Fort Ruger, Fort De-Russy, and Fort Kamehameha all pointed to the south and left the beaches of windward Oahu undefended. We also expected the landing forces to get lots of help from the Japanese-Americans in Hawaii because virtually all had dual citizenship. Those born in the Territory of Hawaii were automatically Americans and had registered at the Japanese Consulate to obtain Japanese citizenship as well. We felt that after carrier air strikes had neutralized our naval and air units, a follow-up ground occupation would be essential to the Japanese if they were going to sever the Pacific air routes and deny Pearl Harbor to us as a naval base. If they could close down Pearl, all naval effort in the Pacific would have to be launched from the west coast of the United States.

This, then, was the gist of the speculation among Air Corps lieutenants at Hickam Field on the eve of the Pearl Harbor attack.

chapter seventeen

DECEMBER 7, 1941

Sunday morning, the 7th of December 1941, started out like any other beautiful day in Hawaii. Lee and I had gone to Honolulu the day before to do some Christmas shopping. We had already gotten our packages off to the States. In Hawaii, you had to shop and mail early because boat travel delayed the arrival of packages to the mainland. On Saturday, 6 December, we bought tree ornaments and presents for our Hawaiian friends. That night, we had gone to a small party at the club, and that fateful Sunday morning, we had decided to goof off.

I got up around 7:45 to go out on the porch to bring in the paper for us to read in bed.

I had just gotten back to the bedroom when we heard airplanes beginning to wind up in power dives. I said, "Here comes the Navy" because when the Navy sent their planes in from carriers to land at Ford Island, they usually made a mock dive-bomb attack. But this was no mock attack. As the airplanes were pulling out of their dives, there were explosions going off. I dashed to the window that faced Pearl Harbor channel and saw a flight of planes flying up the channel, low on the water. They were not American planes. They all had torpedoes strapped to their bellies, and they all carried the big, round, red "meat ball" insignia that marked them as Japanese war planes.

I told Lee, "Honey, it's finally happened. The noise we heard was Japanese bombs going off over in Pearl Harbor, and I just saw a flight of torpedo-bombers heading up the channel. I'm leaving right now for the flight line. You stay here in the house and get under something and don't go outside until I tell you it's okay—I love you!" I put on my khaki shirt and pants over my pajamas, and still wearing my bedroom slippers, took off on a dead run for the flight line.

Lee showed the kind of stuff she was made of at once. Several of the neighborhood wives gathered at our house, and Lee took over. She had the girls take the mattress off our bed and put it on top of the dining room table. She got the electric coffee maker going; turned on the radio to get the news; and took the girls, the radio, and the coffee under the table.

It was a frightening experience for the wives. The Japs not only bombed the ships in Pearl Harbor, but concentrated on the hangars and airplanes on the Hickam Field flight line, with both high-level and dive-bombing. After their bombs were dropped, the planes began strafing the field, including the quarters area. Our home took a number of hits from explosive 20-millimeter machine-gun fire. The power on the base went off shortly, of course, and the radio and coffee maker went dead.

When the attack was over, the decision was made to get wives and families off the field as quickly as possible. I dashed home to give Lee the word and get her under way. I had been hit on the forehead by a bomb fragment while I was on the line. My head was swathed in a huge bandage, and my shirt was blood-soaked, so I must have been quite a sight. Lee took one look at me, and her eyes went big and she asked, "Are you all right?" I told her I was okay, and without further ado, she started packing a few of her things.

Our car, which had been parked behind the house, had taken a few hits, and one round had gone through the gasoline tank, draining the tank. The girls carpooled, and three of the wives who had no place to go went with Lee to stay in the house in Nuuanu Valley, where we had been married.

I waved her goodbye as she headed for the gate, and then went back to the flight line. The word went out that bomb shelters would have to be dug throughout the residential section of the base before the families could return. At least, Lee was safe for now, but who knew when the next attack was coming? I certainly didn't!

chapter eighteen

THE FLIGHT LINE ON
DECEMBER 7, 1941

That day was one I will always remember. To a young lieutenant whose exposure to violent death and mutilating wounds had been limited, it was unreal. The day had a sense of horror and unreality that are hard to convey.

The sky was full of Japanese airplanes. Formations of high-level horizontal bombers were laying down a pattern of bombs on our parked aircraft. Dive-bombers were making individual attacks. Several put bombs into the consolidated barracks and into the flight line hangars as I was running for the line. I saw one dive-bomber go straight into the big Hawaiian Air Depot hangar without appearing to try to pull out.

Fighters and dive-bombers that had released their bombs were making strafing passes over our parked aircraft, up and down the streets and over the quarters area. It was a random operation, without opposition, and they seemed to be having a great time. In open cockpits, they wore cloth helmets, and their faces were clearly visible. Strafing planes were carefully picking off individual men trying to make their way across the parade ground. They also seemed to delight in shooting up parking lots full of cars. Perhaps they were making sure there would be a good post-war market for Datsuns and Toyotas in the United States. Their activity seemed heaviest over Pearl Harbor, especially around Ford Island and battleship row. Muffled explosions were continuous, and huge columns of black smoke poured up.

My little squadron was hard hit. Our wing of the barracks was hit, killing many of my troops sleeping in on Sunday. The Central Mess Hall was hit in the middle of serving breakfast. My first sergeant was killed at his desk in the orderly room. The hangar that housed our aircraft, our operations, and maintenance activities took a direct hit, and I lost my line chief and my operations clerk, both of whom were at work that Sunday morning.

Much had to be done: fires put out, small arms distributed, wounded taken to the hospital, and aircraft dispersed. At various times, I was involved in doing all these things. I couldn't begin to tell you when or in what order certain things were done.

I remember one small man, a Japanese civilian. I don't know what his job was, but he had gone to the yard in front of the hospital where the wounded were beginning to be collected—some horribly mutilated—and this little man had somewhere found a basin of water and a piece of rag and was going from person to person wiping off their faces. It wasn't much, but it was all he could do. For some reason, the memory of him has stayed with me.

I recall taxiing a B-18 across the runway for dispersal. It had one engine knocked out, but the aircraft next to it was on fire, and it needed to be moved. I'd rev up the one engine to the limit, and as the plane would start to circle forward, I'd slam on one brake to make the plane swing back around the other way. We duck-walked across the ramp and the runway that way, with the crew chief pounding me on the shoulder, saying, "Lieutenant, you can't taxi these things on one engine."

There was a squadron of B-17s arriving from the mainland that morning, on the first leg of their journey to the Philippines. They were arriving without any warning in the midst of the attack, and you can imagine the confusion. Most were low on fuel. They had, of course, made the flight without ammunition in their guns to save weight. Some landed at Hickam, with Zeroes trying to shoot them down in the traffic pattern. Some landed at other airfields, and some went to the outer islands. I remember that one landed on the Waianai Golf Course.

One B-17 landed at Hickam with the tires shot up and a fire in the radio compartment. It slid to a stop in the middle of the runway. I was with a group trying to clear the runway, and we ran up to the airplane. The pilot turned out to be a guy I knew named Swenson. He stuck his head out the window and yelled, "Hi, Eddie! Hey, what the hell goes on here?" Under the current conditions, it seemed a pretty reasonable question.

We got him out. He had a couple of wounded on board and a flight surgeon with him who had been killed. I wanted to extinguish the fire in the radio compartment of his plane so we could get it off the runway to clear space for other airplanes to land. We got one of these big pushcart CO_2 fire extinguishers from one of the hangers and rolled it out there. I climbed up and through the pilot's window over the wing and was going back through the bomb bay to the radio compartment. The minute I turned on that rascal, I had CO_2 sprayed all over my hand because the rubber in its nozzle had rotted. It froze my hand, which I didn't realize at the time.

We got the fire out, and I climbed back down. We got wire cutters and cut the control cables because the B-17 had broken in half, in the center. We got a tug and towed the two halves out of the way so others could land. About then, a Japanese airplane went across strafing and dropping fragmentation bombs. I felt a big bang and was knocked out. When I came to, of two guys who were with me, one was very badly wounded, and the other was dead. I felt my head because I couldn't see out of one eye. There was blood running down, and I felt with my frozen hand. It felt like I had a hole in my head big enough to put my fist into. "Well," I thought, "that's all she wrote. That's the end of the road. What can I do? I'll just sit here and wait to die."

I hadn't seen anyone just slightly wounded that day at all. I sat there and waited to die, but nothing seemed to happen. Then, I reached up with the other hand and found out that all I had was a little nick in my head. Feeling very foolish, I got up and went back to work.

chapter nineteen

FIRST CLASS PASSAGE

It was about a week before bomb shelters were dug in the vacant areas throughout the quarters section and wives could come back to the base. There was a curfew after the hours of darkness all over the island. All windows were blacked-out so that no light could show at night. The general had put me on duty in Wing Operations, and Major Roger Ramey (later a major general) set us up on shifts, 24 hours on duty and 12 hours off. Lee was pretty well tied to the base and, of course, couldn't leave the house after dark. Sentries were jittery and were apt to shoot first and ask who you were afterward.

The day before Christmas, it was announced that the *Lurline* had been converted to military use and would sail on Christmas Day from Honolulu for San Francisco with destroyer escort. All wives were ordered to be on it.

I took Lee down to the dock Christmas morning with her luggage to put her on the *Lurline*. They wouldn't let me go onboard to help her get settled, and she was concerned about what kind of conditions would be provided for the girls. "Will we go in steerage?" she asked me. I assured her, with all the confidence and ignorance of a lieutenant, that she was an officer's wife and would go first class. I was right—sort of. She was in a first class cabin, all right, but double bunks had been installed, and she shared the cabin with five other wives.

It was a sad moment, watching Lee go up the gangplank, lugging her suitcases, and not knowing when, if ever, we would see each other again. After all, we had been married just one year and a few days. But the war had been hovering around just over the horizon for quite a while, and even though we tried to ignore it, we both knew that it was there, waiting for us. Although we were both shocked by the suddenness of the parting, we both felt a sense of relief, in a way. Lee knew that I was a soldier and that our country was at war, and there was no question about what I had to do. She also knew that the war zone was no place for wives. And I wasn't real sure just what the future had in store for me, but I knew that pretty soon—

and the sooner the better—I would be on my way to somewhere and would feel better knowing that Lee was safe on the mainland with her mother and dad. The war had looked us in the eye, and we had accepted whatever it might have to offer.

Letter to Mom and Dad, December 24, 1941

This is the day before Christmas. It hardly seems possible. Christmas this year is sure a farce. Writing to you now is almost an impossible job because so much has happened the last couple of weeks, and there is actually so little I can tell you about it. Needless to say, we had a ringside seat. Lee will undoubtedly be home before too long, and she will be able to tell you much more about what went on than I will be able to in a letter. Luck was certainly on my side. I was in the middle of everything and got away almost without a scratch.

My little squadron was hit extra heavy, and my Adjutant, Lt. Green, was killed, among others. It was a horrible thing to go through. There is nothing honorable about being machine-gunned while in bed as so many were. We were so utterly helpless on the ground, and the attack itself was so wanton and ruthless. It wasn't a fight—it was butchery.

Now that we are squared away, things will be different. Cold-bloodedly speaking, it was a cheap lesson because the American people, being what they are, had to have something like this happen before we could get any public sentiment aroused. It's just too bad we, over here, had to be the goats, but now that we are in it, I'm glad I was here. The war is my own personal fight now. You can read about things like that from now until doomsday, and it will never mean as much as to actually have people you know and like blown in half in front of your eyes without chance to defend themselves.

Believe me, it's only a matter of time until every little Jap in the world is either dead or flat on his face in the dirt, and I'm so very happy that my training has suited me for a major role in bringing this to pass. It's up to those of us who know how to take over from here on, and believe me, it will be done. As soon as Lee is safely home, I'll be able to relax and enjoy it.

As a country, we can't help but win. As for me personally, that's in somebody else's hand. I've a job to do that I know how to do, and I'm looking forward to it. However I come out of it myself, you can rest assured I'll have never done anything to make you ashamed of me. The American way of living and doing things is a religion with me and one I've sworn to protect as an officer in the United States Army. I hope this doesn't sound like flag-waving to you because it's not.

Don't worry about me. Now that we are on our feet, nobody is a match for us, and they'll never catch us flat on our backs asleep again. My letters will be few and far between from now on, and they will be none too full of news. Will have lots to talk about when it's all over, which shouldn't be too long.

Remember my love is with you and I'm proud of you both. It won't be long.

chapter twenty

THE SUNSET MESSAGE

After Lee left on her way back to the States, I did a lot of worrying. I was not at all sure that the Navy, with its destroyers, was capable of assuring that the *Lurline*, with its precious load, would have a safe passage. I had several sleepless nights until I got a wire that Lee had arrived safely in San Francisco and that her mother and dad were there to meet her.

Our quarters were dismal and empty without her, but I didn't stay there long. General Rudolph had orders to return to the States and gave me three options. One, to return to the United States as his aide. Two, the general coming in to replace him said he was willing to keep me on as his aide. Three, I could be reassigned to a combat unit. I, of course, took number three. I packed up what little stuff Lee and I owned, including my civilian clothes, and shipped it all to Lee. I also shipped our car. Lee put most of our stuff in storage. I later learned that when she was notified that our car had arrived in San Francisco, she went up and found it sitting on the dock, deserted, with a dead battery, out of gas, and with four flat tires. "There *is* a war on, you know," was the standard excuse anytime something like this happened.

I was assigned to the 26th Squadron of the 11th Group, which had been dispersed up to Wheeler Field, next to Schofield Barracks. I had a B-17 and a crew waiting for me and was billeted with five other officers in a set of family quarters. Our operational schedule was based on a three-day cycle. One day, we would fly a search sector out from Oahu, looking for Japanese carriers and submarines. Missions took off around 5 o'clock in the morning, with a return in the middle of the afternoon. The next day would be a regular day of ground duty and training flights. On the third day, we would preflight our airplanes at about 4:00 A.M. and then stay in the hangar on alert all day long.

In January, on a patrol flight about noon, we spotted a submarine. We knew there were no American subs in the area, so we popped open our bomb bay doors and made a bombing run at 1,000 feet altitude. We sank the sub, leaving a big oil slick. The Navy later confirmed the sinking, based on intercepted Japanese radio traffic. I had a pretty happy crew. The sinking of the submarine made the mainland news, so Lee had a pretty good idea of what I was doing.

Before Lee left, we had worked out a code to be used in our letters. All mail going home was censored, and we were not permitted to discuss anything about military operations, but I told Lee that if I said anything in my letters about a beautiful sunset, that would mean that I was moving out west somewhere. If I mentioned a sunrise, I would be on my way home. In May, a couple of squadrons of B-17s, including the 26th, were directed to fly out to Midway Island. The Navy had been deciphering Japanese coded messages and knew that the battle for Midway was shaping up. The Battle of Midway was the first real American victory. When the news about it broke in the States, Lee knew, although the Navy didn't say so, that some B-17s at Midway had done their bit and that her husband was flying one of them. That was our "sunset" secret.

Letter to Lee, December 31, 1941

The Dutchess [car] is likely to be following you very shortly, but as for the rest of our stuff, I don't know. You'll be glad to see The Dutchess, anyway.

The War is still about the same as when you left. I'm still stuck in the office, and I've about given up hope of getting away in the near future. There's no use butting my head against a stone wall. I might as well get as much fun out of this job as I can and forget about flying.

Tell my folks I think about them all the time, but that spare hours are few and far between. Most of my letter writing will be to you, and you will have to distribute the information to all our families. They will understand.

No news is good news, and when I do write, I can't tell you much. All I do is work, and I can't tell you about that. All you really want to know anyway is that I'm okay, and you can take that for granted if you never get a letter [from the War Department]. You will be the first to know if anything goes wrong, so don't worry if I skip a few days now and then.

Keep your chin up, Darling.

Letter to Lee, January 3, 1942

My boss is going back to the States shortly. I know he dislikes the idea of being relieved, and yet he is honestly happier now that he knows what is what, and his worries will soon be over. Yesterday, he talked to me about it and gave me my choice of going back with him or staying here. He said that I was to feel free to do as I honestly wanted, and he wouldn't hold it against me. If I wanted to stay, he said he'd see that I was assigned to a fighting outfit.

It was tough to pass up a chance to come back and see you and our families, but I had only one thing I could tell him, and I think he knew what I would say. I know you understand, Lee, Sweet. There's nothing I'd rather do in the world than go home and be with you, but we have a job to do, and the sooner we do it, the sooner we can all come home and live a normal life again.

As soon as I finish this, I'm going down and arrange for an allotment to be paid to you directly. It will take a couple of months for it to begin, I think, but I'll tell you all about it after I know [it] myself. We can only allot our base pay less deductions. My base pay is $175, and I have about $10 per month taken out for insurance, so I'll allot $150 a month to you at your mother's address. If you have any left over, you can start a bank account, and if you run short, you can cash checks against our account here. That should work out okay.

I'm enclosing a picture for your scrapbook. Do you recognize my hangar and the tail of my number one airplane? It sure didn't look that way when you used to take me down for night flying.

Oh yes! Clipper mail to and from soldiers and sailors is now only six cents, so don't put too many stamps on your letters.

Letter to Mom and Dad, January 6, 1942

Lee should be there by this time, and she'll be able to tell you much more about what's doing over here. So far, it's a pretty dull war from this point of view, but it will take time for this peacetime military machinery of ours to get rolling and really go to work. We should be in the middle of things when operations really start. Sure hope so, anyway. We all have a long hard job ahead of us before we can relax and live a normal life again. The sooner we start, the sooner it will be over, and I'm glad my previous training has equipped me to take a part in the big cleanup.

My letter writing time is very limited these days, so outside of an occasional note, most of my letters will be written to Lee, and she'll pass on anything. Don't ever worry about me. If anything does happen, you'll hear about it soon enough—so no news will be good news.

Hope everyone received our Christmas cards and bundles okay. We were lucky to have them all off before the War broke. The mail coming the other way *wasn't so lucky. We didn't get any packages through at all and only a half a dozen cards. Christmas sure took an awful wallop this year.*

Give my best regards to everyone in the [Santa Monica] Canyon. It will sure be nice to get back and see them all one of these days. Please don't worry. This is no fun for you, I know, but it won't last forever and it will all be over before we know it.

Take care of Lee for me.

Letter to Lee, January 7, 1942

Still working in the operations office, but I'm still fighting to get turned loose to a fighting outfit, and one of these days, I'll make it.

I went to the Finance Office yesterday and made arrangements. You should get your first check around the 10th of March and every month thereafter. Buy Bonds with whatever you may have to spare each month (if any), and I'll do the same here. If we both do that faithfully, we should have a pretty fair sized little wad of them by the time the war is over.

Tomorrow morning, I'm going over to Wheeler to see the two boys receive their Distinguished Service Crosses they won on the 7th of last month.

Don't let my folks worry about anything because you know this is right down my alley. I sure do miss you, Sweetheart. I'm going to lose that doughnut around my waist now that I'm not eating your cooking. I don't see why you couldn't have stayed on here for a while longer so we could complete one or two little plans of our own.

Letter to Lee, January 13, 1942

Golly, Honey, I hope my letters to you are getting through. Mail at this end has been a joke. Yesterday I got the first mail since you left. It consisted of three Christmas cards.

I'm still living in the front bedroom of our house, but Cod and Cam Sweeney and I are going to live together when the rest of the families leave.

The General is all packed and has been relieved from duty. He's just waiting for the next boat to take him home. He fixed it so I will go to a flying outfit when he leaves for sure, so things are looking up.

The Dutchess will probably be on the way over in a short while. I'll write and tell you when she leaves, and they are supposed to notify you when she gets to Ft. Mason so you can come up and get it. I sure am glad we put those tires on her when we did, or she wouldn't be much good to you.

It will really be fine when I begin to hear from you. Mail is so tied up here now that I don't expect to get any letters from you for another two weeks, and it will probably be at least a month before they finally get around to giving me our Christmas packages. Most of the mail being received now is six weeks old.

I told you in my last letter I was going up to Wheeler to see the two boys who shot down so many Japs get decorated. Remember? Well! The guy who got four of them was the same kid that got tried for pulling the slow roll off the mat the day we were up to see the Peashooters Air Show, so I guess he's squared himself. At the time, I said he would make a good wartime pilot.

Letter to Lee, January 14, 1942

Golly, Honey, so much has happened since I wrote to you yesterday. I don't know where to begin. I received three letters from you today and was so glad to get them! They were so sweet they made it seem as if you were here with me. You are without a doubt the sweetest wife a guy could have. I'm so proud of you. I know the trip home was no fun for you, and I'm so glad you are finally home with our families.

Sorry you are having trouble cashing the pineapple checks back in the States, but you'll get it eventually, and starting the 10th of March, you'll have the $150 a month.

I bought a $50 Bond this month instead of a $25 one. I have so much money now that my wife is gone, I don't know what to do with it all.

Now for the big news. I'm in a tactical outfit. I was transferred to the 26th Squadron today. Mickey Moore is Squadron Commander. I'm his number two man and Squadron Operations Officer. I have a brand-new airplane and my own crew. It's just like heaven. We're stationed at Wheeler Field, but keep on writing to me at Hickam because we are still under them, and they send up our mail every day. I'm living with my navigator and co-pilot. I haven't a worry in the world. (Except my wife.) I feel ten years younger getting away from that office.

I said good-bye to General Rudolph today, and he sure is a swell old guy. He told me he had recommended me for immediate promotion to Captain. He said, "Eddie, you are the finest, most outstanding youngster I've run across in the Army. You have a brilliant future. Never once, while you were my Aide, have you ever displeased me in the slightest. I've written you the highest efficiency report I've ever written in my 34 years in the Army." Wow!!!

He said to give my sweet little wife his love and best wishes. He is a fine man, and I hate to leave him. His last request before he relinquished command was *that I be assigned to a flying outfit, so he took care of me to the last. It seems good to be wearing Air Corps insignia on my collar again.*

Darling, I have a 32 waist and wear a 9¹/₂ shoe, but don't go sending me things. I'm living out of a shoebox and have to throw away some things I would like to keep every time I turn around. Spend your money on yourself, and I'll catch up when I get home.

It sure makes a long day of it when we make these dawn patrol flights. We get up in the middle of the night and take off before day light and get back just before it gets dark. Sure see lots of water during the day, and also sometimes we see little odd bits of life way out in the middle of the ocean. About 1,000 miles out today, we found the badly decomposed body of a dead whale. There were hundreds of birds on it and flying around it eating. Some of the birds were of the big, ocean-going variety, but there were a good many small shore birds that must have climbed aboard when the whale drifted past an island someplace. When they eat so much that the whale's bones finally sink with the last of the carcass, they will sure be in a bad way. Not very important as far as the war is concerned, but quite a deep-sea drama to the birds.

Hawaiian newspaper article sent to Lee, January 1942

Reporter Describes Dawn Patrol in One of Army's Flying Forts

WRITTEN BY LASELLE GILMAN*

The Dawn Patrol, a wartime institution to which Honolulu has now become thoroughly accustomed, is a far different affair from the upside looking down than from the downside looking up, so far as a landsman is concerned. Formerly the giant Flying Fortress of the U.S. Army thundered seaward every morning shortly after sunrise, but when a reporter flew with a reconnaissance plane on a routine search patrol yesterday, the takeoff was made in darkness, because of "war time," and most of Honolulu slept as the motors roared overhead.

The Army shares the ceaseless task of guarding the vast mid-Pacific stretches surrounding this Island stronghold with the Navy, and daily the Fortresses range hundreds of miles over the ocean far from land, to ensure Hawaii against surprise raids, either from the air or the sea.

---

* Duke annotated the article to indicate that Gilman flew as an observer with him and his crew.

The 20-ton planes bristle with guns and carry a varied crew. To the non-flyer they look hugely sedate, but they pack plenty of destruction and the men who fly them know how to dish it out. To most Hawaii folk they are little more than machines of the upper spaces, impersonal symbols of American air power. What goes on inside the massive, streamlined fuse-lages is strange to the observer, but routine day's work to the crew.

They aren't luxurious clippers, by any means. They appear to be roomy, but their interiors are packed with weapons, supplies, gear, and some of the most complicated mechanism known to aviators. The crew's duties are exacting, and these men are skilled fighters who have put in great numbers of hours of flying time.

The patrol plane skirts the Oahu coastline, then strikes directly out to sea. The sole purpose is to hunt Japanese. A previous gunner had scrawled a cheery message across the side of a machine gun mount. It read:

We won't give them anything but bombs, baby; All Japs get is what to them belongs, baby.

That was the main idea of the flight.

The crew of a Fortress is the pick of the Army Air Corps—men selected on the basis of sheer ability, superior intelligence and character. Highly trained in his particular field, each man must also be able to handle the duties of at least one of the other crewmembers.

On yesterday's plane, for instance, the sergeant was gunner and engineer; the pilot, co-pilot and navigator in turn were skilled machine gunners. The Bombardier was a long-trained "egg-layer"; U.S. Army bombardiers are scientifically schooled. Sitting paternally above his precious bombsite, the bombardier was a key man among the crew, and he kept a sharp eye open for anything that might turn up below—besides water.

The pilot admitted that the pickings were lean; the Japanese don't come very close these days. Last week they sighted a whale and mistook it at first for a submarine. Yesterday there was a school of porpoise playing among the whitecaps. That was all. If they had been a sub instead, four sharp warning bells would have sent the crew to battle stations. But, there were no battle stations, unfortunately.

This young pilot conducts the flight mission, yet is only one member of a team, his crew. Important to the teamwork is the navigator. He is a long-range course-plotter. It's a remarkable feat for the navigator on a long over-water flight, such as these all-day hops with no landmarks for guides to plot a course that brings him right back on the nose again at sunset.

The gunners man 50-caliber weapons, and have a tough job, for the flights are long and generally uneventful, with water, water all day long and nothing else to gaze on except an occasional overcast. But they like the work, and regard it as no weary vigil.

This crew has won high marks. Their former squadron mate was the late Capt. Colin Kelly, hero of the Philippine action who was formerly flying in Hawaii.

The Fortress returns to its nest on the Island shortly before sundown. The crew climbed out stiffly yesterday, and the pilot came last.

"So tomorrow's Japanese Empire Day," he observed thoughtfully, making a last notation in his log. "Maybe they're planning a local celebration. We're waiting to help them with it."

Letter to Lee, January 18, 1942

We had a wonderful piece of luck day before yesterday that has done more towards cementing my crew together as a unit than anything else could have done. I have to take my whole crew down to Pearl Harbor and talk to the Admiral about it tomorrow. This war will be lots of fun if it keeps on the way it's going now.

Report from the *Long Beach Press-Telegram*, August 1942 (Delayed)

Santa Monica Ace Extolled by Knox for Hawaiian Feat

Honolulu—The sinking of a Japanese submarine by a U.S. Army bomber, skippered by a youth who batted through the December holocaust in his bedroom slippers, came to light today as the result of a commendation by Secretary of the Navy Knox.

The skipper is First Lieutenant James V. Edmundson, 26, of Santa Monica, Calif., former football star at Santa Monica Junior College, an eager, rugged youth who admitted that he would do almost anything to get to Australia or anywhere else to fight the Japs.

He was decorated with the Order of the Purple Heart, but not for his feat in the air. It was because he was knocked down by a bomb fragment December 7 and got up again to do what he could to stem the Japanese attack. He still carries the scar on his forehead.

Lieutenant Edmundson has flown 40,000 miles on Hawaiian dawn patrol. His heroic career started when he sighted a submarine periscope just breaking the water off the Island of Oahu.

"Yes, I saw it, but it was my crew that got it," he declared. "Those boys really went to town." He interrupted his conversation frequently to watch fighter planes dive at plane-towed targets high over Wheeler Field. The interview was on the line in front of a hangar. We sat in a couple of steel chairs, with the planes overhead drowning the conversation time and time again.

"We were flying along in pretty heavy weather," Lt. Edmundson related. "All of a sudden I happened to see the periscope just breaking the water. Within 45 seconds my crew had flashed word to our base, the bomb doors were opened, the bomb sights adjusted and we had dropped two bombs right at the stern of the submarine." (He failed to mention that it must have taken pretty fast maneuvering on his part to get into position.)

"Every member of the crew was at his station." The Lieutenant continued. "The bombardier and the navigator must have had everything plotted, speed, altitude, wind and drift. There wasn't a second's delay. If there had been we would never have got him, because he would have sighted us first.

"The decks were barely awash when the first two bombs were dropped. The navigator and the gunner told me that some big metal pieces flew up astern when they hit. That's probably why he did not submerge right away. He couldn't; anyway we made another turn and the bombardier dropped three more bombs that practically blanketed him and on the third time around a bomb hit him right on top.

"He just blew up and disintegrated, apparently, and all we could see was a great circle of white foam of sulphuric acid from his batteries. The concussion even shook our plane, a thousand feet above. A few minutes later all there was to see was a big oil slick; and after circling awhile we went home."

And that's the story of the dawn patrol flight, which brought results, and which was the reason Secretary Knox said yesterday in Washington that Edmundson should be cited for keen observation, flying skill and successful attack with bombs.

Letter to Lee, January 20, 1942

All our Christmas presents came yesterday and, Darling, you should have seen them—big boxes just full of pretty packages. It sure made me feel sad to open them all up by myself and to think how much fun it would have been for us both if Christmas had gone according to schedule.

I'm keeping some soap your mother sent and some candy and cookies from my folks. Everything else, I've repacked in a box and am sending right on to you to keep for us. Next Christmas will be different.

Your mother was so sweet. She had a little stocking for Eight Ball with catnip balls and rubber mice and everything. Poor little guy, he sure would have liked Christmas. We will have to have another silly little black kitten when we have our home again, won't we, Sweet.

I'm flying my socks off these days, and it sure feels good again. You and the Dutchess should have quite a time together there as long as her tires hold out. After that, I don't know how you'll manage. Maybe you can have them retreaded, once, anyway. Sure am glad we bought them when we did.

Letter to Mom and Dad, January 25, 1942

Outside of our work, things are dull here. I'm way up at Wheeler where I can't get to town without my car, even if I wanted to. There is nothing to do in town anyway as you can't be on the streets after dark, and the liquor situation is non-existent. There isn't any, and it's against the law to have it anyway. We have a very lopsided existence.

Sounds like you people are busier at home than we are—with all your Air Raid Wardens and First Aid instructors and stuff.

It makes us feel good here to know the folks at home are behind us in so many ways. We, in the service, are so used to having civilians run us down every time they get a chance, but war makes a difference. I'm reminded of Kipling's poem Tommy.

[Following is the poem to which Duke refers.]

Tommy

BY RUDYARD KIPLING

I went into a public-'ouse to get a pint o' beer,
The publican 'e up an' sez, "We serve no red-coats here."
The girls be'ind the bar they laughed an' giggled fit to die,
I outs into the street again an' to myself sez I:

O it's Tommy this, an' Tommy that, an' "Tommy, go away";
But it's "Thank you, Mister Atkins," when the band begins to play,

The band begins to play, my boys, the band begins to play,
O it's "Thank you, Mr. Atkins," when the band begins to play.

I went into a theatre as sober as could be,
They gave a drunk civilian room, but 'adn't none for me;
They sent me to the gallery or round the music-'alls,
But when it comes to fightin', Lord! they'll shove me in the stalls!

For it's Tommy this, an' Tommy that, an' "Tommy, wait outside";
But it's "Special train for Atkins" when the trooper's on the tide,
The troopship's on the tide, my boys, the troopship's on the tide,
O it's "Special train for Atkins" when the trooper's on the tide.

Yes, makin' mock o' uniforms that guard you while you sleep
Is cheaper than them uniforms, an' they're starvation cheap;
An' hustlin' drunken soldiers when they're goin' large a bit
Is five times better business than paradin' in full kit.

Then it's Tommy this, an' Tommy that, an' "Tommy how's yer soul?"
But it's "Thin red line of 'eroes" when the drums begin to roll,
The drums begin to roll, my boys, the drums begin to roll,
O it's "Thin red line of 'eroes" when the drums begin to roll.

We aren't no thin red 'eroes, nor we aren't no blackguards too,
But single men in barricks, most remarkable like you;
An' if sometimes our conduck isn't all your fancy paints:
Why, single men in barricks don't grow into plaster saints;

While it's Tommy this, an' Tommy that, an' "Tommy, fall be'ind,"
But it's "Please to walk in front, sir," when there's trouble in the wind,
There's trouble in the wind, my boys, there's trouble in the wind,
O it's "Please to walk in front, sir," when there's trouble in the wind.

You talk o' better food for us, an' schools, an' fires an' all:
We'll wait for extry rations if you treat us rational.
Don't mess about the cook-room slops, but prove it to our face
The Widow's Uniform is not the soldier-man's disgrace.

For it's Tommy this, an' Tommy that, an' "Chuck him out, the brute!"
But it's "Saviour of 'is country," when the guns begin to shoot;
An' it's Tommy this, an' Tommy that, an' anything you please;
But Tommy ain't a bloomin' fool—you bet that Tommy sees!

82 : *Territory of Hawaii, 1940–42*

Letter to Lee, January 31, 1942

Things up here are still pretty quiet. I'm pulling all the strings I can, trying to transfer into pursuit and it might work. Aaron is letting me fly all the pursuit ships on my days off, so I alternated between the big ones and the little ones. It's a fine set up. It really is fun flying the little peashooters again. My acrobatics are really as good as they ever were right now.

Our furniture is all crated and stacked in front of the house and covered with canvas, and a couple of kids are living in our house.

*Stopped by to see General Rudolph. He isn't feeling very well, and he's still waiting for a boat. He said if he doesn't get a boat in the next few days, he's going to pay his way home on the Clipper.**

I sure am anxious to leave these islands and run over to Tokyo and go to work, but there's so much to consider. People are probably going to be impatient with us before this is over, and now there's no use rushing into anything half equipped. When the time comes for action, we'll get action and action with a bang. Until then, I'll just have to dig in where they put me and wait my time.

You've been gone over a month already, and it seems like years and years. I wish they could arrange this war so I could get home to see you for a couple days out of each month. It won't be too long though, Darling.

Letter to Lee, February 3, 1942

Cod came up to take command of the 26th, and I am his A Flight Commander. He moved into the house with us here, and when we get squared away, we'll be playing Chess and Cribbage every night. We had a fine bridge game last night.

Up here, at Wheeler, we are away from all the higher headquarters, and the Squadron is on its own. Soon we plan on moving to another field, which is being built on this island.

I don't think my pursuit transfer is going through, but I'm still spending my days off flying all the new pursuit ships. I sure have been having fun wringing them out. Acrobatics in these new ships are dynamite, and I love it.

I just sent the Income Tax people $127. You can handle the car insurance, I think. I'm busy buying Defense Bonds hand over fist. I now have $200 worth

---

* The Pan American Clipper, a plane, carried mail (which was then stamped "Via Clipper") and a few passengers.

for us, and I'll keep on buying them as fast as I can and still keep a respectable balance in the bank.

Letter to Mom and Dad, February 5, 1942

Your son will have at least one pretty medal to wear home. Orders came out today awarding me the Order of the Purple Heart, which is a mighty pretty little ribbon. It is given to all soldiers who are wounded in enemy action. They kind of over-estimated my little crease in the forehead, but I won't argue with them.

Lee has pictures of what all the U.S. Medals look like, so she can show you pictures of my Purple Heart and anything else I may pick up before the whole mess is over. I may even collect an Order of the Rising Sun when we get to Tokyo. It won't be long.

I have a prize crew—all youngsters and full of fight. My senior radioman lost his dad in the last war, and my tail gunner had a brother killed at Pearl Harbor. We really operate as a unit and have real confidence in each other. We've had a session of fun or two, and they sure are with me. Two of them turned down promotions last week because it meant they would be taken out of my crew and put on ground jobs. Americans are the best fighting men in the world—bar none!

Letter to Lee, February 5, 1942

Received a letter from you yesterday, Sweet. I'm so proud of you. Don't work unless you want to, Hon. If you have nothing else to do and you want to, it will be good, but don't work too hard and don't work if it isn't fun. You have to take care of my sweet little wife for me. The hell with licking the Japs, I can do that by myself.

Letter to Lee, February 25, 1942

I took my crew down to the Royal Hawaiian Hotel on our day off. The Royal is kind of a YMCA now for all Army and Navy officers and men who are on active combat crews. It cost $1.00 for officers and 25 cents for men, including rooms and meals for 24 hours.

Liquor came back yesterday, and everyone is sure happy about the whole thing. They are really fining the people who are caught drunk, however. $500 fine for getting caught drunk. Wow!!

Don't worry about my rank, Honey. I'll be a Lieutenant for the rest of my life. The War Department is making no more promotions. They are all made locally, and they are giving us the bad end of the deal, as usual. Good old Army red tape.

Darling, I'll send you Postal money orders from time to time so you can buy Defense Bonds over there, if it's okay with you. It's next to impossible to get them here these days.

My mustache is gone, Sweet. It never did amount to much, and I whipped it off soon after you left. You are sure a darling to send my news on to my folks. They both mention how sweet you are about that whenever they write.

Darling, I can't imagine anything more perfect than looking forward to the day when we have our own little house again. Coming home to you every night after work is the most wonderful thing that could happen to anybody.

Letter to Lee, March 1, 1942

Don't worry about the censors reading what you write, Doll. They only read a very small percentage of our incoming mail. I haven't gotten a single one of our letters yet that had been opened.

I'll bet you look swell in all your new clothes, Sweet. You'll be so fat and pretty when I come home I won't know you. Your mother says you've really picked up since you arrived. I didn't send you home in very good condition. I hope they don't hold it against me.

Things are about the same here. We have a fine little household. Cod and Al Sewart and Ed Lanigan, my navigator, and I play quite a bit of bridge. Tonight we made a big batch of biscuits for the four of us with honey.

A couple nights ago, we bought two enormous T-bones, and Cod cooked them perfectly. We had French fries and everything with them. I sure do miss your cooking though, Darling. I can't tell you how much I miss you and everything about you.

Letter to Lee, March 14, 1942

Don't worry about having talked strongly to Bobbie [her sister-in-law], Honey. If I had been there, I would have lit into her first. She is very narrow in her outlook and completely fails to understand about 90 percent of what goes on around her. You were absolutely right, Doll. Those people don't know what goes on. All the war means to them is worrying about where their next set of tires will come from.

Sweet, you, having been here, have a much better idea of what a war really means than they ever will have. They'd stop pampering those God Damn Japs over there if they'd seen our men blown to pieces in front of them or taken a walk through the morgue, as I had to on the second day of the war trying to identify any members of my squadron that were there. Stick to your guns, Sweet. You are a fighting man's wife, and that's something they'll never understand. I'm proud of you.

Letter to Mom and Dad, March 17, 1942

The old war is in a bad way at present, but what has happened amounts to more than the toss of the coin to decide who looks into the sun for the first half. The real game hasn't started yet.

Dad, you said in your letter that it was fine to be here in the Service if we had to have a war. That, I think, is the wrong attitude. We do have to have one, and the less we say about any other alternatives, the better. People should stop talking about "after the war" and "if we weren't at war" because the job is so big that we can't even let ourselves think about anything else.

If you could only hear, as I have, first hand stories of how the Japs have been treating our people over yonder, you'd know that this is more of a crusade than a war. It is a nasty business, but it is absolutely necessary now.

War does terrible things, but it also brings out the best in people who are fighting for something they believe in. It doesn't take much contact with these Japs to know that the American way of living is worth any personal sacrifice that we, as soldiers, can make. Of course, we all want to live through the war, but that is very secondary to insuring victory for our way of life over the unspeakably horrible things our little friends stand for.

War is a nasty business, but it is the ultimate in competitive sport. America has become what it is because it has grown rugged men who were willing to fight and die for their beliefs. People, as a nation, do not stand still; they either advance or retrogress. As long as the old Romans were on the march, they were rulers of the world, and when they relaxed to sit on their laurels, they didn't last long. I hope America hasn't waited too long now because what we stand for will mean the salvation of the world if we have the will and the strength to stand behind our ideas.

I'm not trying to argue that war is a good thing because it's not, but it is a necessary state of affairs and will be until we can wipe out those we are now fighting with, and believe me—this time, we'll do a complete job of it. If there hadn't been such a stress on peace and pacifism in America during the last few years, we wouldn't have our backs to the wall now, and it's those of us in the front line who will take the rap for our people going to sleep.

We should all realize now that war is the only way to preserve our democratic life, and it will have to be a tough, rugged, bloody war. When you are in the right and know it, war is the ultimate in giving for a cause. It turns tramps into heroes and sinners into saints. It is an experience that will make a man of anyone who gets into it and lives through it.

Wow! Enough soap box oratory. It is a useless thing to try and instill front line spirit into the folks at home, and I hope that the front line is never moved back to where you will need it. Lee had quite a session with Bobbie, from what she tells me, along the same lines, but she's wasting her time. Until people have actually seen what goes on, the war will only mean cutting down on tires and attending defense lectures once in a while.

I sure have held forth at great length, but we all feel so strongly about this thing over here. We are all in a hot spot, and we know it, and there isn't one of us who wouldn't gladly die fighting for our beliefs, but we hate to see signs of softness and indecision in the States.

Letter to Mom and Dad, March 26, 1942

Sure is swell that they have gotten General [Douglas] MacArthur out where he can do some good. He'll be our next president (after F.D.R. winds up his third term). His message to the Governor of California after your submarine-shelling incident was the prize story of the war to date. He said, "Hold out for 30 days and we'll send you reinforcements."* That even beats the Wake Marines request for more Japs.

Letter to Lee, March 30, 1942

Darling, I'm just about stumped as to what to get you for your birthday. I wish you could give me an idea or two as to what I could send you. Here's an idea. Congress has just voted a 10% pay increase for all officers in the combat zone. It is effective from December 7, and on our April pay, which I get on May 1st, I will get all the accrued money. It will be just about $100, and I can send

---

* On the morning of February 23, 1942, a Japanese submarine fired 20 rounds aiming for the oil tanks at the Ellwood oil fields just west of Santa Barbara, California. They were unsuccessful. When they saw planes coming, they submerged. On their way back to Japan, they sank two merchant ships.

you a money order for that amount and let you go on a shopping spree. You should be able to buy yourself a birthday dress or two.

Letter to Lee, April 5, 1942

It's Easter night, Darling. It sure is hard to believe. I'm an awful husband because I should have sent you an Easter radiogram or something, but I just couldn't. I've been on duty for the last 72 hours in a row including flying and standing by on the alert. This is my first time away from my airplane in three days. You know that I'm thinking of you and loving you on Easter as well as on every other day of my life, and I don't have to send you a special message to tell you so.

It's been raining like bloody blue blazes all day long, and it's doing it tonight, too. We came in this evening and cooked up a big pot of beans and Boston brown bread, and then the four of us sat around the fire and drank hot buttered rums and chewed the fat. It's been a very pleasant evening but, Darling, I miss you so. I have an awfully hard time telling you how much through the mail.

There hasn't been a clipper in for six days, so it's been quite a while since I've heard from you. Ever since the Navy's taken over the Clipper schedule, we never know what to expect. Some day those boys will do something right.

Sweet, a new order came out today on what we can say through the mail. No more locations can be given. From now on, I'll tell you about going to that certain city and seeing Mr. Blank on _____ street.* We went to _____ and saw _____ and when we decided _____ I came home to _____ and went to bed. What a lot of foolishness. By the time the war's over, I won't even be able to sign my name to my letters. They'll assign me a number. Even if I move from here, I'll never be able to tell you where I am. I don't know who they think they're kidding, but if it makes the censors happy, that's all that matters.

Letter to Lee, April 9, 1942

Happy Birthday Sweetheart ~
No way of knowing how long it will take for this to get to you, but I hope you get it in time for your birthday [April 28]. The bond is for our rapidly growing collection, and the money order is for you to spend on yourself.

---

* The blank lines in this paragraph represent redactions by the military censors.

The clipper schedule is all fouled up again, My Sweet, and I haven't received a letter from you for well over a week. Suppose it's all tied up going back, too, so you probably haven't been hearing from me either. It sure is tough, Darling, when I don't have your letters to keep me going. I miss you so very, very much it hardly seems as though I'll be able to get along much longer without you.

All the love in the world to you on your birthday, and on your next one, I'll be with you to help you celebrate.

Letter to Mom and Dad, April 17, 1942

About sinking the sub—That is sure a good example of being ready to make the most of your opportunities. It was just fool luck that he popped up when he did and we happened to see him, but if we hadn't been ready to act when the minute arrived, it would have been a different story. It sure makes a fatalist of one when you realize what a narrow margin exists between a big success and a dismal failure. A half an inch more or less is the difference between a scratched man and a dead man when it comes to bomb fragments, and a half a mile more or less is the difference between stumbling across a sub or letting him by to raise havoc in the middle of a big convoy.

Letter to Lee, April 17, 1942

Thirteen letters this afternoon!! Wow!! Seven from my darling sweetheart and all masterpieces. Darling, nobody in the whole wide world could ever be as wonderful as you are, and I love you so much it chokes me all up inside. Today is the best day I've had since you left. I've been gobbling up your letters all afternoon.

Darling, I'm kind of interested in how badly my letters home are being censored. I wish you'd tell me in your next letter whether any of my letters have been opened and taped together or whether any of them have had parts cut out.

Cod and I are carrying on as usual. They are rationing our liquor now, but we laid up a pretty good stock while it was wide open, so we haven't felt the pinch yet. You and Patty are the main topic of conversation when we get started. It just doesn't seem right to settle down to an evening of drinking and playing bridge without you two. We always begin with and end every evening with a toast, "To The Ladies." We always toast the president and the Air Corps and the Army and the squadron and dozens of others in the course of an evening, but we always begin and end with a toast to our sweethearts.

Letter to Lee, April 20, 1942

Well, Sweet, the promotions finally came through from Washington for the Pineapple Army, and your husband is now a Captain. Wow!! Went down and got myself all sworn in this morning, so it's all legal and everything. That means a pretty nice raise. The first chance I get, I'll go down the hill and have your monthly allotment increased another $50. What are you going to do with all the money, my Darling? I can't begin to spend my half of the money as you can tell by the rate I've been sending you Defense Bonds.

No mail in the last couple of days. Oh Well! I can still read the last batch I got over and over and over. Golly, they were swell.

Letter to Lee, April 21, 1942

I made arrangements to talk to you via telephone on your birthday, Sweet. You sure do have to put in your reservation early. The transpacific operator called me about an hour ago and said that she had contacted you and the call was all set up.

I'm going to start now making a list of things I want to say to you so I won't be too lost in case it turns out that we can understand each other this time. The list of rules they give you covering what you can talk about and what you can't mention is really something.

I've a new pleasure out of life these days, Sweet. It may sound small to you but I sure enjoy it. I've rigged a super aerial for our little radio outside the house, and now I can pick up the all night stations in the States. After years of closing up shop at 10:30, it is wonderful to go to bed and listen to good music nearly all night long. The new will wear off in a few days, I guess. You wouldn't know our little radio the way it is performing these days.

P.S. Kate Smith is just singing a new song, "A Soldier Dreams of You Tonight." He sure does, Darling.

Letter to Mom and Dad, April 29, 1942

Dad, you would probably be interested in knowing that our squadron has signed to buy $8,000 worth of bonds for next month. I can't tell you the Squadron strength or anything, but that is quite a record for one month from an organization the size of ours. Some setup when the men who fight the war want to finance it, too. I can't imagine that happening in any other country.

It sure sounds as though your various activities are keeping you both busy—air raid warden, first aid classes, sugar rationing board. Wow! Now if

Mom goes to work at Douglas [Aircraft plant], that will surely be a full schedule. Lee enjoys working so much. It makes her feel as though she is doing her part to help (which she is), and it makes her happier to feel that she is making airplanes for me to fly.

I have to take my last CENSORED *shot today. Soon we'll have more serum than blood in our veins. I've been inoculated now for small pox, yellow fever, typhoid fever, epidemic typhus, pneumonia, tetanus, and cholera. That still leaves bubonic plague and several others that I can't think of now. If they could make us impervious to bullets, sort of puncture proof, they would really have something.*

Letter to Lee, May 25, 1942

This afternoon is the first breather I've had and I'm spending it catching up on my letter writing. Darling, we are really busy and no doubt about it. I can't tell you anything, My Sweet, but you'll understand. We've been on duty 16 hours a day, every day, and that doesn't leave much spare time.

No mail from anyone for four days, so I can't answer any of your queries this time. That makes it tougher than usual because I have to dream up all my conversation from this end, and not much of our activity is released for discussion. What a life!!

The radio is playing a bunch of Hawaiian music now, Sweetheart, and it sure makes me think about us and how much fun we've had here. This place has changed so much it's just as if I wasn't in the Islands anymore.

Letter to Lee, May 28, 1942

Sure is a cheerful household around here when the mail is in. Darling, your letters are the most wonderful things in the world. They make me feel on the top of the world for days afterwards. They make me want you and miss you terribly, and yet I couldn't do without them.

Sweetheart, the day I see you again and hold you in my arms will be the finest day of my life, even far better than the day we were married. It's been over five months since you left. Another five will kill me. People just can't begin to realize how terribly much they love a person until they are kept apart the way we have been. It's certainly something I never want to have to go through again.

Letter to Lee, May 29, 1942

Your idea of loading the Dutchess up and driving her as far as we can and then packing way, way back into the mountains for a long stay sounds perfect.

I know just the place, my Sweet. We'll get a couple of horses and a burro and go way up into the real fishing country and sleep under the stars. You'll have to cook over an open fire, but I'll help you, Sweet. We'll probably both forget to ever come back. You have a date for one of these days when the war is over.

Don't expect to hear from me for about a week, my darling. We're awfully busy these days, and I just won't be able to write. I'll tell you all about it one of these days, so please, Sweetheart, don't worry and above all, don't forget how much this old husband of yours worships you and loves you and wants to be with you.

Letter to Lee, June 3, 1942

We got in late last night after flying 40 hours out of the last 72. We really were a tired outfit. I hadn't washed, shaved, or taken my clothes off in three days and nights, and I've had five hours of sleep in the three days and nights.

We're keeping busy, and it's sure fine. Our outfit is a real fighting outfit. I'm sure proud of our squadron and especially so of my own crew. I can't tell you where we've been or what we've been doing, but it doesn't really matter. This old ocean is plenty big and plenty wet, and there's not much difference between one part of it and another.

Don't ever worry if I happen to skip several days between letters. We never know where we'll be from one day to the next. I have a hunch this will be my last letter for another few days, but as I said, we never know until an hour or so before.

Letter to Lee, June 8, 1942

Here's your husband again after all this time, Darling. Did you think you were the forgotten woman?

Sweet, we got back here again late last night all tired out and dirty again, and I just could stay awake long enough to take a shower before going to bed. We sure have been busy, but I can't tell you anything (as usual). You have no doubt read in the papers about our activity around here* and guessed our part in it.

It sure was an experience, and they've really had us going for the last couple of weeks. I've slept on the ground under the wing of my plane for so many nights lately it doesn't seem natural to get into a bed.

---

* The Battle of Midway, June 4–7, 1942.

As usual, my little angel had letters waiting for me when I got in this time and not one, but three. What a wife!! Darling, coming home to your letters is the next best thing to coming home to you.

Here it is the 8th of the month, and I have 75 hours of flying time already. Not bad! I was kind of glad to come back this time because for the last couple of days, I've been flying my ship with no brakes, and I've had to ground loop it to stop it every time I land; not dangerous at all but hardly conducive to a carefree attitude. My poor Tail Gunner is black and blue from being slapped around in these ground-looping landings.* It sure is a helpless feeling to have 50,000 pounds of machinery rolling along the ground at 100 miles per hour and no way of getting it stopped.

Don't ever worry about anything, my pet. Cod and everyone you know is still fine. This business of ours is like going to war in a bulletproof rocking chair.

My precious wife, I miss you now more and more as the days go by. I didn't think I could ever miss you more than I did the day I put you on that boat, but it keeps getting worse instead of letting up.

Letter to Lee, June 9, 1942

Your last letter was very cute, Darling, when you spoke about how you enjoyed shopping with me and needed an efficiency expert around to help you manage things. You sounded as if you'd almost forgotten how mad you used to get when you went shopping with me because I was too direct about it and didn't shop around forever with no results. You used to trot along with me as fast as your little legs would take you—fuming and fussing to yourself because things weren't being done casually and indirectly enough and mainly, I guess, because it wasn't a woman's way of doing things and you just plain old didn't like it. Remember?? You little dickens. You are so cute when you work yourself into that frustrated mood of yours.

And when I'd suggest that you do the ironing once and forget it for the rest of the week instead of piddling around and ironing seven days a week. Wow!! It was just like sticking my head into an electric fan! You want to make the most

---

* A ground loop landing is usually an unintended turn on ground that very quickly becomes uncontrollable unless stopped in short order. After landing, and with the airplane's weight largely on ground, the pilot immediately applies hard rudder and then rams on full throttle to generate immediate prop wash across the rudder so that the rudder can help prevent an uncontrollable turn.

of your chance now to do things your own way without a husband to butt in and spoil your routine.

Sweetheart, your box of English toffee came today, and it is still as fresh and crisp as can be. You are such an angel to always keep sending me things. Nobody else in the world has a wonderful wife like you. I miss you so much I don't know how I'll ever be able to get along another day without you.

We are lucky, Darling, to be able to write as often as we do. I talked the other day to an old friend of mine who was going back through from the other side— pretty well shot up. He finally got a phone call through to his wife from here although he couldn't tell her where he was or that he was on his way home. She said she hoped he'd been getting her letters because she'd written every day. He said he wondered where his mail had gone because he hadn't heard from her since the middle of November. He'd been moving around so much that his mail just hadn't caught up with him.

Letter to Lee, July 24, 1942

The sun is setting. Tomorrow will be a long day, too. I wish I could tell you how terribly happy I am about how things are working out or even tell you what is going on but it just can't be done.

I haven't named my airplane yet, but we got the Squadron painter to put a little black submarine with a red cross through it up on the side under my window. We saved room for additions underneath it.

Duke as a Sea Scout.
Santa Monica, California,
1931. (See Chapter 2)

Cadet Edmundson
in Texas, 1938.
(See Chapter 1)

Graduation program from Kelly Field, Texas, 1938. (See Chapter 1)

A-17s in formation, March AFB, 1939. (See Chapter 1)

Lee and Duke, Waikiki Beach, Oahu, Territory of Hawaii, 1940. (See Chapter 4)

Formation of B-18s flying over Diamond Head, 1940. (See Chapter 4)

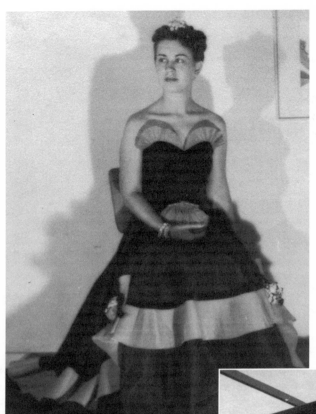

Lee at the Royal
Hawaiian Hotel,
Oahu, 1940.
(See Chapter 13)

Lee boarding
the *Lurline*, 1940.
(See Chapter 8)

B-18 crash landing in a sugar cane field, Territory of Hawaii, 1940. (See Chapter 8)

Lee and Duke's wedding day, November 21, 1940, Oahu. Reverend Judd is at left. (See Chapter 10)

"Sunday Driver" by Corporal Bill Grimm, Hickam Field, Territory of Hawaii, 1941. Lee didn't think it was a bit funny. (See Chapter 14)

— THIS IS THE FINAL TEST- IF LT. EDMUNDSON'S WIFE CAN'T TEAR IT UP IN FIVE MINUTES, THEY'RE GOING TO BUY IT FOR GROUND DEFENSE ! "

Duke's exploits recounted in the *Minneapolis Star Journal*. (See Chapter 17)

AWARD REVEALS SAGA OF DAWN PATROL:

Wounded Flier Battles Four Days in His Slippers

By WENDELL WEBB

HONOLULU—(UP)—The sinking of a Japanese submarine by a United States bomber, skippered by a youth who battled for four days through the December holocaust in his bedroom slippers, came to light today as the result of a communication by Secretary of Navy Knox.

The skipper was Lt. James V. Edmundson, 26, of Santa Monica, Calif., former football star at Santa Monica Junior college, an eager rugged youth who "would do almost anything to get to Australia or anywhere else to fight."

He was decorated with the Order of the Purple Heart today, but not for his feat in the air.

It was because he was knocked down by a bomb fragment Dec. 7 and got up again to do what he could to stem the Japanese attack.

He still carries the scar on his forehead.

* * *

Lieutenant Edmundson has flown more than 40,000 miles on Hawaiian dawn patrol, but the highlight of his career came when he sighted a submarine periscope just breaking the water off the island of Oahu a few weeks ago.

"Yes, I saw it, BUT IT WAS MY CREW THAT GOT IT," he declared. "THOSE BOYS REALLY WENT TO TOWN."

He interrupted his conversation frequently to watch fighter planes dive at plane-towed targets high over Wheeler field. The interview was "on the line" in front of a hangar. We sat in a couple of steel chairs, with the planes overhead drowning the conversation time and again.

* * *

"We were flying along in pretty heavy weather," Lieutenant Edmundson related. "All of a sudden I happened to see the periscope just breaking water. And within 45 seconds my crew had flashed word to our base, the bomb doors were opened, the bomb sights adjusted, and we had dropped two bombs right at the stern of the submarine."

(He failed to mention it must have taken pretty fast maneuvering on his part to get into position.)

"Every member of the crew was at his station," the lieutenant continued. "The bombardier and the navigator must have had everything plotted — speed, altitude, wind and drift. There wasn't a second's delay. If there had been, we would never have got him.

* * *

"The decks were barely awash when the first two bombs were dropped. Big metal pieces flew up astern when they hit. That's probably why he did not submerge right away. He couldn't.

"Anyway, we made another turn and the bombardier dropped three more bombs that practically blanketed him, and on the third time around a bomb hit him right on top. HE JUST BLEW UP AND DISINTEGRATED, APPARENTLY. The concussion even shook our plane 1,000 feet above."

* * *

And that's the story of the dawn patrol flight which brought results and which was the reason Secretary Knox said in Washington that Edmundson should be cited for "keen observation, flying skill and successful attack with bombs."

Bombs weren't anything new to Edmundson. He was on the receiving end of them Dec. 7.

Fragments went right through the house where he lived with his wife, the former Lee Turner, who now is with her parents, Mr. and Mrs. Lomax Turner of Long Beach, Calif.

He was stationed at Hickam field then, and saw his buddies struck down right and left.

* * *

Edmundson was born in Hollywood June 12, 1915. He attended University of California at Los Angeles, and later was timekeeper at the Douglas aircraft plant in Los Angeles.

"I saw all those planes coming out and knew someone would have to fly them," he recalled, "so I wrote to the war department asking where the schools were."

In 1937 he went to Randolph and Kelly fields in Texas and later had a tour of duty at Lowry field in Denver. He came to Hawaii in 1939. He was married here Thanksgiving day, 1940.

* * *

Of the Dec. 7 attack by the Japanese, he recalled:

"I heard planes, and looked out the window, to see the enemy streaking toward Pearl Harbor. I got on what clothes I could and went out, I CERTAINLY WORE OUT THOSE BEDROOM SLIPPERS BEFORE I GOT HOME FOUR NIGHTS LATER."

Edmundson insisted his crew was more to be credited than he for the destruction of the Japanese submarine off Oahu.

They were:

Co-Pilot Lt. Arnold Johnson (address unavailable); Bombardier Master Sergeant Joe Wilderman of Oklahoma City; Navigator Lt. Edwin Lanigan of Boston; Engineer Technical Sgt. Frank Bowen of San Antonio, Texas; Radio Operator Corp. Russell Hultgren of LaVerne, Calif.; Assistant Radio Operator Sgt. E. F. Smith of Columbus, Neb.; Gunner Staff Sgt. Leonard Tallaferro of Arlington, Ga.

THE SECRETARY OF THE NAVY.

WASHINGTON.

The President of the United States takes pleasure in presenting the DISTINGUISHED FLYING CROSS to

MAJOR JAMES V. EDMUNDSON, UNITED STATES ARMY

for service as set forth in the following

CITATION:

"For heroic and extraordinary achievement while participating in an aerial flight as pilot of a B-17 Flying Fortress in action against enemy Japanese forces in the vicinity of Tulagi, Solomon Islands on August 19, 1942. Flying at perilously low altitude through a bursting hail of anti-aircraft fire, Major Edmundson, with cool courage and utter disregard for his own personal safety, scored a 500-pound-bomb hit just abaft the after turret of a Japanese cruiser, setting up a series of violent explosions aboard the vessel and leaving her in a rage of flames. His superb airmanship and loyal devotion to the accomplishment of a highly important objective contributed materially to the success of our forces in the campaign of the Solomon Islands."

For the President,

Frank Knox

Secretary of the Navy.

Duke's Distinguished Flying Cross citation from Secretary of the Navy Frank Knox. (See Chapter 20)

"Heroes of Democracy." (See Chapter 20)

Flying Fortress with newly painted sub on the fuselage. (See Chapter 20)

United Press correspondent Bill Tyree with Duke, October 1942. (See Chapter 23)

Duke and the crew of his B-17, the Flying Fortress, October 1942. (See Chapter 23)

Duke in Salina, Kansas, 1944.
(See Chapter 30)

Duke in India, 1944. The fast
pace of operations, the extreme
temperature and humidity, and
primitive living conditions both
in India and China account for
Duke's weight loss in the few
months between these photos.
(See Chapter 31)

The haircut. The barber is Clink and
the victim is Duke. India, May 17,
1944. (See Chapter 32)

Clink and Sally
in India, 1944.
(See Chapter 32)

Lee and Ed in Long Beach,
California, May 14, 1944.
(See Chapter 32)

The B-29 Superfortress. (See Chapter 32)

Lord Louis Mountbatten (*left*) with the crew of *O'Reilly's Daughter*, Kharagpur, India, 1945. (See Chapter 33)

B-29 with bomb bay doors open, 1944. (See Chapter 33)

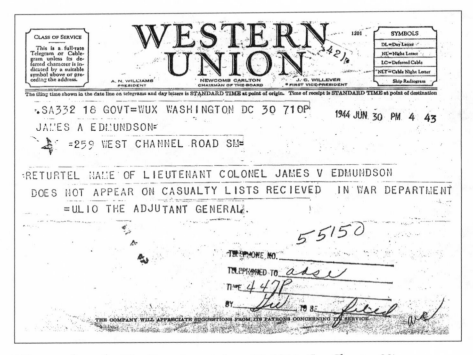

Telegram from the War Department, June 30, 1944. (See Chapter 33)

General Curtis
LeMay and Duke
in India, 1944.
(See Chapter 33)

O'Reilly's Daughter and crew, India, 1944. (See Chapter 33)

Lee in Long Beach,
California, 1945.
(See Chapter 33)

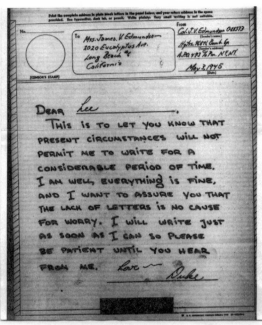

Example of a V-Mail
to Lee, May 3, 1945.
(See Chapter 23 for the
first mention of V-Mail)

part three

THE SOUTH PACIFIC, 1942–43

chapter twenty-one

FROM LONG BEACH
TO GUADALCANAL

Soon after we returned to Hawaii from Midway, the 11th Group was alerted for movement to the South Pacific. I had been promoted to captain, which I could tell Lee about, but there was no way I could let her know that we were headed south. She found out eventually, though, because we flew a lot of missions, and some were successful enough to make the news. We did most of our early flying and fighting out of Espiritu Santo, an island in the New Hebrides. As soon as the airstrip on Guadalcanal was secured and made long enough for B-17s, we moved there.

Soon after we arrived in the South Pacific, the commander of the 431st Squadron failed to return from a combat mission. Colonel Blondie Saunders,* commander of our 11th Group, moved me over to command the squadron. With the new job, I was promoted to major.

Lee lived in Long Beach, California, with her mother and father. Her two brothers were away from home serving in the Navy. Lee went to work at the Douglas Long Beach plant building C-54s. I had never met Lee's parents, but I got to know them through Lee's letters. Her mother proudly flew her flag in the front of the house with three blue stars on it.† This is just an indication of how Americans faced the problems of war together. My mother went to work in the Douglas Santa Monica plant building airplanes. My dad was an Air Raid Warden. Gasoline was rationed at five gallons per week. My little sweetheart was part of what made America great. She was many thousands of miles away, but she felt close to me, and we shared the wonder of togetherness when we were half a world

---

* Colonel (later Brigadier General) LaVerne G. "Blondie" Saunders.

† Families with a member in active duty flew Service Star Banners. Each blue star represented one member. Lee's two brothers were both in the Navy and in active duty. A gold star was displayed if a family member was killed in action or otherwise died in service.

apart. Our love was entwined with our love of our country and all the things about America that were good and clean. We were a part of it all, Lee and I. I realize I don't tell the story very well, but our love and the life that we shared, even at that great distance, were a part of America and its glorious history. It brought pride to both of us and made our very private and very wonderful love even closer. The distance between Long Beach and Guadalcanal was many thousands of miles, but Lee and I were never apart.

chapter twenty-two

HOW TO WIN

WHILE LOSING, II

Our first station down south was on one of the southern islands in the New Hebrides, called Efate, near the capital city of Vila. Our flying field consisted of one very narrow strip, covered with pierced steel planking and carved out of the jungle. The jungle was very close to the runway, and it was a scary place to land in a crosswind. Airplanes were parked by backing them with a tug into notches carved out of the jungle along the length of the strip. We were bombing targets on Guadalcanal and Tulagi, softening them up for the coming Marine landing. It was a long way up to Guadalcanal from Efate, and they were preparing another runway on one of the northern New Hebrides islands, Espiritu Santo. This would put us much closer to our work and permit us to carry much larger bomb loads. In the meantime, Efate was home.

The islands just north of the New Hebrides were the Santa Cruz group, and the northernmost of these was a little spot of land called Nupani. This islet was actually the tip of an extinct volcano, and the walls were broken in on one side, so the crater was open to the sea and formed a snug little harbor. Intelligence reports reached us that the Japs were using Nupani as a base for a couple of flying boats, which they were refueling from submarines during the night and during the early morning hours. This looked like too good an opportunity to pass up, and my boss said, "Eddie, go get them! If you take off about 3:00 tonight, you should catch them at it around daybreak."

I said, "Yes, sir," and we began hoisting up a load of bombs. There were a few difficulties. Our runway was awfully narrow, and the strip had no lights. We decided that if we parked a couple of jeeps at the end of the runway with their headlights pointed back up the strip, they would provide all the light we needed for take-off. We had overlooked the fact that there was a hump in the runway, so when we lined up for take-off, the jeep lights would be hidden, and we would not be able to see them until we were halfway down the runway.

By the time I lined up at 3:00 A.M., it was too late to chicken out, so I began feeding in take-off power to my trusty B-17, and we started to roll. We were just beginning to pick up speed when I felt a jolt and realized that I had hooked a tree with my right wingtip. I pulled off the power and slammed on the brakes, and we slid around to our right and skidded to a stop, nose to nose with another B-17, which was parked in one of the revetments. I'd lost a wingtip, of course, but there was little damage done to the two B-17s rubbing noses except for a bit of broken Plexiglas; nonetheless, it made an awful racket. There was one casualty. A navigator had been sleeping in the nose of the other plane. He woke up in the dark with all that noise and was sure the world was coming to an end. He scrambled out of the nose hatch as fast as he could; the only problem was that the forward hatch in the B-17 was about 11 feet in the air. He sprained his back when he hit the ground and had to be taken to the hospital. If there was any enemy activity up at Nupani that night, we were no threat to them, and it took several days to get our two B-17s back in operation.

After this heroic mess that I had made out of what should have been a simple mission, I knew by now just what to expect. They promoted me to major and made me commander of the 431st Bomb Squadron. What else was I to expect?

Letter to Lee, August 7, 1942

Golly, it's been nearly a month since I've written to you and what a month. Wow!! I've been more places and seen and done more things than you could ever believe possible. I'll sure have some stories to tell when we are together again. God only knows when this letter will reach you or if it ever will. Mail delivery out here where we are is non-existent. The boys who have been here a while are still patiently waiting for their April mail, so it's going to be a tough old row to hoe for a while, but actually I'm much closer to home here than I was up where I was.

This old stuff can't possibly last forever, and there's only one place to go when we are through but home. Time has been flying because we've been so damn busy. Yesterday and today have been our first rest periods since we got here, and we've been going 24 hours a day since then.

Yesterday I got my first shower and shave in 10 days, and took my clothes off for the first time in four days, and went to bed and slept the clock around twice.

Today things are normal again, and I can finally write to you, and tomorrow we'll be back at them again. It's a wonderful feeling to be doing something at last, and believe me, we are sure having a time. Of course, I can't begin to tell you where I am or what is going on, but you have no doubt seen Cod by this time, and he will have given you a rough idea.

This is an impossible letter to write because there is so terribly much I want to tell you and so little I'm actually able to. It will just have to suffice for me to tell you that I'm well and healthier than ever and busy and having a time I'll never forget and as happy as I can possibly be.

I'll try to write my folks soon, but let them know what you can. You can't even begin to realize how hard it is to find time to write. We only eat one meal a day because we are so cramped for time. Above all, don't worry about me for an instant because it's a waste of time, and just remember it can't last forever.

Report from the Associated Press, August 1942 (Mission of 3 August in the Solomon Islands)

Edmundson Hero in New Saga of Air

Maneuvers Bomber in Amazing Manner

From a jungle-hidden airfield in the Solomon Islands, Santa Monica's air hero, Maj. James V. Edmundson, 27, zoomed his four motored American Army bomber into the sky in the opening dogfights for mastery of the air over the Solomons and, with skill and daring to amaze his seasoned comrades, was instrumental in shooting down four speedy Japanese Zero fighter planes, it was reported today from the Associated Press.

Recognition first came to Major Edmundson at Pearl Harbor when he was commended by the War Department for sinking a Japanese submarine off the Hawaiian coast.

With customary modesty, Major Edmundson said of his latest exploit: "We were just coming in from our bombing run when seven float type Zeros showed up about 1000 feet above us and off our right wing. There were three bombers in my element.

"Those Zeros stayed up there, riding alongside us for about five minutes. After they'd figured out a plan of attack, or maybe they were drawing straws to see which one got to hit us first, they started peeling off to make a semi-hidden head on attack.

"The first one aimed at my plane, it being the lead plane. My gunners worked him over and think they got him. The Jap was smoking heavily when he went down below. At least he never came back.

"Then the second Zero attacked my wingman. That Zero caught on fire and crashed. Credit that to one Lt. McDonald.

"The third Zero veered off and attacked from behind. The gunners got him. They said he hit the water and exploded.

"The fourth Zero hit us from behind and below. They're good climbers and this bird must have thought he would show off, because he pulled up in front of us and that was when, I guess, I got mad.

"I put the bomber in a wing-over and started diving after the Jap. My left wingman didn't know what was up, but he pulled his plane over and started to follow.

"Well, we followed that Jap Zero down for about 4,000 feet. The Zero was running, all right. I imagine he wondered 'What the hell,' when he saw a bomber dog fighting him.

"Anyway, when we got close to him my plane nosed up slightly, giving the gunner a chance to work the Jap over. The gunner did a good job getting the Zero, according to his story. I couldn't see the results myself."

Major Jim, as his fellow pilots call him, indicated his wing planes and his own gunners deserved all the credit for any Zeros shot down.

"The pilot just sits up there like an old man in a rocking chair," he said. "It's the gunners who do the real work during combat. That day, they were 1000 percenters, in my book. They probably looked that way to those other three Jap Zeros, too, because numbers five, six and seven stayed out of range from then on.

"We went right on with our bombing run. We were about 400 feet lower than we meant to be, but it didn't make much difference, apparently. I think our bombs scored all right."

Letter to Mom and Dad, August 12, 1942

I've had a chance to come home because I've been away so long, but I kind of feel that if everyone does that, the war will hang on and hang on. I like to roll up my sleeves and pitch in, and maybe my small effort will bring the end that much nearer. There's nothing I'd rather do than come back and see you all and be with Lee, but my conscience just won't let me as long as there's so much to be done and actually so few to do it. It's kind of hard to explain, I guess, maybe you get an inkling of what I mean. The Government has fed me and paid me for five years just so I can do the job I'm doing now, and the least I can do is to put out. It isn't so bad, really, because I enjoy it in a way. As much as it is possible for anyone to enjoy a war. I must have had a latent primitive streak in me because I actually get a kick out of combat. Of course, I have a funny feeling in my stomach sometimes; anyone who says he doesn't is an out and out liar. But there is also an exhilaration and lift from it that compensates for a lot. I pity the boys in this who don't have the tough, rugged competitive attitude because it must be sheer hell for them.

I expect to get a squadron of my own here shortly. One squadron commander failed to return a couple days ago, and as soon as a reasonable time has elapsed to make sure he isn't drifting around somewhere in a rubber boat, I'm slated to take over. Sure tough, but fortunes of war and all that sort of stuff.

Now that I think of it, I haven't written to you since I made Major. It came through the day before I left my last station after a long delay. It was dated back to March 1st so although I'll miss the pay for that period, I'll have credit on the books for those months of service as a Major. I hope I never get promoted again because the next one will promote me right out of an airplane and out of combat duty and put me behind a desk with the fuddy-duds.

chapter twenty-three

MISSION OF 19 AUGUST 1942

Early in August, we began operations from Espiritu Santo, an island in the northern New Hebrides and closer to the action in the Solomons. Our base on Espiritu Santo was extremely primitive, just a runway chopped out of a copra plantation and covered with pierced steel planking (PCP). There was no taxiway structure. Our B-17s were parked in hardstands off of the runway. Later, the group operated out of a collection of Quonset huts, and each squadron established a tent camp in the coconut palms. To begin with, though, there were no structures of any kind. Flight and ground crews slept under their airplanes. Actually, it wasn't too bad. With the flaps down and bomb bay doors open, the B-17 provided quite a bit of protection against the rain. Also, the underside of the airplane provided a structure to which we could anchor our mosquito nets.

The Solomon Islands were a long way from the New Hebrides. It was about 500 miles from Espiritu Santo to Guadalcanal and another 150 miles from Efate to the Canal. Our mission during July and early August was to bomb Japanese targets on Guadalcanal as well as on Gavutu and Tanambogo. We also flew reconnaissance missions as far north as Buin Harbor on Bougainville. These missions were in preparation for the Marine landing on Guadalcanal, scheduled for 7 August 1942. In order to operate at these distances, we established a standard practice of carrying one bomb bay tank. This gave us the fuel to extend our range, but it cut our bomb load in half, leaving us only the bomb stations on one side of the bomb bay.

On 18 August, flying out of Espiritu Santo, we flew a mission to bomb Tulagi. We got back to the base late in the afternoon and checked our airplane over, fueled and bombed up, and cleaned and loaded our guns. Refueling was accomplished with a hand pump from 50-gallon drums in the back of a truck; we strained the fuel through a chamois skin. Bomb loading was equally primitive. They would dump off our four 500-pound bombs at our hardstand, and we would roll them into position under the bomb bay and hoist them up to the racks with a manual hoist that was built into the B-17. It was well after dark before our airplane was ready to go. We each wolfed down a box of K-rations, set up our cots and mosquito nets, and hit the sack.

The first thing I knew on the morning of 19 August was someone shaking me awake. I opened my eyes and saw that it was Colonel Blondie Saunders, our Group Commander. I jumped out of bed in a hurry. Colonel Saunders had Admiral John S. McCain with him, and that really woke me up. This was the grandfather of our present senator from Arizona, and the man in charge of our air operations. His headquarters was aboard his flagship, the *USS Curtis*, anchored in Segun Channel between Espiritu Santo and Malekula, the next island to the south. It seemed that the admiral had received an urgent message that a group of Marines ashore on Guadalcanal were pinned down on Lunga Beach by a Japanese warship that was shelling them heavily while staying out of range of Marine weapons. They urgently requested air support. Admiral McCain came ashore to see Colonel Saunders and find out what the B-17s could do to help. It turned out that ours was the only B-17 on Espiritu Santo that was in commission, fueled up, loaded with bombs and with ammunition in our guns, ready to go. Colonel Saunders said, "Go get "em, Eddie." In 15 minutes, we were on our way.

It took us about two and a half hours to get to Guadalcanal, and sure enough, the situation was just as reported. A ship that appeared to be about the size of a cruiser was steaming back and forth throwing shells onto the beach, where there was a lot of smoke and some fires burning. We were determined not to waste our four 500-pound bombs because if we didn't stop what was going on, there wasn't anyone else who could. My bombardier, Lieutenant Al Thom, could do wonders with a Norden bombsight, and I decided to bomb from a low altitude to give the ship minimum time to take evasive action. We decided to bomb from 5,000 feet and knew that at that altitude, the flak would be thick, so we didn't want to fly through it any more times than we had to. We decided to make one run only and drop our four bombs in minimum train. This setting would release our bombs within a fraction of a second of each other—just far enough apart so that they would not bump into each other and detonate in the air on the way down.

We lined up for our run from the ship's stern. This reduced the ship's relative speed and also put it in a position where evasive action in either direction would not present a complex bombing equation. I gave Al as steady a bombing platform as I could, and his corrections were precise and minimal. The flak was quite heavy, but they had overestimated our altitude, and most was bursting above us. When I felt the airplane shudder and lurch upward as the 2,000 pounds of bombs were released from the racks and Al called, "Bombs away!" over the interphone, I cranked it hard left and put the nose down to pick up speed and get out of there. When you hear that "Bombs away!" call, you are no longer working for Uncle Sam, and your primary concern becomes your wife and family.

I could hear the waist gunners yell over the interphone when the bombs hit and knew we'd made a good drop. The ship had made a tight left-hand evasive turn as the bombs arrived. They were so close together that it looked, to the gunners, like one explosion. The number 2 and 3 bombs in the string hit him in the fantail, just behind his aft turret. The number 1 and 4 bombs were near misses, one on each side and detonating under water. They may well have done as much damage as the bombs that made direct hits. We continued losing altitude, staying out of range and watching to see what went on. We had caught him in a tight turn, and the near misses must have jammed his rudder because he continued to steam in a tight circle and burned, with occasional explosions and lots of fire and smoke. One of my waist gunners had a handheld camera and took pictures out of the waist gunner's hatch.

We decided to fly down along the beach to see how the troops were doing. They had been under heavy direct fire for several hours, and we wondered what their situation was, so as to include it in our mission report. I let my exuberance get the better of me, and we made a pass along the beach just a few feet off of the water, rocking our wings in salute to those guys who had taken so much. To our surprise, there were a lot of men on the beach, jumping up and down and waving and yelling. They couldn't hear it, but my crew was yelling just as hard, over the interphone. We all had a very warm and a very happy feeling and a long flight ahead.

Our fuel was running a little low, and we had to head back to Espiritu Santo. When we arrived, we found that a report from Guadalcanal had beaten us there, and Colonel Saunders and Admiral McCain were standing by to meet us. When the tug had backed us into our hardstand, my crew left the plane smartly and drew up at attention in front of number 1 and 2 engines. The admiral went down the line shaking the hand of every crew member, thanking him for the job he had done. Colonel Saunders had a big smile on his Irish face. We were all sitting on Cloud Nine.

Letter to Mom and Dad, September 23, 1942

Dad, you have suggested several times that I should keep a diary. I've thought about it too, but am afraid maybe it wouldn't be a good idea. In the first place, nobody is allowed to keep such a thing in the combat zone because it would contain much secret information and might fall into enemy hands. It's true that I won't be able to remember all the little details of what has happened, but much of what I have seen I really don't want to remember. Most of the high spots will be impossible to forget, and the rest will be just a blur, which is, perhaps, the best way for it to be.

I'd hate to be as unable to break the bonds of this affair when it's over as some people I've met who were in the last war and never outgrew it. Lots of major adjustments will be necessary when it's over, and if I can live with this thing now from day to day and wring what satisfaction I can from it and then forget it, I'll be better off than trying to save up a bunch of data to pore over when its finished. Six months after the war is over, nobody will care who was in it and who did what or where, and anyone who can't brush this old business off in a hurry and start all over again will be seriously handicapped in adjusting himself to post-war conditions.

Mom, you were talking about its being a morale booster if I could come home to be decorated. That is 100% wrong. Nothing makes the fellows madder than to see newspaper pictures of these so-called "national heroes" at parties with the movie stars when boys out here are doing more in a day than the glamour boys have done in the whole war. If and when something like that develops, they should decorate them where they are and leave them there to fight where they will do some good. I would refuse to return to the States under those conditions because it wouldn't be right and because it would do me more harm than good. When my outfit is sent home, I'll go home with it, but that is the only honorable way to return. What we need are fighters, not grandstand players, and when things are run into the ground the way they are now, it hurts our national effort. It's 99% luck anyway. You can't kill Japs by waving press notices or medals under their noses.

Letter to Lee, September 30, 1942

Another letter from your seldom heard from husband—no need to tell you I've been busy as ever, and writing has been out of the question. You know that already. Anyhow, I have my outfit out at another base for a few days doing another job in a little different corner of the war. We'll be back in the old stomping ground again shortly.

Your letters are coming through in fine style, and it is so good of you to write as often as you do. Your letters are all so sweet and dear, and they are read and reread until they are just about worn out. They are the only thing that keeps me going and mean more than you can ever possibly realize.

The old war down here progresses. That's about all I can tell you about it. I'm getting prouder of this squadron of mine every day. The boys are doing an unbelievable fine piece of work, and their spirit is something to see. We sure have a fighting outfit. With units like it scattered all over the world, working like my boys are, we can't possibly lose. It's only a matter of time. The American soldier is unsurpassed when it comes to being able to take punishment and to give it out. You just have to make him mad first, and then he's unbeatable.

You wouldn't recognize the fighting army of today as the same organization you knew in peacetime, with its formality and red tape and social life. Maybe some day it will revert to its old status, and I guess, even now, things haven't changed too much in the States. Out here, however, it's a fighting machine, and that's all. If some of the taxpayers could only get an inkling of the job these boys are doing—see how they are living and the conditions they have to put up with—and if they could see the courage and guts they show in combat, it would be an education to them.

Letter to Lee, October 8, 1942

Your letters are coming through quite frequently. Sometimes one will get on an airplane and come right through in two weeks, and sometimes it will take them two months to get here. It doesn't really matter because they all tell me what I want to know—that you are happy and busy and that you still love me.

I told you how I felt about camping out when our time came. Thank all the nice people who offered us cabins for me and tell them that I've had enough of life in the raw to do me for a while. You and I are going to run off by ourselves but will do it where we can have lights and music and hot water and beds and real food and a martini before dinner. OK??

Darling, I don't think you'll know your husband when you see him again. Everyone here looks several years older than they did three months ago, and I'm no exception. In addition, I've lost about twenty pounds and feel much better for it, but it will sure make my clothes hang on me like a scarecrow's. I've also let my mustache grow in again, and after a couple months, it is quite respectable. You'd be surprised.

Letter to Mom and Dad, October 11, 1942

Two days ago, they had a little ceremony out here, and Admiral [Aubrey] Fitch came over and gave a Distinguished Flying Cross (DFC) to my bombardier and me for a mission* we pulled last month. It was just a small affair, but there were some reporters around taking pictures and stuff, so you may hear about it. I'll be ashamed to come home if this keeps up. Somehow I always get the publicity, and there are any number of boys out here who've done a much better job than I have. Folks will begin to think I spend all my time getting my picture taken while everyone else fights the war. It just seems to happen that way. At least it's the only way I can let you know what I'm doing. I can't tell you in my letters, but they can put it in the papers. Seems foolish, doesn't it?

The medal is a beauty. They were going to give me the Navy Cross but gave me this instead, and the Army has me in for a DFC also, which means I'll have an Oak Leaf Cluster to pin on it some day. All very fine to show off after the war, but right now, they aren't worth a dime a dozen.

The last few days have been the most rugged since I arrived in these parts. We flew on a mission that was really a dilly. It so happened I had a war correspondent with me. He's down here to give a picture of what the boys are doing and how they are living. His name is Bill Tyree of the United Press, and he's a mighty fine gent. His wife and baby daughter live in Westwood, right near Santa Monica. We sure made a Christian out of him on this trip, and he is busy now writing what he says is the best story yet from down here. He says he is the first correspondent to ever go out on a raid with a Flying Fortress crew. I don't know what he'll have to say, but you'll enjoy reading it because he really knows whereof he speaks, and he should be able to give a pretty accurate picture if they let him print much of it. He had his photographer take pictures of our whole crew. You may see those in your paper, too.

Report from the United Press, October 12, 1942 (Delayed)

United Press Correspondent Accompanies Maj. Edmundson of Santa Monica on Air Raid

BY WILLIAM TYREE

Slugs from a Zero's 7.7 machinegun smashed the navigator's window and ricocheted through the nose of our Flying Fortress.

---

* The mission of 19 August.

Another Zero in front of us speeded to rake our formation. I thought of saying the Lord's Prayer but there wasn't time. As I stared at the oncoming Zero a stream of tracers burst from the tailgun of the Fortress ahead and the Japanese plane crashed, exploding on what our bombs had left of the Buka airfield.

This engagement was a part of two air battles that proved to me that it takes a special kind of courage to fly over Japanese-infested territory in the northern Solomons, batter their major airfield at Buka with heavy bombs, and then roar down and smash a concentration of 38 enemy ships at Shortland harbor. I know, because I rode with them all the way through a flock of Zeros and antiaircraft fire. And I found out that these boys who fly the big B-17s have what it takes.

The task of the flight with which I hitched a ride was to cripple Japan's massed air and sea power attempting to wrest the Solomons from the Marines. Everyone expected trouble.

As we approached Buka, the first objective, we took a last cigarette before putting on oxygen masks. Mine tasted bitter. Pilot Maj. James V. Edmundson of Santa Monica, Cal., smiled reassuringly at me, and asked if I was scared.

I was petrified.

Second Lt. Hulbert Burroughs of Los Angeles, son of the author Edgar Rice Burroughs, hoisted himself onto the catwalk in the bomb bay. We skimmed across Buka passage, a narrow strip of water separating Bougainville and Buka Islands. It was 9:01 as we started the bombing run and Sgt. Albert Durham of McMinnville, Tenn. patted me on the back and said, "Here we go, Chum." Down below I saw three Zeros taking off from the sandy runway. Bursts of antiaircraft fire blossomed in the sun 100 feet ahead.

Lt. Albert N. Thom, of Noblesville, Ind., the bombardier, jammed his head into the sight. Seconds later our bombs fell. Explosions ripped the runway, throwing up geysers of sand and dirt. One apparently hit a fuel dump, for black smoke gushed up. Then the Zeros hit us.

Speeding straight down Bougainville Island, our formation roared toward Shortland harbor where the Japanese has massed a fleet including two battleships, cruisers, destroyers and transports.

The battleships appeared much fatter. They saw us coming and opened up with ack-ack* that piled up higher and higher as they found the range. I could see orange flames bursting from the guns below.

---

* Anti-aircraft fire.

One shell exploded below the bomber in which I was a passenger and the concussion blew us up 100 feet.

Then we dropped our bombs. Several hit a cargo ship; a cruiser circling nearby got a bomb and another cargo ship blazed in the tropical sunshine.

All our planes went through the shrapnel-speckled sky safely, but there still was more trouble facing us. Ten more Zeros swooped out of the clouds, coming from all directions. This time we felt like a cat about to lose its ninth life.

Our guns chattered again. One of the attackers exploded, and another seemed to disintegrate. Still they came. Then large cumulous clouds loomed ahead, and we ducked into them just ahead of the Zeros on our tail. When we came out, the Zeros were waiting for another pass at us, but we made it into another cloud and lost them.

Back at our own field early in the afternoon, we learned that at least five Zeros had been shot down by our formation in the battle over the harbor. All our planes returned, but in one of them were a dead navigator and two wounded crewmen.

Corp. Howard Cantor of Mount Vernon, N.Y.; Pvt. V. M. Uriegas of Austin, Tex.; Pvt. William Beckham, Dublin, Ga.; and Corp. Samuel Salvo, Pittston, Pa., crawled out of the gun turrets of my plane, grinning.

"Boy, it sure is good to still be alive, isn't it?" Cantor asked me. I agreed.

Letter to Lee, October 18, 1942

Here I sit, sweltering in the heat with the flies crawling all over me. Not very inspirational, but I'll do as well as I can with this letter under the circumstances.

Received four letters from you yesterday. One regular letter about a month old and three V-Mail* letters almost two months old. It seems that the V-Mail has been taking longer to get here than normal mail. The delay is all in getting photographed in the States before it gets under way. It's a good idea, but Army red tape, as usual, has spoiled all the advantage they may have had. I, too, feel

---

* A one-sided piece of paper with space for the recipient's name and address and a message from the sender. Once completed, it was censored and photographed onto 16mm film. The filmstrip was sent to the addressee's general location, and each individual message was printed onto a piece of 5 × 4–inch paper. These were put into envelopes and were then ready for the mailbag delivery. Regular mail had to compete for airplane space with food, fuel, ammunition, and other supplies, and, as a result, was often left off cargo flights. V-Mail was designed to improve mail service, thereby boosting morale.

as you do that the letters lose their personal touch, which is the reason I haven't written to you that way. I'd rather get one real letter from you than a dozen of the others, and all the other boys out here feel the same way. They take longer in coming, and they aren't nearly as nice when they get here.

Darling, don't do too much for Christmas for me. I won't be able to send a single thing home to anyone, and I won't be there myself, either. This is going to be the most dismal holiday season I've ever had, but we'll just have to bear up and make our own plans for Christmas 1943. I might possibly be home by then, but don't count on it.

Things are moving so darn fast down here, and I'm so busy that I can't begin to write a respectable letter. Some day I'll be able to tell you the whole story. In the meantime, I'll just have to send you my love—all of it and forever and ever.

Letter to Lee, October 22, 1942

Two letters from you yesterday dated July 10th and 12th. They have probably been following me around from one stop to another all this time. Most of our mail however has been more recent than that. I've already gotten a couple of letters from you dated in September. I miss you more and more every day. Your letters are all that keeps me going.

Letter to Lee, October 26, 1942

Sure am proud of this Squadron of mine. We had a really tough mission yesterday. Bad weather all day, tough opposition over the target, home after dark in bad weather, and a landing with almost no lights in a poor field in the rain. They all performed like veterans. They stuck on my wing like flies, and the whole thing was a perfect piece of work from start to finish. As long as we can keep it up that way and with reasonable luck, I'll stand a good chance of seeing you all again. It sure is great to have boys behind you that you can depend on.

Letter to Mom and Dad, October 26, 1942

Just had an interruption while three reporters came into the tent and wanted to hear the story of yesterday's mission. Had quite a time, and I had my usual lucky horseshoe wrapped around my neck. Sure hope I can get out of here before I use up all my luck.

History is being made down here by our little bunch, but it will be a long time before it leaks out, and the real story will never get into print. Heads would sure roll if it did. Hope you get to read enough scraps about us down here in the papers to have some kind of an idea of what a job we're doing.

Sure makes my mouth water to hear you talking about Ted's steaks. It will be a big moment when I get my first real meal with fresh meat and vegetables and maybe a salad. Haven't tasted milk for four months.

You probably won't know me when you see me again. I've grown a mustache and lost about 20 pounds and feel about 50 years older although I only show about five of them. This will make an old man out of a guy in a short time—but then, you can't live forever.

chapter twenty-four

MISSION OF
25 OCTOBER 1942

With the capture of Henderson Field on Guadalcanal and its improvement so that it could accommodate B-17s, the scope of the 11th Group operations was considerably broadened. Reconnaissance missions for Henderson made it possible to locate Japanese naval forces. Also, strike efforts could be launched from there against enemy naval units as well as against Japanese bases in the northern Solomons. It became standard practice to keep a sizable number of aircraft and crews forward on Henderson, rotating them back to Espiritu Santo for major maintenance or short periods of crew rest.

Living conditions on Guadalcanal were less than ideal. We lived in a tent camp down by the Lunga River that was always deep in mud and bred the largest mosquitoes I've ever seen. Most of the crews accepted these conditions philosophically because as primitive as they were, they were an improvement on living conditions endured by the Marine ground troops.

Nights on Guadalcanal were periods of little or no sleep because of the constant harassment by nine Japanese bombers, referred to as "Washing Machine Charlie." These aircraft would circle over Henderson Field all night long dropping bombs with just sufficient frequency to keep everyone awake and out in the slit trenches where the mosquitoes could get to us.

We were also subjected to sporadic, night naval shelling. Daylight bombings by high altitude formations were quite frequent.

The mission of 25 October was a six-ship effort. We took off late in the afternoon from Henderson Field. Because Henderson was closed during the hours of darkness, we knew we would have to land at Espiritu Santo. The weather was extremely bad, and after forming up at low altitude over the field, I climbed out on instruments with my wingman holding tight formation in order to stay in visual contact.

Our target was a naval task force just south of Ramos Island in the northern Solomons. The weather cleared as we proceeded north, and we spotted the task force right where a submarine had reported them to be. We made our run at 12,500 feet and selected the largest vessel—a heavy cruiser—as our target. All the ships began taking violent evasive action and throwing flak upstairs thick enough to walk on. Our target went into a tight turn to the left, and Al Thom, my bombardier, with his usual skill, made the proper adjustment. Our bomb pattern was tight and completely covered the cruiser, making perhaps six or eight direct hits and many near misses.

The ship was later confirmed as sunk. The return to Espiritu Santo at night and through bad weather was a tribute to the celestial navigation ability of my navigator, Lt. Bill Adams. It was great to get on the ground.

Letter to Lee, October 30, 1942

Tomorrow is Halloween. That sure doesn't mean a thing down here. Remember Halloween last year? We ate over at Pattie's and had a jack-o'-lantern all carved in a pumpkin with four faces. If I remember correctly, Cod had just found out he was going to the States on a ferry trip, and I was quite jealous. What I wouldn't give for a trip like that right now.

Only three weeks until our second anniversary, Sweetheart. Sorry I can't send you anything, but you know I haven't forgotten it. We'll have to postpone our celebration until I get home, but we have a date. The first party we go to on my return, no matter what the date, will automatically become our anniversary, and we will celebrate accordingly. Darling, I hope you never have to put up with another year of married life like your second one has been. This is one of the things we're fighting for. We have to clean up this world once and for all so that we can come home and spend our time making our wives happy and raising families.

Hope we have enough money to pay our taxes in March. The way I figure it, they will come to well over $1,000. I can't understand why you haven't gotten the money I've sent you. You should have received $900 worth of money orders by this time.

The old war goes on as usual. Sometimes things look as black as the dickens, and sometimes it seems as though we are out of the woods, but we just keep slugging along and hope for the best.

You've heard the song the boys in the P.I. [Philippine Islands] are singing.

"We're Battling Bastards of Bataan,
No mama, no papa, no Uncle Sam"

[Following is the song to which Duke refers.]]

We're Battling Bastards of Bataan
No mama, no papa, no Uncle Sam
No aunts, no uncles, no cousins, no nieces,
No pills, no planes, no artillery pieces,
And nobody gives a damn!

FRANK HEWLETT, 1942

That's about how we feel sometimes. It sure makes you proud of the American fighting men to see how the boys are doing—the Navy and Air Force and especially the Marines. If the brains running this show were as good as the boys who are fighting it, the whole thing would have been over by now. Someday "the brains" will have a plan so our boys can fight without 5-to-1 odds against them, and then the world will see how really good the American boys are.

Letter to Lee, November 5, 1942

Hi Sweetheart!! I've been thinking about you so much lately—more even than usual. If I don't get to see you pretty soon, I'll go over the hill. We are now going into our 11th month apart, and that is much too long. Nearly a year.

I've changed location for a short while again. I had to take my airplane back while it was put in shape to fly again, so my whole crew and I are getting three or four days of much needed rest. Then we'll be back at it hot and heavy again.

No mail through to us in nearly a month, so I'm way behind in my news of your comings and goings.

Letter to Lee, November 22, 1942

Yesterday was our anniversary, Sweetheart, and what a farce it was for us to celebrate our second year so far apart. You were so close to me all day. I kept thinking about us. Remembering how beautiful you were in your wedding dress and how sweet your pikaki lei smelled and about our little house over in Kailua. That was the finest day of my life, but I honestly believe that the day we are together again will be a more wonderful day for the two of us. I hope, my darling, that we live to celebrate 75 wedding anniversaries and that we never have to observe another one while we are separated. For that matter, you'll have a pretty tough time getting away from me again when I once get my hands on you. I sent a cable from here, which should have reached you on the big day. I hope it came through all right. Not much to it but just a few words to let you know that you still have a husband way out here someplace who loves you more than anything else in the world.

A happy marriage is the most wonderful thing that can happen to any two people, and you and I certainly have that. After the war is over (which shouldn't be too terribly long now), we'll have a chance to cash in on some of our happiness and will both always be better in our hearts for having taken the part that we have in this thing. It will make our appreciation of life much greater for having gone through all we have, and neither of us will have anything to be ashamed of. That means a lot to a man.

Darling, it's been nearly 11 months since I've seen you. It seems longer, but it takes more than time and distance to separate us. I've read that in books before, but it's true nevertheless. You are as close to me now as you ever have been. A dozen times a day, I'll see something or think of something and turn around to tell you about it, fully expecting to see you right beside me smiling up at me, and it always comes as a shock to find you aren't there.

This is an awfully sentimental letter. I hope you'll forgive me, but that's just the way I feel. Wish I could tell you where I am and all about what it's like and what I've been doing, but that will have to wait. Someday we'll be able to talk the whole thing over.

Please tell my parents that I am in the rear [Auckland, New Zealand] having a rest and am doing just fine. We've been eating steaks and eggs three meals a day ever since we got here with ice cream thrown in between meals, and I'm getting back some weight.

Letter to Lee, November 29, 1942

When I got here yesterday, there were about 20 letters from you waiting for me, and I've been reading constantly ever since. Sweetheart, you are perfect. Without you to love, this old war wouldn't be worth fighting.

I'm glad you've decided to stop using the V-Mail. It isn't as much fun to get, and it takes two to three weeks longer to come through.

Letter to Lee, December 5, 1942

As you can see from the return address, I've lost my squadron. Col. Saunders pulled me up into his group staff as Executive Officer. It's a step up, in a way, *but I sure don't like it. It means that my days of combat flying are practically over. The only time I'll get to go out now will be when I go along with somebody else. I argued about it until I was blue in the face, but it did no good. I'll just have to start figuring and working again like I did right after the war until I can get back on a combat assignment, but in the meantime, I'll have to make the best of my present job. It will be interesting although, of course, I'd rather be flying.*

Col. Saunders has been in need of someone on his staff who has combat experience, and it's really quite an honor because it makes me second in command of the Group. Might as well look on the bright side.

We had a big party last night in the squadron to mark my leaving. I sure hate to leave the outfit and that crew of mine.

Letter to Lee, December 9, 1942

Darling, it should be pretty close to Christmas by the time this letter reaches you. Golly, that's hard to realize. We used to get so darn much fun out of the Christmas season, and this year it won't mean a solitary thing. Next year will be much different.

Just received an order issued in Hawaii in September saying that I had been given an Air Medal for sinking that sub last January. Fine time to find out. The Air Medal is a new one, and nobody has ever seen it or knows what it looks like yet. As soon as they design it, I'll get one. Lots of recommendations have been made from this area, and if they go through, we'll all look like a 5-and-10-cent store window. The old red tape appears to be well wrapped around our medals, however, and we'll probably never get any from here. MacArthur gives his to his men direct, but ours have to chase twice around the world with stopovers at 400 desks before they are approved.

Capt. Eddie Rickenbacker was in last night and most of today. He sure is a wonderful man. I spent a large part of the morning just listening to him talk about his auto racing days and his adventures in the last war and his latest adventure floating for 21 days in a rubber boat. I sure do like him. We've had many so-called big shots go through here on "tours of inspection," but he is far and away the finest of the crop.

Letter to Lee, December 18, 1942

Nearly Christmas—it's hard to believe, but it's time. Some of the boys got down to civilization to arrange for presents to be delivered back home, but I got there too late and, of course, from here I won't even be able to send a cable or anything. Don't think for a minute you are forgotten, My Sweet. Our next Christmas will be a record breaker with a beautiful tree and presents and stockings by the fireplace and Tom & Jerrys and all the rest of the fancy trimmings. Christmas has always been such a big day for me that I hate to let one go by, but at that, we are both alive and can look forward to being together again in six months or so. At least it's a better prospect than we had last Christmas.

Glad you got my wire, Angel. I was lucky to be where I could send you one on our day.

Haven't been writing very often because I'm just about out of stamps, and I have to make them last. They are just about impossible to get, and the only stationery I have left is this Air Mail stationery you sent me, which can't be used for anything but Air Mail, and that has to be stamped. Free mail has to go in plain envelopes. What a situation!

Letter from Dad, December 21, 1942

Nora and I are most happy about your being chosen by Colonel Saunders because of your ability, enthusiasm and complete devotion to the idea of doing your utmost. We feel sure that this position will afford you far greater opportunity to help bring about a quicker victory with all the resultant saving of pain and sorrow.

Your zeal, ability and experience will give the needed support to the boys in your outfit and a big boost to the accomplishments of your Group. Also it gives you the chance to do the really big thing of sacrificing your personal inclinations to the much more important and vital, if not so colorful, phases of the service.

That was a happy thought—you letting us know what to send you—two boxes of Roi-Tan cigars have been on their way for two days. Am enclosing 50 Air Mail stamps. Anything else you want, let us know. I told you that Mr. and Mrs. Burges gave me a buck to spend for something to send you, so you can consider that they gave you one of those boxes of cigars.

Yesterday Lee was up here, and we had a nice visit. Lee is looking swell—she is certainly a wonderful girl—so much to her—very clever—genuine and fine principles. Along with your country—she is plenty to fight for.

Letter to Lee, December 20, 1942

You were talking about wearing your Army wings. The next time you go to the field at Long Beach, you should stop at the P.X. [Post Exchange] and buy *yourself a pair of Senior Pilot wings—the ones with the star on top. They have cut the Senior Pilot requirements down to five years service and 2,000 hours flying time, so I am now a Senior Pilot, and I wear the wings with the star, so you, too are entitled to them.*

Letter to Mom and Dad, December 20, 1942

They are planning a big decoration ceremony here in a few days. Nobody knows who's going to get what yet, but at least some of the stuff has caught up with us. If medals and press notices could only win the war, but somehow the Japs never seem to read the stuff our reporters write, and they never get to see how impressive our medals are because we never wear them. However, just like the frosting on a cake, all the fancy trimmings serve their purpose. They make the boys feel like somebody appreciates them, but it can be easily overdone. Eddie Rickenbacker said the toughest thing he's had to do throughout his life is to keep from believing all he read about himself. He sure is a swell gent, and it's hard to believe that anyone as quiet and unassuming as he is has been a public hero for 30 years. Woe be unto the guy who starts taking himself seriously.

Letter to Lee, December 22, 1942

We had a big ceremony here this morning, and there were a bunch of Generals and Admirals wandering around pinning ribbons and medals on everybody. I got my share. The box office score is now Purple Heart, Air Medal with an Oak Leaf Cluster, Silver Star, and Distinguished Flying Cross with two Oak Leaf Clusters. You can look them up on that chart I gave you and see what they look like. We aren't allowed to receive more than one of any particular medal. In lieu of second and third awards, we receive a little metal Oak Leaf Cluster to pin on it, so for all intents and purposes, I have two Air Medals and three DFCs. The Air Medal hasn't been cast yet, but we received the bar ribbon, and it is quite pretty, blue and gold. It won't be on your chart. That makes seven awards in the first year of the war, which isn't bad. If the next two or three years are as kind to me, I'll sure look like an old soldier when it's over. As one of the boys said, the decoration he wants to wear home after the war is his own skin, and I think he has something there. There really isn't much more I can get anyway, except the Distinguished Service Medal and the Soldier's Medal, which are all too high awards for me to shoot at. They are nearly all of the posthumous variety.

Chances of our getting home within the next six months are beginning to look slimmer all the time. I talked to some of the boys in the know today, and from what they had to say, I just don't see it in the cards. I may be wrong, of course, but it looks like a long, hard winter. Keep your little chin up, Sweetheart, it can't last forever.

We still have an awful lot to do here, and I'll be able to come home with a much cleaner conscience if I feel the job has been done. Col. Saunders is a wonderful guy, and I want to stay with him as long as I can. Possibly he and I will return together, and he'll keep me on with him so we can go out together to some other corner of the world and fight.

There's one way to look at this, Darling. There is no such thing as coming home to stay. We come home and get one month's leave, spend two months training new units, and we're off again. Therefore, we aren't really losing any time together because I'll only be home with you a month anyway. If I had come home a month ago, I'd be on my way out somewhere else again, and our wonderful dream would be over. At least, this way, we still have it to look forward to, and this is all that keeps me going. Does this make sense?

Letter to Lee, December 27, 1942

On the afternoon of the 23rd, I found I was going to be gone from here on Christmas, so I opened the packages that evening. Sweetheart, you sent me just exactly what I wanted. The socks are beautiful. I'm going to save them for my homecoming. Everything else was badly needed—razor blades, soap, shaving cream, tooth brushes, and Air Mail stamps. They were pretty well glued together, but by careful work with a razor blade, I split them apart and didn't spoil a single one.

My darling, you are so sweet and thoughtful about everything I can hardly wait for our next Christmas to come so I can shower you with presents and spoil you rotten.

I left here early in the morning on the day before Christmas and was gone until today. I sure was a dirty, tired specimen when I returned. It was a very poor Christmas day. Hope we never have another like it.

Letter to Mom and Dad, January 11, 1943

Col. Saunders has been made a General and returned to the States, which leaves me, for the time being, in command of the 11th Group. Quite some job.

Of course, it will only last for a very short time. Sure did hate to see Col.
Saunders go. He's a fine soldier, and I sure enjoy working for him.

Letter from Dad, January 18, 1943

Perhaps you do not know the new postal rules about letters and packages
coming from us. V-Mail letters are to be the only ones that will be sure of going
by air. Also, we cannot mail packages without showing a request from the soldier
and the consent of his commanding officer for the item mailed. All of which, I
suppose is well justified by the importance of "passing the food and ammu-
nition" first. Anyway, just before the rules went into effect, I mailed you a box
of Roi-Tans.

chapter twenty-five

HOW TO WIN
WHILE LOSING, III

Being a major and commander of a B-17 squadron was pretty tall cotton for a knuckle-headed kid who was just barely smart enough to find his way from his tent down to his airplane and back. I kind of enjoyed it except for those unpleasant periods when very unfriendly people were either trying to shoot you out of the sky or blow you up on the ground.

Eventually, the field on Espiritu Santo was completed. It was much more habitable than Efate and a much shorter run up to where most of our targets were. When the Marines had pretty well secured the airfield on Guadalcanal, it was renamed Henderson Field, and we began staging B-17s into Henderson, where we were even closer to our work.

Early in 1943, I was in command of the advanced B-17 party at Henderson. Those were busy days. We'd go out and bomb them in the daytime, and every night, they'd send in a lone bomber that we called "Washing Machine Charlie" because of how his engines sounded to drop bombs on us all night long. Every so often, a Japanese battleship would come whistling down The Slot (New Georgia Sound) in the middle of the night and lob 16-inch shells in at us. We didn't really get an awful lot of sleep, which wasn't too bad, but it kept us out from under our mosquito nets for most of the nights—and the mosquitoes on Guadalcanal were as big as hummingbirds. Also, they carried malaria, and the Atabrine* they were giving us wouldn't protect us from malaria—it just kept the symptoms under control so we could fly. Most of us were far from the hearty beach boys that had come down from Honolulu. I weighed about 120, and I was one of the fat guys.

---

* A synthetic drug in the form of an extremely bitter pill. Because the correct dosage had not been determined, its effect on combating malaria was minimal. Side effects included nausea, headaches, vomiting, and a yellow hue to the skin.

Around the middle of February, another squadron commander flew up to Henderson to relieve me, and it was my turn to head south to Espiritu Santo for a while, where you could get a bit more sleep and the food was almost civilized. Captain Jack Thornhill and his crew were scheduled to ferry a B-17 back to Espiritu Santo that had been pretty well shot up and needed fixing. I decided to go along as commander. It had a number 4 engine that was in bad shape, but we could use it at about half throttle for take-off. After we were airborne, with the gear and flaps up, we could feather it and continue on our way with the other three. The only things I had with me, other than the uniform I was wearing and my .45 (which I wore even when I went to bed) were my shaving kit and a ton of dirty clothes. I loaded my laundry and kit into a B-4 bag and dumped it into the back of the airplane.

We launched as scheduled, feathered* number 4, and everything was looking fine until along the coast of an island named San Cristobal in the southern Solomons, the number 2 engine began to cough and sputter and was feathered. This left us with two engines, and we weren't about to get very far in that condition, so we did a quick 180-degree turn and headed back toward Henderson. Just a couple of minutes later, number 3 coughed and quit, and we had no place to go but down. With only one engine pulling power, we made a beautiful splash landing in calm, protected water a few hundred yards off the northern shore of San Cristobal. Other than getting wet, the only harm done to the airplane was to tear the tail cone off as we dragged in for a touchdown. We immediately climbed out the hatches onto the top of the fuselage, extracted and inflated the rubber life rafts, climbed aboard, and watched our airplane settle into the water. As it was getting ready for the last plunge toward the shallow bottom, the old B-17 burped and bubbled quite a bit—and just before it sank, my B-4 bag came floating peacefully out the waist gunner's hatch. I figured, "Why not?" and picked it up.

A New Zealand fisherman in his boat had seen us ditch. While we were still on the beach wondering what to do, he came by and told us that if we would give him our two rubber life rafts, he would take us down the island a little way to an Australian Coast Watcher Station. Among other facilities available here was a radio on which we could report in. It sounded like a

---

* Feathering alters the pitch of the blades and is used to reduce propeller drag and airflow resistance.

bargain, so we climbed aboard. In a few hours, we were with the coast watcher. He had quite an establishment, with a native Micronesian staff that kept his house, manned his radio, took care of first aid problems, cooked his meals, and ran the Australian flag up in the morning and down at night with considerable ceremony.

They took good care of us and fed us well. When they found out what was in my B-4 bag, my mess of dirty uniforms was washed and ironed as never before. In about three days, a Navy PBY landed in the bay to pick us up. The native men paddled us out to the PBY in a huge, hand-carved war canoe. The Navy flew us back to civilization. When we came marching back into Group Headquarters on Espiritu Santo, me with my B-4 bag full of sparkling-clean laundry, there was no question in my mind what would happen next. Sure enough! They shipped me back to the United States and promoted me to lieutenant colonel.

part four

WASHINGTON, D.C.;
MARIETTA, GEORGIA;
SALINA, KANSAS,
1943

chapter twenty-six

TOGETHER AGAIN

In the spring of 1943, the 11th Group was returned to Hawaii to remain, reequip, and return to the Pacific war. All of us old B-17 guys were returned to the U.S.—"Uncle Sugar," as we called it. I was flown back to Mather Field, next to Sacramento, California. I shipped ahead what baggage I had and began scrambling to find myself a flight to Long Beach.

When I arrived, Lee's mother met me with a smile and told me, "I feel as though I know you already, Jim. Just like my own boys when they were away at school. When they came home, the first I would see of them was a big bag of dirty laundry." Sure enough, my barracks bag of dirty uniforms had beaten me there. Meeting Lee's mother gave me a chance to appreciate where Lee got all her warmth and charm.

It was wonderful being with Lee again. She kidded me about my gold leaves and said that the only majors she had known were old fuddy-duds and that I had no business being a major. I gave her the only excuse I could come up with: "There's a war on, you know. They aren't putting the stuff into majors any more that they used to." We spent a few days in Long Beach with her folks and drove up to Santa Monica and spent a few days with mine, but the time was all too short. I received orders assigning me to the Air Staff at Army Headquarters in Washington, D.C. After a couple of weeks of rest and relaxation, we packed up the things we had, stowed it in our same little car, got a special issue of gasoline ration stamps to get us across the country, and were on our way.

Crossing the United States by automobile during the war was an adventure. There were none of the interstate highways and freeways that we have today. And because there was hardly any traffic on the road, we took our time, stopping to visit friends along the way. We made the most of it because we were getting into strange waters. We knew nothing about Washington, D.C., or what a staff assignment there would be like. We did know that, eventually, we would find out all about these things and would do it together. The war was still on. My buddies were flying and fighting and getting shot down all around the world, but Lee and I had a reprieve, a little bit of togetherness. We knew it wasn't going to last very long, but in the meantime, we were together.

Lee's letter to Mom and Dad, March 4, 1943

In unpacking my suitcases—I found the little poem I spoke to you about at one time. Here it is.

The Returned

BY ELMA DEAN

War is a paper word, a sound on air and still not touching us.
We are quite free to make our songs and slogans
And to wear our colors on our cloths for all to see.

But he was there.
He knows how very small men are
Or else how big when faced with death.

He knows some will run,
Some hold the failing wall
Only with courage and their final breath.

He has new quietness that seems to say:
The spirit's size is all there is to man
That boasting mouths will ultimately pray
And if we must, kill, die or starve, we can.

There is gentleness upon his face
As though he sees us from a far-off place.

chapter twenty-seven

WHERE'S THE PENTAGON?

We arrived in Washington on a cold, blustery day in March. I found a building that was marked WAR AND NAVY DEPARTMENT BUILDING, and with my orders in my hand, I strode in the door to report for duty. I saw nothing but Navy uniforms around, and everybody looked at me kind of funny. When I showed them my orders, I was quickly told that this building was only a Navy Annex now and that I needed to go to the Pentagon building. I asked where that was, and I was told, "Across the river, in Virginia." I went back out to the car to give Lee the news, and we set off, in the snow, to look for the Pentagon. It was a new building, reported to be the world's largest office building, and while it was still under construction, the War Department—and to some extent, the Navy Department—was already moving in. It wasn't shown on our map, but Lee and I were sure we could find it.

Those of you who have been there know that the Pentagon is surrounded by a maze of highways, off-ramps, on-ramps, traffic circles, overpasses, underpasses, and blind alleys. And none of this was yet on any map. We crossed the Potomac River on the 14th Street Bridge and could see the Pentagon looming large and white through the snow, up ahead of us. Now that we had it located, the next problem was figuring out how to get there.

Every time we found a road that seemed to be leading toward the Pentagon, it would suddenly make a big sweeping turn and dump us on a highway leading away from the Pentagon, and we'd have to drive for miles before we could get turned around. We made several tries with similar results. We finally decided that we'd try taking a road that seemed to lead away from the Pentagon and see what happened. We tried it, and it worked. Our road took a big loop, doubled back under itself, and dumped us in a big parking lot in the shadow of the big building. We parked and sat there in the snow and wondered what to do next. Now that we had located that darn Pentagon and found out how to get to it, the next thing was to figure out how to get into it. We decided that in Washington, nothing was going to be easy.

I told Lee to sit tight. There was a heater in the car, and she had a book to read. I told her that I shouldn't be gone too long, and I set off trudging through the snow. I figured that if I started walking around the building, I'd eventually come to a door. I started out counterclockwise and had walked the length of three sides before I found a place where the buses were going in. I followed them, climbed some stairs, and found myself in a sort of indoor mall.

I found some ramps and took them and walked forever before I found the Office of the Air Adjutant General. I showed some guy my orders and told him I'd like to have at least a week's leave to find a place to live and get squared away. He looked me in the eye and said, "Major, there's a war on, you know. Here's your assignment, and here's the room number where you are to report. You have two days." I said, "Fine. Now, how do I get out of this building?" He gave me instructions, but it was a different door from the one I had used coming in. I had no idea where the car was, so I picked clockwise this time and eventually found it. Lee had almost given up on me, asking, "What happened?" I told her that I had gotten lost, and we had two days to find a place to live. She said, "What!" I said, "Welcome to Washington," and gave her a kiss.

Lee's letter to Mom and Dad, March 3, 1943

Arrived in the capital this a.m. Hit a snow storm about 12 miles out. A thrilling sight for us, but golly, it is cold!! We are loving it.

The Dutchess and I are waiting in front of the Pentagon Building where Duke is reporting in. We have had a wonderful trip—will write very soon and tell you all. We are looking forward with enthusiasm to our Washington experience.

chapter twenty-eight

WASHINGTON DUTY

We found a house. It was a nice little place. We had delightful neighbors across the street and were only a couple of blocks away from a bus line where I could ride to work and let the bus drivers worry about finding the Pentagon for me. I found a pleasant boss, an empty desk, and some nice guys to work with (some of whom I knew), and it seemed that my job had something to do with airplanes. I wasn't quite sure about that, but I figured I could learn.

I quickly found out that I was a strange duck in the building. I was one of only a handful of guys who had pulled a combat tour and come home. I was supposed to have a lot more answers than I did. I also learned that they were always sending me off someplace to work on a problem. When I had to go someplace, they would phone over to Bolling Field and reserve an airplane to fly to wherever I was supposed to go. I never knew what kind of an airplane I was going to get. If it was an airplane I hadn't flown before, the crew chief would show me where all the important handles were, and I'd be on my way. Among other places, I went to Alaska and Greenland, and I had an extended trip to England and got in a couple of B-17 missions with the Eighth Air Force. It was really kind of an odd sort of a job.

Lee and I both knew that this was not the sort of place for us. We were together, and that was great, but I didn't feel happy sitting at my desk while I had so many good friends overseas getting shot at. Lee understood, bless her heart. She realized that I couldn't live with myself until I got back out again. Our life together was going to have to wait until the war was over.

I got to work one morning, and my boss told me that I had been promoted and to go downstairs and buy myself some silver leaves because I was now a lieutenant colonel. Lee had never been with me for a promotion. I was a second lieutenant when we met, but I got my silver bars while she was away on the mainland on a business trip. I made captain in Hawaii after she had gone home, and major in the South Pacific. I could hardly wait to get off that bus and walk home and show Lee my new lieutenant colonel leaves. She didn't even notice them. I finally asked her if she could see anything different about me. She looked me over and said that I looked about the same to her. "Didn't you see these?" I asked, pointing to my shoulders. "Oh, that," she said. "I just thought your gold major's leaves needed to be polished." I strongly suspected she was pulling my leg, but she never did admit it. She was a foxy little rascal.

Blondie Saunders, who had commanded the 11th Group in the South Pacific as a colonel, was assigned to the Pentagon, too. He was now a brigadier general. He called me into his office one day and asked me if I would like to go back to war in the B-29. It was a new, big bomber that was still under development, and nobody knew much about it. I told General Saunders that I sure would. Blondie told me that he had just gotten word that he was in the B-29 program, and he could get me in. He said, "Eddie, grab an airplane and tour the United States and see how many of the old 11th Group you can find and how many of them would like to go back to war. You can't tell them where they will be going or what they will be flying, but you can tell them that you and I will be in the outfit. If they decide to go, tell them they can expect orders to Marietta, Georgia, within two weeks." I grabbed a B-26, made about a ten-day loop of the United States, and found about 50 of our old South Pacific 11th Group gang who wanted to go with us.

Blondie had said that things were going to happen quickly, and he was right. I got my orders to Marietta in a few days, and Lee and I loaded up the car and hit the road. The guys in the office where I worked couldn't figure out how I got sprung from the five-sided building for a second tour when they hadn't yet gotten out for their first one. "Just lucky!" I told them. "Besides, there's a war on. You know?" If Lee hadn't been a good soldier, she never would have put up with it, but she knew something like this was coming, and she was prepared for it. And to make things even more difficult for her, she was pregnant.

Lee's Letter to Mom and Dad, March 9, 1943

It has been almost impossible to write sooner. We have been on the go every minute we've been here. First, looking for a place to live and, miraculously enough, finding a house the second day—a very dirty one. Both Duke and I have been digging away at the dirt—getting it livable.

Duke is to be stationed here permanently—that is, as permanent as anything is these days. Isn't that wonderful news? He really just started to work yesterday, and everything is a bit new just now. But it seems that he may be making little trips around—so we have a flying salesman in the family. He may be gone a week or two on such trips—maybe less and sometimes even more, but anyway, he won't be gone for so long a time as this past separation.

I'm supposed to pick Duke up from work, but the Dutchess won't budge. She says it's just too darn cold. We've had one snowstorm since our first day.

Our little house is brick, as are so many here. It has two bedrooms, bath, kitchen, dining room, living room with a fireplace, and a large basement with adjoining bedroom. It is furnished, after a fashion, except for linens. We had fun shopping for sheets, blankets, towels, etc. We found two blankets, 50% wool and 50% cotton. They will tide us over until ours come.

Am just so busy getting our establishment organized and thinking up good things to cook—I hardly know what the front of our house looks like. I'm having too much fun inside—and we love it!

Lee's letter to Mom and Dad, March 12, 1942

It's 8 a.m.—Duke has just left for the office. The dishes can wait and so can the bed, the picking up and the dusting and a hundred other little things. I want to chat with you this morning.

Duke usually leaves about this time and has been getting home between 6:30 and 7 in the evenings. We don't know just yet how his Sundays will work out. Seems so many of the boys work that day too—taking one Sunday off every two months or every three or four months. Duke is finding his work very interesting. He is in a position where he has access to all the available inside information concerning the war—from all fronts all over the world—what our Allies and we are doing, as well as what our enemy has done, etc.

Today he has to talk to the Civilian Defense in Washington about Black-outs, Dim-outs, etc. And too, he will make a trip to talk with the group of men who compile weather maps of the world to give them information from the part of the world where he has been.

He hasn't been too pleased with what is termed "The Washington Attitude." I'm not quite sure that I just understand what that means, but these last few days, he has been so interested and busy in his work that "The Washington Attitude" hasn't been mentioned.

Letter to Mom and Dad, April 13, 1943

It has been quite a revelation to me to see all that goes on around here. It's kind of aggravating to see so many officers riding the gravy train, and yet it has certainly been interesting because I've gotten a look into some of the big plans as well.

This is quite a place and is really interesting, but I'd hate to stay here too long. They are in the midst of a big reorganization right now, and no telling where I'll be or what I'll be doing when I go back to work. Sure hope I can get away from here in a few months and get back into action again. I'm not cut out to be a desk pilot.

Sure haven't been able to get in very much flying, but what flying I have done has all been in little ships, so I'm getting back in form on my acrobatics. Kind of fun for a change.

Lee's letter to Mom and Dad, June 3, 1943

Now, for a big bit of news. Please sit down because this is big news. How are you both going to like being called Grandmother and Grandfather come this December? Sounds grand to us! We are so happy about it. Thought we could keep it a secret and really surprise you, but we just couldn't. We have to share our happiness, and who would we better share with than our dear family? I feel like I have a one-track mind these days. This gives us much to look forward to and much to get ready for.

Letter to Lee from Dad, June 7, 1943

Our precious daughter—thanks for your sweet and clever letter and the wonderful news! Everyone is thrilled to death and very happy. The homestead is in an uproar. Uncle Al at once remembered having seen a particularly swell blanket somewhere—Elsie has a special pattern for something or other—Nora knows an old lady who is famous for making such wonderful so-and-sos. Everybody is plotting and planning!

Lee's letter to Mom and Dad, June 20, 1943

Our Duke is wandering again. This time he's in Greenland!! Isn't that something! He expects to be back this Tuesday or Wednesday, depending on the weather.

*The night before he left, we had dinner again with Capt. George Putnam,
Amelia Earhart's husband, a publisher in his own right. He loaned me several
books to read while Duke was away—two of his own. One is* Wide Margins,
his autobiography, and the other is Soaring Wings, *his biography of Amelia.
In his writings, I've run across two familiar names, Waldo Waterman and
David Malcomson. Mums wrote that you might be spending today with them.
I'm wondering if that is where you all are, and I'm very much tempted to phone
and say hello. Would, too, if restrictions on long distance calls weren't so that it
would be practically impossible to convince the operator that my call was an
important one.*

chapter twenty-nine

MARIETTA, GEORGIA

In 1943, Marietta, Georgia, was a quiet little southern country town, clustered around a town square. Today, Atlanta has spread out like an amoeba and engulfed Marietta completely. The airport, just out of town, was a small one, where a big hangar had been built as the first installment of the Lockheed factory that was coming. The B-29 Project was housed in a farmhouse in the back reaches of the field. Offices had been set up in the farmhouse, and this was the temporary home of the budding 58th Bomb Wing. Planning was under way there for four B-29 groups to be activated on four bases in Kansas. After the four groups were in place, the 58th Wing planned to move to Kansas and expand into an active Bombardment Wing Headquarters. We had one YB-29 there in Marietta in which we could check out.

Lee and I found a house on the outskirts of Marietta, where we rented a room and a bath. We ate all our meals at a little restaurant on the town square that we referred to as "The Greasy Spoon." Lee and I soon learned that no other officers in the B-29 Project were bringing their wives to Marietta. Lee was the only wife in the outfit. Three young bachelors found rooms in the house across the street from us, and Lee took on the role of a mother hen. She seldom went anyplace without multiple escorts, and as her pregnancy advanced, she became the object of affection to what was probably the largest male harem in Georgia.

General K. B. Wolfe was the commander of the 58th Wing. He had an engineering background and had been a pivotal figure in the development of the B-29. General Saunders was G-3, Director of Operations, but it was clear that when the B-29 Program moved from the developmental to the combat phase, he would be moving up to the commander's spot. Blondie had promised to release me from the headquarters after the fourth group was in place, and I could have a squadron in the last group.

By fall of 1943, the four groups had been activated in Kansas, and the wing headquarters was ready to leave Marietta. It was the parting of the ways, once more, for Lee and me. She was warned against flying in her condition, and I took her to the railroad station in Atlanta and got her on a train headed for Long Beach. The trip was long and tiresome for her. She had a long layover in New Orleans, and a kindly hotel there that was full to the brim found a place for her to get a few hours of sleep between trains.

I took off for Smoky Hill Army Airfield at Salina, Kansas, where the 468th Group was being assembled. It was a relief to know that Lee was back with her folks and would probably be there until the end of the war.

Things were not yet clear what the future had in store for me. We were manning the outfit, equipping it with B-29s that were still going through testing and had no idea how long it would take us to get combat ready, nor to what part of the world we would be sent after we were ready.

chapter thirty

SALINA, KANSAS

My tour at Smoky Hill Army Airfield was short but busy. The days were about 48 hours long. New assignees would, walk in each day, and they would be greeted and put to work. Our job was to get combat ready in B-29s while they were still inventing the airplanes. We had one B-29 per squadron, most of the time. The majority of our training was done in B-17s and B-26s. During our months in Salina, I checked out all 15 of my pilots in B-29s, myself. It was a cold and snowy winter, and we lived in temporary barracks, heated with coal stoves.

On November 30, I received a phone call from Lee's mother, telling me that Lee had just given birth to a healthy baby boy. We had agreed on the name, Edwin James, after my B-17 navigator, Edwin J. Lannigan, who was killed in the South Pacific. I got to talk to Lee a couple of days later, and she sounded happy. She had located a house to rent, not too far from her folks, and she had found a lady to come in and help with Ed. I was extremely proud of her.

I took a few days off over Christmas and flew out to see her and to meet Ed. It was quite an event. It really wasn't a fancy Christmas, but it was pretty wonderful for Lee and me. It ended all too quickly. I went back to Kansas to continue getting ready to take the B-29s into combat, and Lee went back to the job of being the best little mother in the world and waiting for the war to be over.

Letter to Mom and Dad, September 27, 1943

I hope you both don't feel too bad about my getting into a combat outfit again and preparing to move out once more. Please understand that I'm just not able to stay in the States and take it easy as long as this war is still going on. We have much to do before it is all over for good, and I just have to be in there swinging. I wish it could be otherwise, but it can't be. I am now the Squadron Commander of the 792nd Squadron. I have a swell bunch of kids, all eager and good pilots. I'm as happy as I can be with the job. I feel sure that in the next few months, I'll be able to teach them some tricks that I wish someone had taught me before I went out the first time, and I feel sure that we'll be able to do a real job with this airplane of ours. It's a pilot's dream ship. I've never flown anything like it before.

It's a big relief to me to know that Lee has found herself a home and will be able to settle down for a while. Without a family, she could have followed me around over the country, living in hotel rooms and eating in restaurants as some of the wives are doing, but we wanted a family enough to make the sacrifices that are necessary. I'm glad she's back there where she can be near you and where I can fly out and see you all every month or so.

This is sure the wrong way to have a child. I should be around to help her over the rough spots, but it's this way or not at all. She is sure a swell little soldier about it all. Not many people would be able to understand how I feel about this war and be able to put up with all it brings forth the way she does.

One of these days it will all be over, and then we will be able to live the way we want to again. That's the one bright spot—it can't last forever.

Letter to Mom and Dad, October 7, 1943

Lee tells me you are taking good care of her in the way of baby equipment. She sure is a brick to carry on the way she is, ands she sure appreciates all the help you are giving her.

I hope to get out there for a day in a couple of weeks—if I can swing the deal.

Everything here is going according to schedule. I'm as happy as a lark with my Squadron, and the new airplane of ours is a dream. It will sure do a job in a hurry. I've flown 32 hours in the last four days, so you can see how we are hitting the ball.

Letter to Lee, December 1, 1943

I love you, I love you, I love you. At this point I'm so completely overwhelmed I can't think of anything else. Golly, Honey, you sure came through with a surprise, and I just can't seem to realize it. This business of being so far away from you when this happens is the bunk. Sweetheart, it takes all the willpower I have not to go down and climb into an airplane and come out to see you.

Your mother was awfully tired when she phoned me and quite a little confused. I had an awful time finding out from her how you were and how bad it had been for you and whether everything was okay. I sort of gathered that all *was well, or she would have told me so, but it was awfully unsatisfactory. I'll never be so far away from you again at a time like this.*

Darling, forget everything I've ever said about little babies not being pretty. I just know he's beautiful. He'd have to be, being yours. I can't wait to see you both, my Darling.

Golly, I was in a storm yesterday when your mother called. It was about 1 o'clock in the afternoon and her call left me in a complete spin. It just so happened that I had loaned Clink some money and just had bought $20 worth of whisky, and I was stone-broke. It was the last day of the month, and I didn't have a cent. I borrowed $20 from one of the boys and borrowed Clink's car (the Dutchess is out of gas and has a dead battery) and went to Salina. I sent you two dozen roses and went to about 50 drug stores until I found a guy who would sell me a box of cigars. I had enough money left to send you a telegram, and I was broke again. I got paid today and sent some telegrams right off.

Everyone was so happy about it all. We had a big celebration party at the club last night that lasted until 2:30 this morning, and I don't feel so sharp today, but you don't become a father just every day.

My Darling, I'm still so completely overwhelmed and breathless I can't get things down so they make sense. It's just too wonderful to believe.

As soon as you can, my Sweetheart, telephone me and tell me how you are and what he looks like and all about everything.

All my love to you, my darling wife, and to Ed. May he be as sweet as his mother. You explain to him that his old man will be home again someday and to stay!

part five

CHINA-BURMA-INDIA, 1944–45

chapter thirty-one

CIGARS AND MUSTACHE WAX

In March of 1944, we began receiving the B-29s. These were the first we had seen with operational remote control gunnery systems and operational pressurization systems. We had to change all engines, across the board, to the new combat-ready engines. The Ground Echelon of our group had already left to travel to our destination by boat, and the combat crews changed the 240 engines in the 60 B-29s of our group. It was a relief to be finally on our way. And we finally learned where we were going: to the China-Burma-India Theater.

We flew from Salina to Goose Bay, Labrador; across the Atlantic to Marrakech, Morocco; over northern Africa to Cairo, Egypt; through the Middle East to Karachi, India; to what was going to be our home base, Kharagpur, India. It was quite a trip.

Our base in Kharagpur, about 125 miles west of Calcutta, was pretty primitive. We lived in *bashas*, which are thatched huts with concrete floors. We arrived at the beginning of the monsoon season, when the temperature would level off at 120 degrees during the day and cool down to about 100 at night. During the monsoon season, it rained every day from 10 o'clock in the morning to 4 o'clock in the afternoon. The humidity was so high that mildew formed in our shoes every night while we slept. We also had a base in interior China, in the Chengtu Valley. We slept in tents in China. Our base was called Pengshan.

Much of our effort went into flying bombs and gasoline over the Himalaya Mountains, past Mount Everest. It took 12 round trips over the Hump* to get enough fuel and bombs forward to support one combat sortie out of China. From Pengshan, we hit targets in Taiwan, China, Manchuria, and the Japanese home islands. From our base in India, we flew combat missions against targets in Bangkok, Thailand; Kuala Lumpur, Malaya; and Singapore. On the longest combat mission of World War II,

---

* The east end of the Himalayas.

we staged out of Trincomalee, Ceylon, and bombed the oil refinery in Palembang, Sumatra. In August, our group commander, Ted Faulkner, was shot down over Singapore. General Curtis LeMay moved me up to command the group; three months later, I was promoted to full colonel.

Lee and I wrote religiously. She was hard pressed to find much to write about except Ed's progress, but news from home was still pretty wonderful. Mail, when it came, was the biggest event in any of our lives. Much of what we were doing couldn't be written about, and our letters home were all heavily censored, so there wasn't much for me to tell her.

Even under these conditions, Lee and I found things to write about that made us chuckle. The government was generous in making cigarettes available in the P.X. Every man had a ration of a carton a week, at a dollar a carton. But cigars were hard to come by, and at that time, I was a cigar smoker. Lee would, from time to time, send me a box of assorted cigars from home, and she had hilarious stories to tell about her adventures in patrolling all the drug stores in Long Beach, buying cigars, one and two at a time, to send to her husband in India. And for lack of something better to do, I decided to grow a bushy British-type mustache. I found that it was hard to control in the tropics and asked Lee to see if she could find some mustache wax. Mustache wax was about as plentiful as dinosaur eggs. Lee could write a book about her experiences tracking down a tube of mustache wax for me. Whenever I'd find myself telling about how tough things were in India, Lee would usually tell me, "You think you had it tough! Did you ever go out and shop for mustache wax?"

chapter thirty-two

HOW TO WIN
WHILE LOSING, IV

It was a real relief when the people on top decided there were better ways to use my special talent, and they assigned me to the B-29 program. The B-29 was a big, new bomber they were inventing with a pressurized cabin, remote control turrets, and a lot of other goodies that, we were told, would make her the queen of the skies. They were right, of course, but there was still a lot of inventing to do.

The first B-29 unit was the 58th Wing, which consisted of four groups, each group with four squadrons. I found my place as one of the 16 squadron commanders. Each group trained on one of the four Kansas bases. We trained hard, but before we had trained enough to count for much and way before they were through inventing the airplanes, they shipped us off to war so they could start training the next wing. We were on our way to the China-Burma-India Theater (CBI), where General Arnold had made a commitment to The Generalissimo, Chiang Kai-shek. Our route out was interesting. It took us from Kansas to Goose Bay, Labrador; Marrakech, Morocco; Cairo, Egypt; Karachi, India; and then on to our final Indian bases about 150 miles west of Calcutta. Our group's base was a place called Kharagpur.

The B-29 had two huge bomb bays and could carry a respectable bomb load, but for our trip out, we were placed in a special configuration. There were 600-gallon fuel drop tanks that could be carried in the bomb bays, two tanks to a bay. In order to stretch our range, three of these 600-gallon tanks were installed in the front bomb bay, two side by side and the third tank flat across the bottom. The only problem was that this was a fixed installation and could not be jettisoned. In the rear bay, they installed loading platforms, on which were stowed a lot of spare parts and an extra 3350 engine, in case they were needed en route. The load in the rear bay could be jettisoned in the event we got into trouble. It all looked great to us, and in the spring of 1944, we said goodbye to Kansas and launched ourselves on the way to the CBI.

It was quite a trip. Here were 240 B-29s still in the process of being invented, in the hands of a bunch of kids who averaged about 50 hours apiece in B-29s, on their way to a place most of them had never seen before. There were, indeed, a lot of unexpected and bone-jarring experiences along the way for a lot of the troops. My airplane was named *O'Reilly's Daughter*, in honor of the heroine of a rather bawdy song I had learned in the South Pacific and taught to my crew. My crew and I, in *O'Reilly's Daughter*, had smooth sailing until we arrived at Karachi, India, which is now part of Pakistan.

We got into Karachi in good shape. We were hung up there for a few days because there were reports that a take-off accident in Cairo had been caused by contaminated fuel. The powers that be eventually solved the problem, and the daisy chain of B-29s that stretched from Kansas to India was put in motion, again.

Take-offs from Karachi were scheduled between midnight and 3:00 A.M. to permit arrival at our East Indian bases after daylight and before 10:00 A.M. The monsoon season was just beginning in that part of the world. The weather closed in, and the rains began as regular as clockwork at 10 in the morning.

On the day before we were scheduled to take off, a sandstorm moved in on Karachi that was so thick, the birds were walking on solid ground at 1,000 feet. Visibility was less than 50 feet. We lost a B-29 coming in from Cairo that afternoon. There was a low-frequency radio station a couple of miles off the end of the Karachi runway, and this poor guy made half a dozen passes at the field, coming in over the radio station and trying to find the runway. The visibility was just too bad for him to see anything, and he finally ran out of gas and crashed about half a mile from the end of the runway.

We decided to go ahead with our midnight take-off because we knew that the top of the sand was at about 3,000 feet, and after we had climbed out on top, we would have good flying weather all the way to Kharagpur. We could see two lights ahead down the runway, so we had no trouble taking off through the murk, but we had just broken ground, retracted the gear, and were milking the flaps when the number 1 engine's propeller ran away with a roar, and the number 1 tachometer went way past the red line. We were unable to bring it under control and had no choice but to feather number 1. We were immediately in serious trouble because we had managed to get only 150 or 200 feet of altitude, and it took rated (maximum) power out of the three good engines to maintain our altitude. The engines soon began to overheat. We were at very heavy weight but couldn't jettison the three 600-gallon tanks fixed in the forward bomb bay. And if we dropped the loading platform and spare engine in the rear bay, our center of gravity would move so far forward that the airplane would become uncontrollable. Further, I was never able to claw myself high enough that I could order the crew to bail out. I limped around over the radio station on the proper heading toward the runway but couldn't see a darn thing. I called the control tower on the radio to see if they had seen us go over. The control tower officer answered that they hadn't seen anything, but that they had heard an aircraft of our type pass over at a very low altitude. I asked him what part of the field we had passed over, and he told me that it had sounded as though we had passed directly down the runway. The sky was the color of sand, the ground was the color of sand, and I couldn't tell where one ended and the other began.

Our engines were badly overheated, and I knew that our flying time was limited, so we circled around again, oriented ourselves over the radio station, passed through its cone of silence, took up the heading for the runway, extended the gear and flaps, pulled back a bit on the power to set up a slow rate of descent, and peered ahead into the blowing sand for a glimpse of the field.

We hit the field all right, with a good hard thump, but we had missed the runway by a couple hundred yards. The field was rough, and the roughest part was when we bounced over the cross-runway. We finally came to a stop a couple hundred feet short of a little building where they stored explosives, which would have contributed to a beautiful fire if we had hit it. I chopped the power on my three good engines, breathed a sigh of relief, and threw open my cockpit window. The landing had been so rough that my navigator was convinced we had made a belly landing. When I opened my window, he climbed across my lap and dove out the window, expecting to be close to the ground. Instead he found himself about 12 feet in the air, and when he hit the ground, he broke his leg. He was our only casualty.

My crew chief, who was with us, checked the airplane over and found nothing wrong with it but a malfunctioning propeller governor on the number 1 engine. When he replaced it, the engine checked out fine. In a couple of days, the sand stopped blowing, and we got our navigator out of the hospital, loaded him aboard, splint and all, and proceeded with an uneventful flight to Kharagpur.

It was almost automatic that as we got involved in the war against the Japanese from our bases in India and China, the excitement of our little episode in Karachi paid off. We hadn't been there very long when our group commander was evacuated home with a serious health problem. The deputy group commander took command of the group, and I was moved up from my squadron commander slot to be deputy group commander. Our new group commander was shot down over Singapore on his first mission as our commander, and I moved up to take his place. Promotion to the rank of colonel followed three months later.

Letter to Lee, March 30, 1944

You should see me these days, Honey. I have had all my hair cut off except a real short bristle, and several of the other boys are doing the same thing. It doesn't look so hot, but it sure does feel good. I've started letting my mustache grow in preparation for using the wax, and it is sure an unkempt looking thing at present. In another couple of weeks, it will be long enough to wax, and then I'll have something!

We are all working like fiends on our airplanes. They are really coming right along. I'm in love with mine already. We can't paint names on them until after we leave the country, but we are getting pictures ready now to paint on them and names lined up. Our crew still wants to name our ship O'Reilly's Daughter, *and a painter down at the Depot is designing for us a lovely, thinly clad, little red-headed wench to go on the nose beside the name. I think it's a pretty good name for an airplane. Cactus is naming his* The Cactus Special, *and Shelley is naming his* The Limber Dugan. *The rest of the crews are in the throes of dreaming up names for theirs.*

Letter to Lee, April 30, 1944

I'll write to you, My Sweet, just as often as it is possible and tell you all they will let me tell you. Due to the nature of our operations, there are apt to be gaps of several days or even weeks, but don't worry. No news will be good news, and your worthless husband is going to take good care of himself so the two of us will have at least 70 years of married life together after this war is won.

I've squared away with the censors here and found out their rules on what I can tell you about our trip, and they are quite big-hearted. I can tell you now much that I haven't in our previous letters, so you can get out our maps and see just about where we went. I can't tell you where any of the bases are where we stopped, but that shouldn't matter too much. I also can't tell you just where I am now, but you should know that already.

Now, about our trip. . . .*

I'll tell you a little about our base here and bring this lengthy travelogue to a close. Things here are far better than I could have hoped for. I have a fine room that I will share with Cactus when he arrives. We have a chest of drawers, a desk, and a little clothes cabinet between us and, believe it or not, Darling, I have a regular ³/₄ bed with a Simmons inner-spring mattress. It's unbelievable! I sure sleep in luxury under my mosquito net.

I hope you haven't forgotten that I love you, Sweetheart of mine. Not an hour goes by that I don't wish you were here to see something or wonder what you would think of something that was happening. Or maybe I'll just close my eyes for a moment or two and try to imagine how you look. Time will pass quickly for us even apart as we are, because we both will be busy, and one of these days the war will be won, and I'll be home to stay with you forever and ever. I guess I tell you that in almost every letter, but it's a thought that's constantly in my mind and one I couldn't go on without knowing—that sooner or later, our turn will come.

Letter to Lee, May 4, 1944

Cactus arrived day before yesterday, and we are all squared away in our quarters. We are actually much more comfortably situated than we were in Salina. We have a bearer who works for us named Papaya, and he does every-thing from making our beds to shining shoes. He's quite a nice guy, and although he doesn't know much English, we get ourselves understood. He calls us Major Sahib and Colonel Sahib.

We are expecting Clink and Sally (his dog) in sometime today. Col. Engler should get here before long, too. We'll soon be a real going concern.

Letter to Lee, May 6, 1944

We had a major project on our hands this afternoon. The hot weather has been too much for Sally, and we clipped her today. It took the four of us about

---

* The next page and a half of this letter were redacted by the military censors.

two hours to do it, and it isn't too sharp a job, but she will be much cooler now anyway. She's still a little self-conscious about the way she looks, but she'll get over it.

Cactus and I fired our bearer, Papaya, today. He was working for about eight officers around here, not doing much for us, and was making more money than we are.

You said I should write and ask for anything that I want—so here goes. I would sure appreciate you sending me a batch of little 25-cent pocketbooks [paperbacks], the mystery type, preferably. There is nothing whatsoever over here in the way of reading matter, and those little books are handy. I sure would like some snack supplies. The food here is okay, but not really too good, and every so often, we hit meals that are completely inedible. Crackers in tins, jars of sandwich spreads, cheese, and peanut butter, or stuff of that nature would sure taste good. Anything you send should be in a jar or a tin so the rats can't get it. I don't know how much you'll be able to send, but you said to let you know.

Letter to Lee, May 11, 1944

This is sure a hot, dirty country, Sweet, but it is quite interesting. Just driving around our airdrome in my jeep, I see some amazing sights. They are busy pouring concrete and laying taxi strips now, and it is sure something to see—an endless parade of Indian women walking up to a line-up of big concrete mixers, each with a little basket of sand or a jug of water on her head to dump in the machine. There are thousands and thousands of natives working around here, and it is all so primitive. You wonder how they ever get anything accomplished, but they seem to.

We've been getting some pretty good local fruit here lately—coconuts, mangos, and lychee nuts. You would get a big kick out of the little Indian who sells fruit on the post. He can't speak any English, but the soldiers have taught him enough to enable him to peddle his wares. Not really understanding himself what he is saying, he was rather at their mercy. It's very funny to see him wandering around the post hollering at the top of his voice, "No damn good coconuts for sale! Rotten tangerines, no damn good bananas! Too expensive!" He's always good for a laugh whenever he comes around.

I'd like to send you a photo of our Post Tailor Shop. It's about four feet square with a thatched roof, and the Indian tailor sits cross-legged on the floor of the little porch in front. The big sign over the door reading "Post Tailor" is the crowning touch. He is, however, quite a big dog to the local natives. He has *the neatest piece of transportation I've seen in quite a while. It's built like a bicycle except instead of a hind wheel, it has a little cab and seat with a top on it kind of like a rickshaw where he sits. He has another Indian who rides the bicycle and pumps him around. It looks kind of like this.*

Kind of rough but maybe you can get the idea. He cuts quite a figure riding around in this rig and he sure seems proud of himself

Letter to Lee, May 17, 1944

Honey, your husband is sure a sight these days. I let Clink and Cactus give me a haircut, and they clipped my hair off all over my head right down to the skull except for a strip about an inch wide right down the middle from front to back that bristles up about an inch high. I look like an Iroquois Indian. After wearing it that way for a day, I prevailed on them to clip it all off, and now I am as bald as an eagle. My mustache now is quite a bushy affair with waxed points about an inch long, and the combination of the mustache and the bald head is quite something. I hardly think you would approve of it as a steady thing.

Letter to Lee, May 29, 1944

My precious wife, your letters are so sweet. They tell me all the things I want to know. All about what you are doing and how you and Ed are. Life here is awfully drab and dull except when it does get exciting, and then it's too much so. All is going well, however, and we are going to do our job as well as we can. I think we will all be able to feel that this little outfit of ours has had a part in shortening the war, and that was our reason for coming here.

Maybe I misread your letter, but you seemed a mite sad, My Sweet. Please don't be. We are now on the last leg of our separation, and each day that passes brings our final and everlasting reunion closer.

I've trimmed my mustache back down to normal again. It got to be just too darn much trouble, and it was awfully hot on my face. It was a lot of fun while it lasted. I'm enclosing a little snapshot of your ever-loving husband that George Putnam took right after Cactus and Clink finished giving me the haircut. You can see Clink, the smiling barber, in the background. If anyone ever asks you what your husband looks like, you can proudly show them this!

Report from the *Los Angeles Times*, June 1944

Palmer Putnam with B-29 Unit in West China

Superfortress Base, Western China

Major George Palmer Putnam, of North Hollywood, Cal., former publisher and husband of the late Amelia Earhart, is now Intelligence Officer for a Superfortress Group, which has been pounding Japan.

Putnam, more than 50 years of age, said, "This is the most interesting job an older man could get in the Air Forces. I feel lucky to be associated with a crowd like this."

Putnam said that with only one exception every man in his command is "young enough to be my son."

"That keeps an old fellow like me on his toes," he declared.

He introduced to newspaper correspondents several key officers, in his group including Lt. Col. James Edmundson, Santa Monica, Cal., and Maj. James Van Horne, Tucson, Ariz.

Letter to Lee, June 2, 1944

We have been a busy bunch. Don't be surprised if you begin reading about us in your papers before long. We are still the hush-hush outfit, but I believe by the time you receive this letter, the papers will have been given all the dope about us it will hit the front page.

The evenings are the only time we have to read or write letters, and the lighting situation is so bad we can't do anything then. When I write a letter, I have to take some time off through the day, and that is awfully hard to do, as busy as we've been.

O'Reilly's Daughter has been behaving beautifully. She is a perfect lady. We have boxing gloves I got for Ed mounted up in the pilot's compartment, and they seem to have brought us good luck so far.

Don't stop writing, Honey. Your letters are bound to come through after a while.

Letter to Lee, June 9, 1944

I sure am sorry the censor chopped my letter to pieces telling about our trip over here. Everything I told you in it was authorized by our Group censor, but the Base censor must play by his own rules. Cactus had his letter to Louise chopped up in the same manner. These damn censors never seem to get together on their regulations. I believe you can understand the type of guy that usually winds up as a base censor anyway, so no explanation is necessary. Their one glory is the authority to chop up other people's mail.

Last night, Cactus, George Putnam, and I went in to the local town to a little club the British have there. We had some pleasant conversation and a couple of most welcome drinks (British style, no ice). It was my first real relaxation since arriving here, and it was a welcome change. We are all so busy with our job, and our job gets so much bigger every day, that we forget to knock off every once in a while. The place has been overrun with various and sundry news correspondents, so it may be that one of these days we will cease to be such a hush-hush bunch of people.

Letter to Lee, June 10, 1944

Golly, Honey, my mail has really caught up with me with a bang. Yesterday and today, I received 21 letters from you. Wow! They are dated everywhere from April 11th to May 29th. Sweetheart, they are wonderful. All of them. I spent yesterday evening reading them all through twice, and it took the entire evening and burned out two sets of flashlight batteries. It was just like sitting down and having a long talk with you, My Darling. Each and every one of them is a little masterpiece. I'll have a glow inside for many many days just from thinking about your letters. The pictures are especially welcome. Ed is sure growing. I've been showing the pictures off ever since they arrived.

The house and the yard must look swell by now. You sure seem to do a lot of work in the yard. It's hard work, but it's kind of fun in a way, isn't it? I wish I were there to help you.

Letter to Lee, June 22, 1944

Well, Honey, I'm finally back to our India Base and can write to you again. It's been quite a while since the last time I wrote, and much has happened. Now that we have started to work and the papers have announced our activities, censorship restrictions have been greatly lifted. We can now come right out and say that we are flying B-29s, and we can admit we go to China. This has been very taboo up until now. We can also tell about flying "the Hump" and a little about our first mission on Japan proper.

I think you would like China, My Sweet. The climate there is very cool and pleasant compared to here in India where it is unbearably hot. You would also like the Chinese. They are dirty and disease ridden to nearly the same extent that the Indians are, but they are smiling and cheerful and friendly. A welcome relief after the sullen Indians. Our base in China was all built by the Chinese by hand, and it's an amazing piece of work. They are sure an ingenious bunch of people. They have never seen any white people in our section of the country, and when we go to the little local town, they flock around us by the hundreds— pointing and laughing and talking. They are interested in everything we have, and it all fascinates them. Watches, matches, almost anything we have in our pockets is a source of amazement to them. I have sure seen some interesting things over there, and I'll take China any day over India. It's nice to be able to tell you about it now because up until now the fact that we ever went to China was a secret.

I bought a couple of things over there that I will send home as soon as I can. I got you a piece of embroidered silk for $2,800 and myself a silver water pipe for $900. Perhaps, at this point, I should explain that Chinese currency has inflated until it now takes 200 Chinese Yuan to equal 1 American dollar. In other words, the silk cost $14 and the pipe $4.50. I'm enclosing a 100–Chinese Yuan bill for you as a souvenir. You don't need to tell anyone that it's actually worth 50 cents.

The flight from India to China, which I have made several times, is one of the most beautiful in the world. The mountains in Northern Burma and Tibet are higher and more rugged than it's possible to believe without seeing. We call it "The Hump," and believe me, it is sure the hump of the world.

There is not much to tell you about our mission that you don't already know. Our target was the Imperial Iron and Steel Works in Yawata, Japan, and we knocked the devil out of it. O'Reilly's Daughter behaved beautifully, and it was a most pleasant trip all the way around. I've waited a long time to bomb Japan proper, and it sure was a satisfaction. I hope we can do it again, frequently.

On June 26, 1944, *Time* magazine reported that the previous week the secret B-29 Superfortress flying out of China attacked the Japanese Empire. The target was the Imperial Iron & Steel Works in Yawata. Known as Japan's Pittsburgh, it was the source of one-fifth of all Japanese war steel.

This mission was unlike the Doolittle raid two years before, in April 1942. Flying B-24s, the single attack on Japan was launched from the aircraft carrier *Hornet*. The more recent mission was not a single strike. The long-ranging B-29s left from bases that had been "painfully carved out of the fields of western China by nearly 500,000 coolies." While this was the first major strike, it would not be the last.

The Chief of the Twentieth Air Force Bomber Command, Brigadier General Kenneth B. Wolfe, selected Brigadier General LaVerne Saunders to lead the mission. Saunders was nicknamed "Blondie" despite his being "rugged, black-browed, [and] hairy-chested." At one time an All-America tackle at West Point, Saunders was a veteran airman with a spectacular record in B-17 Flying Fortress operations around the South Pacific.

Reports indicated that the target hit was accurate, although there was ground-to-air flak and resistance from Japanese fighters. Four aircraft and crews were lost during this attack, one of them downed by enemy flak over the target.

This experimental attack went as planned. The B-29s hit the target before midnight. They were not in formation but lined up singly, with eight planes leading the way. The fire from their hits identified the target for those who followed.

For successful raids like this one, the challenge was getting the supplies where they are needed. The materiel (bombs, fuel, and technical equipment) had be carried by the B-29s from bases in India to the takeoff point in China. Those flights over the "Hump" were critical in bringing the war to Japan's homeland.

chapter thirty-three

TOKYO ROSE

One incident that occurred during my year in India and China was a chapter of the war that Lee and I never forgot. In June 1944, we flew our first mission out of China against the Japanese home islands. We bombed the steel mill in Yawata, on the island of Kyushu. It was a tough mission, and we lost several airplanes and crews. It was the first time that Japan itself had been hit since the Doolittle Raid, and we tried to make the most of it.

The Japanese had a propaganda broadcast that they put on the air every night pointed at the American troops. Most of us listened to it for a couple of reasons. It was usually good for a laugh, and it played good music. The announcer on the program was a young Japanese woman called "Tokyo Rose." She spoke excellent English, and was, in fact, a young lady who had lived in California for a number of years and had graduated from UCLA.

After the Yawata mission, Tokyo Rose announced that several B-29s had been shot down and listed six crew members, by name, who had been identified and buried. My name was among those she listed. It was sort of a joke to us, but of course, the broadcast was picked up in the United States, and this came as a shock to my little Lee. She got in touch with my folks, who were also shocked. My father got off a wire to the War Department asking for confirmation. In China, we were on the end of a long pipeline that extended three-quarters of the way around the world. In those days, there were no satellite relays, and it took an ungodly long time to pass the word back and forth between Washington and China.

I wrote Lee a letter right after the mission, and when she received it about two weeks later, it was the first word she had that I was still alive. To show how thoughtful some people can be, Lee's postman was aware of Lee's being on her own while her husband was in China, and he went out of his way whenever he had a letter to deliver from me—and he knew that I had been reported missing. He was sorting mail in the post office one morning when he came across my letter written after the mission, and he stopped sorting and made a special trip to bring Lee the letter.

This was a harrowing experience for Lee, as the Japanese propaganda mongers intended it to be, but the truth finally came out, and Lee had the strength and courage to see it through. If the Japanese lie did anything, it brought us closer together.

Report from the *West Los Angeles Tribune*, June 23, 1944

Japs Report Death of Col. Edmundson

War Department Casts Doubt Upon Nipponese Claims;
Washington Authorities Suspect Tokyo Angling for Information

Lt. Col. James V. Edmundson, Santa Monica's most famous flying ace, was listed in a Tokyo radio report broadcast at midnight last night. The report picked up by the United Press in San Francisco, named him as a member of a crew of one of the B-29 Superfortress which made a raid on the Yawata Steel Works in Japan on June 16, but James A. Edmundson, the pilot's father, today reported that members of the family have not received any word from the War Department to confirm the Tokyo announcement.

Wire dispatches from Washington indicated that the War Department doubted the truth of the Tokyo broadcast, describing it as "Axis propaganda designed to feel us out."

Puzzling Factors Cited: "We don't know any more than you," the Colonel's father told a reporter. "We know he was in that area, and the probabilities are that he was on the flights," the father added, however.

Puzzling to Santa Monicans who heard the broadcast or read the report of the enemy message was the fact that six Lieutenant Colonels and one Major were named as having been aboard one plane. Except under extraordinary conditions, it was considered unlikely that so many officers of such high rank would be on one ship.

The radio message, as heard by Glenn Knox, head of a Santa Monica escrow firm at midnight last night, gave the names and home addresses of seven men out of the eleven men who were supposed to have been on a Superfortress downed by anti-aircraft fire explaining that the names of the other four could not be identified from a partially burned list found in the plane's wreckage.

Wounded First Day: Colonel Edmundson, who ranked as an Eagle Scout here before he joined the Army Air Force, won the Purple Heart decoration on the first day of the war when he was slightly wounded by shrapnel in the Japanese sneak attack on Hickam Field near Pearl Harbor, but he avenged that attack in more than 100 flight missions in the South Pacific.

Singled out by the President for special mention after he sank a Japanese submarine, he also participated in the bombing of other Japanese naval units and had the distinction of having been given the Distinguished Flying Cross three times, twice by the Navy and once by the Army, participating in some of the toughest air fighting which marked the campaign that finally stopped the Japanese hordes on their southward march toward Australia.

May Be Prisoner: Two peculiar aspects of the Tokyo announcement, which were noted by the Edmundsons, were that a special dispatch from a Chinese airbase dated June 16, mentioned Edmundson as one of the key officers at the Superfortress base.

If the message was sent out on the date given, the boys father pointed out, the writer must have known Edmundson's fate, and probably would not have mentioned his name before War Department advised members of his family of his death.

Even more significance was attached to a March of Time report heard here last night, which indicated that one of the Superfortresses had been forced down in occupied China, and that the crew of this ship had been captured by the Japanese.

The Tokyo radio listed Edmundson's age as 29 and since his 29th birthday occurred only on June 18, members of the family incline to the belief that he may have been among the airmen captured in China, rather than among any who might have lost over the target in Japan. Surviving the crash, they argued, he naturally would have given his new age to the Japanese, rather than the age he was on the flight of the raid in which he was said to have been killed.

In another radio report recorded by the United Press in San Francisco, the Japanese reported that Japanese military authorities had cremated and buried all of the crewmen of B29s allegedly shot down in the June 16 raid "in accordance with the code of Bushido."

Report from the *Evening Herald-Express*, June 1944

Japs Bury B-29 Dead

American fliers who were killed when Japanese anti-aircraft and fighter planes allegedly shot down B-29 Super-Flying Fortresses raiding northern Kyushu Island June 16 have been cremated and buried in accordance with the Bushido code, Tokyo radio claimed Friday.

The broadcast quoted the caption under the picture as reading: "In accordance with the code of Bushido, the Japanese military authorities cremated all the crew of B-29s downed at dawn on June 16 and laid these ill-fated American fliers to eternal rest. The grave posts on which are written the names of the American fliers were erected on the mounds by the members of the Japanese Anti-aircraft Corps."

Report from the *Los Angeles Times*, June 24, 1944

Wife Receives No Report on Col. Edmundson

Although the Tokyo radio listed Lt. Col. James V. Edmundson as a member of the crew of a B-29 Superfortress shot down over Northern Kyushu Island June 16, his wife has received no word that he is missing, she said yesterday.

The Japs claim to have compiled a partial list of the names of 11 men they say were aboard the B-29 when it was shot down. Names of all the crew were not confirmed, the broadcast concluded, because a list found in the plane was partly burned away.

He holds the Purple Heart for a bomb fragment wound at Pearl Harbor; the Air Medal (and several Oak Leaf Clusters) for blasting a Jap submarine off Hawaii; the Distinguished Flying Cross (also with Clusters) for sinking Nip cruiser in a low altitude Flying Fortress attack off Tulagi, for scoring hits on Jap transports and scarring up enemy airfields, and the Silver Star for gallantry in action.

Boyish-looking and quiet-spoken, the former Santa Monica Junior College grid star also is credited with dog fighting a Fortress against attacking Zeros and with flying more than 40,000 miles on Hawaiian dawn patrol.

Tokyo Rose : 161

Report from the *Los Angeles Times*, June 24, 1944

Edmundson Family Given Ray of Hope

War Department Does Not List Him Dead

New hope for the safety of Lt. Col. Edmundson, famous Santa Monica pilot reported killed by the Japs in the B-29 raid on Japan, came to Colonel Edmundson's family last night in the form of a telegram from Gen. James A. Ulio, head of the Adjutant General's office, Washington, D.C.

The message, in response to an inquiry sent by the boy's father, simply advised the Edmundsons that "the name of Lt. Col. James V. Edmundson does not appear on casualty lists received in War Department."

Although this report did not exclude the possibility that reports on the B-29 raid had not yet been received, members of the family considered it "very encouraging."

Mrs. Edmundson was reported in Long Beach.

Report from the *West Los Angeles Tribune*, July 3, 1944

Col. Edmundson Alive; Jap Report Proved False

Air Hero Writes to Wife; Letter Describes Superforts' Raid

Lt. Col. James V. Edmundson, reported by the Tokyo radio as one of the American pilots killed in the B-29 raid on Japan's Yawata Steel Works, is alive and safe, according to a message received from the famous Santa Monica flier early today.

Ending weeks of anxiety and uncertainty inspired by the lying tongues of the Japanese, a message in Colonel Edmundson's own handwriting this morning reached his wife in Long Beach and was relayed promptly from there to his parent's home at 259 West Channel Road, Santa Monica Canyon.

Unaware of Worry: Seemingly unaware of the confusion inspired by the Tokyo radio report in regard to his safety, Colonel Edmundson, who now ranks as a key officer of the new 20th Air Force, described for his wife the long trip which his Superfortress made from China to the target, and spoke of the satisfaction he felt at being able "to take a whack at the Japs" on their own ground after having "waited a long time" for that privilege.

Colonel Edmundson was injured by shrapnel on the first day of the war when the Japanese made their sneak raid on Hickam Field near Pearl Harbor.

"We gave them a good pasting," he added, expressing the hope that he "would be able to do it again and do it often."

Axis Propaganda: Mr. and Mrs. James A. Edmundson, the pilot's parents, have been receiving messages of condolence from far and near from persons who heard or read of the original Tokyo radio message, but failed to note subsequent messages sent out by the War Department which described the Tokyo broadcast as "Axis propaganda, designed to feel us out."

His wife, the former Miss Lee Turner, has been writing to him regularly, refusing to give any credence to the Japanese report. She never had mentioned the Tokyo message to him because she did not want him to worry.

Report from the *West Los Angeles Tribune*, July 28, 1944

Col. Edmundson Safe in China: Tokyo Won't Talk

June 16—B-29 Superfortresses raid Japan.

June 23—Tokyo radio reports Lt. Col. James V. Edmundson of Long Beach killed in B-29 shot down June 16 over Northern Kyushu Island.

July 3—Mrs. Edmundson receives letter from her husband dated China, June 22: "It was a most pleasant trip . . . Our target was the Imperial Iron and Steel works at Yawata. . . . We knocked the devil out of it . . . O'Reilly's Daughter (the Colonel's Superfort) behaved beautifully."

July 3—Tokyo radio . . . no comment.

Letter to Lee, June 24, 1944

Last night, Radio Tokyo announced that I had been shot down over Japan on our last mission and that the honorable Japanese had cremated me. A little later they gave my name as being a prisoner of war in Japan.

Honey, I can just about guarantee that neither of those stories is true. Of course, I might not be a very good authority, but I'm relatively certain they aren't right. What do you think? All kidding aside, Sweetheart, I sure hope word of this report hasn't reached you. As soon as I heard it, I contacted Bomber Command. They sent a radio message to Washington denying the statement and asking the War Department to notify all concerned immediately that it wasn't true. That was the fastest way I could think of to stop your worrying in case you had heard the story. Bomber Command told us to write to our next of kin as soon as possible and deny the story as well. I hope you didn't hear it, and I hope, Honey, that you never let anything you hear through the Japs bother you.

Letter to Lee, July 6, 1944

I received a very sweet letter from my darling wife today. It was dated the 27th of June, and I know it was a hard letter for you to write. You see, the wife of one of the boys in the Squadron sent him a clipping from the LA paper dated the 24th which gave Tokyo's account of knocking me down over Yawata.

I had hoped that would never reach you, and I had assurance from General Wolfe that you would be immediately notified that it was a false report. I could tell by your letter that you had heard the report and also that you hadn't yet received word that it wasn't true. It must have been a tough letter to write, Darling. I know by this time that you know better and your worries are over. You are a wonderfully brave little soldier to carry on that way without a peep. I love you so much. You must have known in your heart it wasn't true, and yet the doubt was still there. My Sweetheart, never, never believe anything you hear from Jap sources, and don't worry for a single instant about me. Everything is okay and will continue to be that way. O'Reilly's Daughter is getting to be an old hand at this business, and she'll take care of things.

Report from the *West Los Angeles Tribune*, July 28, 1944

Don't Believe Japs, Edmundson Writes

Tokyo Reports Usually False, Flier Says

Col. James V. Edmundson, famed B-29 pilot, has written to relatives here, giving the lie to the Japanese propaganda reports which identified him as one of the casualties in the first big Superfortress raid on the Yawata Steel works in Japan.

"Never, never believe anything that you hear from the Jap sources," Colonel Edmundson said in a letter to his parents. "And don't worry for a single instant about me," he added. "It's wasted time because everything is okay and will continue to be that way. 'O'Reilly's Daughter' is getting to be an old hand at this business, and she'll take care of things."

Pleased by Raid: "O'Reilly's Daughter," Colonel Edmundson's father, James A. Edmundson of Santa Monica Canyon explained, is the B-29 that he is piloting after having won top honors for his flying exploits during the early months of the war in the South Pacific.

"Just returned yesterday afternoon from another little trip," the latest message received here by Colonel Edmundson's parents read. "There was a swell letter from each of you waiting for me. You can believe that there was a lot of personal satisfaction connected with my participation, and I hope to do it many more times.

"Things are running along fine over here," Colonel Edmundson reported. "Everyone is much happier now that we are getting down to business. The sooner we get this show on the road, the sooner the war will be over, and we can all come home."

In Primitive Area: "Operating out of this part of the country is quite interesting. This is a much more out-of-the-way corner of the world than the South Pacific. I never cease to wonder at what the Chinese have done to their country with their bare hands. Whole mountain systems in China are completely terraced into rice paddies, and their method of doing everything from building airfields and irrigating their land, to their mode of transportation and method of grinding their flour is as primitive as possible, but surprisingly effective."

In another letter, Colonel Edmundson wrote that he was based in an area where few white men had ever been seen, and that even the simplest items of equipment, such as matches and watches worn by the American pilots, were a source of wonder to the natives.

Crowds of Chinese from the village, he said, followed the men about, smiling, pointing, and shouting the Chinese equivalent of "Good Luck" to the fliers.

The B-29 pilot also wrote that a pipe, which he has received as a gift from his brother, Al, made the trip with him on the raid to Yawata. As evidence of the wartime inflation, which has gripped China, he reported that he has recently purchased a souvenir for $900, which sounded like a lot of money, but turned out to amount to only $4.50 in American coin.

Jap Stories Unreliable: Referring again to the Japanese radio report of his death, Edmundson said, "I hoped you wouldn't have heard it, and been saved the worry, because there was no basis of truth in the report whatsoever. In the future, I hope you will be spared the bother of having to hear such reports put out by our little yellow brothers, but in case they do come through with any wild stories, you will know that you can't believe them. I don't know what they expect to gain by such tactics, but their only aim can be to cause you worry and pain, so please don't let them."

Letter to Lee, July 15, 1944

George P.P. [Putnam] sends you his best wishes and says to tell you he'll be seeing you in three or four months. He hasn't been feeling too well since he arrived here. It's kind of a rough life for a man of his age, and he is going to get a Medical Discharge and return to the States within the next few months. He says that you will be one of the first people he will look up.

We've had a visiting dignitary with us the last couple of days. Vincent Sheehan, now a Lt. Col., is around here gathering material for another book. We have one of his books at home, Not Peace But the Sword, *which I enjoyed reading very much. He is a very likeable sort of a guy, as you will gather by reading his book. He's going from here to Saipan.*

Letter to Lee, July 20, 1944

Everything is well under control here and rolling right along. Nothing special has happened since the last letter I wrote you. Yesterday evening George P.P. and I spent playing chess, and I smoked up my last cigar. Col. Engler has acquired an icebox run by kerosene, and it sure is nice to be able to keep our canteens of water nice and cold. We are also receiving rations of canned fruit juice now, which is greatly improved by being cooled off. I mailed your Chinese silk yesterday in the cigar box I just emptied. I don't know what you'll be able to use the silk for, but it is sure pretty.

Letter to Lee, July 24, 1944

Got a picture from the Washington Star *yesterday of O'Reilly's Daughter and some of the crew. They are standing in front of the nose, and you can see her name painted on the side quite clearly. She is still behaving like a perfect lady. She's received a facial—that is, two new engines—and we took her out for a whirl yesterday to see how she felt about them. Quite an improvement. She sure has turned out to be a fine piece of machinery. Maybe Ed's boxing gloves have something to do with it. At any rate, they are still hanging in the cockpit.*

George P.P. and I had a chess tournament again last night, and I whipped him two games out of three. After that, I think he's just about to give up chess.

Letter to Lee, July 25, 1944

Lots of hurrying and scurrying around to do most of this morning, and then George P.P. and I had a couple of games of chess. We each had a turn at winning, and we let it go at that. This afternoon, I've spent the last couple of hours reading over some of the material George has for his book, and very good it is, too. It is sure a book you will want to read, My Sweet, when he gets it out, because it will tell so many of the things we have done. He comes to me for technical advice, and he likes to talk over parts of it with me. I have no idea of how the whole thing will fit together, but the separate pieces of it that I have seen have been excellent.

After I wrote you yesterday, the mail came in, and there were four wonderful letters from you. It seems we are all squared away, now, on the fact that I'm still alive. Even the newspapers agree with us, so I guess there's nothing else to worry about. Also today came two fine mystery books from you. A fine batch of funny papers were also in the mail yesterday, and they sure caused a furor in camp. They were the first any of us have seen since we left the States, and I had a waiting list a mile long trying to find out how "Dagwood" and "Terry and the Pirates" were doing. The Indian bearers were sure impressed with the funnies. They gathered around and oh-ed and ah-ed and pointed and chattered to themselves. They had never seen anything like it before. Darling, you are so sweet and thoughtful!

Letter to Lee, August 3, 1944

Returned to our base in India day before yesterday and have been going full blast ever since. As you no doubt read, we pulled a daylight formation mission on the Showa Steel works in Anshan, just south of Mukden in Manchuria. It was a big success and a lot of fun. I had a Newsweek correspondent with me on the trip named Mr. Harold Izaacs, so read Newsweek if you want a full account of my doings for the past few days.

Sweetheart, it is now the next day. While I was writing this letter, they called me in for a meeting, and some big changes have been made. Col. Engler has been pulled out of the Group and upstairs to a bigger job, and Ted Faulkner has taken over the Group. I have lost my Squadron and been made Deputy Group Commander. Bill Savoie now has my outfit. I sure am unhappy about it all. It means I won't get to fly quite so much in the future. I'll still be able to fly quite often, but I'll fly with all the Squadrons and a different crew each time. I lost my old crew, and O'Reilly's Daughter is no longer my airplane. Golly, Darling,

*it's an unhappy world right at this point. My mail now will come to Head-
quarters 468th Group instead of 792 Squadron. It's all for the best, I guess, but
it sure is hard to take.*

*Got another batch of funnies from you yesterday, my sweetheart. They are a
real event around here and sure are greatly appreciated by the entire post.
Everyone waits to read them.*

Report from *Newsweek*, August 7, 1944*

Job by Experts

Nineteen minutes ago the bombardier waved his hand and turned his
bald head around. "They're away," he said smiling broadly. Craning my
neck over the Pilot's head a few seconds later I saw a great sheet of flame
and black smoke begin to billow skyward. Over the interphone from all
corners of this great ship came congratulations for Capt. Louie Wedel, the
Bombardier. Gunners and other who also had an even better vision of the
target announced direct hits.

Lt. Col. James V. Edmundson, our Pilot and leader of the Squadron,
ducked the plane lightly away from the few bursts of flak that appeared on
both sides of us. As we pulled away we heard the rather pensive voice of
Staff Sgt. Jim Meehan, the Left Gunner; "Looks like Pittsburgh, don't it?"
We swung around and started for home, passing other Squadrons of
B-29s on their way in.

Resistance Nil: Ours was the first Group to hit the industrial center at
Anshan southwest of Mukden in the first daylight formation precision
bombing raid by the Superfortress.

We sighted only one fighter, a ship climbing vainly toward the upper
sky, but it never got within the Gunners' reach. Later elements obviously
encountered more flak, but resistance over the target was virtually nil.

We still have to cross half of Asia to get to home base. Most of the way
is enemy-occupied territory dotted with airfields. But the atmosphere in
this ship is not much different from that in a regular airliner just out of
Kansas City. The most relaxing thing is to be able to get out from under

the weight of the chute and flak suit, in which I was barely able to stand during target run. The whole operation was a smooth, easygoing job by experts.

Behind a mission like this, however, were weeks of laborious preparation—the flying of fantastic distances by combat crews and combat planes freighting every bomb and every gallon of gas over the highest mountain barrier in the world to West China bases, whence they strike at the enemy. Thursday morning I was in India; Thursday night in West China.

Today just before noon I was over Manchuria and tonight I expect a transport plane to drop me at Chungking. Some 4,000 miles in less than three days is rather a small sample of the kind of flying the men of the Twentieth Bomber Command are doing all the time.

Bombs Away: The take-off this morning was in the face of a blood red dawn. Colonel Edmundson raced the ship over a runway built by hand by half a million Chinese men and women, most of whom probably never had seen a railroad, much less planes like these. He lifted it smoothly over rice paddies and started climbing toward the West China Mountains. Our tight formation flew for hours over the terraced hillsides of China.

Then navigator Donald O'Brien (Obie to the crew) announced briefly: "We are over enemy territory." From a great altitude I began to see Japanese-held cities and airfields dotted with fighters, but there was no interception. Just before eleven the ship headed in over target. "She is yours, Louie," Edmundson said. The interphone crackled with orders. The ship and all the men aboard her prepared to perform the function for which she was created and they were trained, and both acted with perfect precision. At 11:05 the bombs were away.

The men who fly the B-29s are the most carefully selected crews in the Air Force. This was Colonel Edmundson's 81st mission. He flew 78 of them during the grueling days at Guadalcanal, where he was credited with two Japanese cruisers. His co-pilot, Eddie Winkler, has 2,200 flying hours in his log. Navigator O'Brien is also a veteran of South Pacific missions, as is Tech. Sgt. Red Heffernan. Possibly the most exacting job aboard, not allowing a single moment of relaxation, is that of Lt. Casimer (Casey) Stelmach, Flight Engineer who sits before his own panel of instruments, nursing the flow of power through the four 2,200 horsepower engines.

For Limber Dugan: Throughout the Twentieth you encounter crews in which every man is top-trained in at least two distinct specialized jobs.

Every one is a veteran. It is apparent in the more mature level of men when you see them enmasse at Mess. But maturity has nothing to do with age in the Air Force. Colonel Edmundson, who commanded the famous Eleventh Bomber Group at Guadalcanal is 29. O'Brien is 28, Wedel is 27, and Winkler 24. Some Enlisted Men are younger, but in the constant flow of quiet reports coming from Gunners and Radio Specialists is the confidence of men who know precisely what they are about.

These men are scornful of attempts to glamorize them. Edmundson, who obviously loves flying said: "The only way to get it over is to get out and get it over. The happiest day of my life will be when nobody's shooting at me any more. It scares me."

I flew with the same Group and same Squadron that Newsweek's correspondent Bill Shenkel, flew with to Yawata six weeks ago. Bill and the plane are now listed as missing. But chalked on one of bombs I saw in the Bomb Bay before the take-off were the words: "For the boys of Limber Dugan." That was the name of the missing plane.

Letter to Lee, August 14, 1944

Just returned home yesterday afternoon late, and there were two fine letters waiting for me from you. They were just what the doctor ordered. I just can't tell you, My Sweetheart, how much your letters mean to me and how wonderful it is to get them. A nice packet of funny papers and the Ellery Queen magazine arrived this morning. Honey, with reading matter at its present minimum, I could sell the funnies at $5 per sheet. Their arrival is really an event!

This place is getting quite civilized these days. We have a P.X. here now where we can buy soap and toothbrushes, matches, pipe tobacco, and stationery so you won't have to send me any more of these items. Cigars, however, are still almost impossible to obtain. Guess it's the same back home now, too.

I take great pleasure in showing off the latest picture of Ed you sent me. I've been carrying that picture in my shirt pocket ever since it arrived, and by now, it's rather the worse for wear. You are a wonderful wife to keep me so well supplied with pictures. Incidentally, a nice new big picture of my wife would be appreciated more than I can tell you. How about it, Kid?

All the love in the world to you, Sweetheart. Keep your chin up, and I'll be home before you know it. On looking at the date, I see that tomorrow will make exactly four months since I left the States. That, Precious One, is 1/3 of a year and quite some considerable chunk of what this tour will undoubtedly be. Time seems to be going faster than it did when I was in the South Pacific. It can't last forever.

Letter to Lee, August 23, 1944

We all got back from China yesterday, and it was nice to return, even to India. Everyone was pretty tired this time, and it's quiet here even if it is hot. We had a good mission—a daylight attack on Yawata that really should have given the Japs something to think about. It sure is a pleasure to be able to hit them where it hurts. Now that I'm up at Group, I can't fly in the same airplane with the same crew all the time, but must swap around. This time, I led the second flight in Clink's Squadron in Doc Schanlau's airplane, The Great Speckled Bird, *with Doc's crew and Doc as my copilot. We had a very satisfactory trip. You'll remember Doc from Salina. We used his car one night when the Dutchess was out of gas.*

Notifications have gone to the next of kin now, and the casualty reports have been submitted so I can tell you that Clink was knocked down over the target. Sally, of course, was with him. Also, O'Reilly's Daughter *failed to return with my entire old crew. Bill Savoie took over my airplane and crew when he took my squadron. We are all hoping that they may show up someplace as nobody saw what happened to them.*

Letter to Lee, September 1, 1944

As you can see, the new stationery you sent has arrived and it sure is swell stuff. All I can say is I hope I don't have to stay out here until I've used it all up, My Sweet, because there must be about a three years' supply! Guess that's a very subtle way of telling me that I haven't been writing often enough and, at that, you are perfectly correct. The frequency of my letters, however, can't begin to tell you how much you are loved and how many hundreds of times a day you are thought about. Golly, Sweetheart, it's going to be so wonderful when we are together again, finally and for keeps. This old war just can't last forever, and every day that passes brings the final finish just one day closer. I have to hurry up and get home so I can play ball with Ed on the front lawn and mix martinis for my wife and, oh, dozens of other things.

No doubt you have read in the papers by now that General Saunders was hurt in a crack-up a few weeks ago. He wasn't flying a B-29. He has been in a very serious condition for a considerable time, but now he is showing marked signs of improvement. He is a swell guy and always asked about you whenever I'd see him.

Darling Girl, I won't be able to write to you again for about a week, so don't be alarmed if there is a slight lapse in your mail. Some day, we won't have to worry about these things.

Today is a beautiful day. It is still uncomfortably hot, but there is a definite feel of fall in the air, and I can't help feeling like there should be pumpkins and cornstalks and football games and Halloween and all the other things that come with this time of year. Certain things I have always enjoyed so much are definitely childish, and I haven't been able to pitch into them in the last few years because I have supposedly outgrown them, but now, with Ed growing up, I'm going to feel perfectly free to forget my dignity and take part in his celebrations.

I'll get to carve jack-o'-lanterns and trim Christmas trees and dye Easter eggs to my heart's content. The more I think about it, the more convinced I am that this business of having a family is the only sure way of having fun yourself. Golly, when Ed gets a few years older, I might even be able to get him an electric train for me to play with.

Give Ed a big hug from his old man and take especially good care of his beautiful, young mother for me. I love her very much.

Letter from Dad, September 10, 1944

We enjoyed having Ed and Lee with us and were lonely for them when they went home. Ed developed a lot the few days that he was here. He first started to crawl while they were here. He got to know Nora and me quite well. When I would open the door into the kitchen in the morning where Lee would be feeding him, his face would light up with a big smile of recognition. I did all the crazy clowning that I could conjure up. Ed must have thought that plenty of fuss was made over him.

Someone said about some other time in history—"These are times that try men's souls"—and I suppose that the test is in keeping the old chin up regardless. There is a quotation from Shakespeare I often think of—I have just spent a half hour trying to find it but I couldn't smoke it out. Something like—"In peace there's nothing so becomes a man as gentle quiet and tranquility, but when the blasts of war blow in your ears, then imitate the tiger— disguise fair nature with foul fiendish rage." If anyone wants to argue with Shakespeare about whether or not that is the proper procedure in these modern times, then, at that point is revealed just why Shakespeare was pretty smart. He just had one of his characters say that. He isn't out on the limb himself. He is at perfect liberty to have someone else declare, in equally forceful fashion, just the opposite.

I thought you said that since you were now Deputy Group Commander, you would only fly half the missions. As far as I can see, you haven't missed one. As one of my friends said, if it weren't for the fellows that want to fly the missions, the rest of us would be in a H--- of a fix. Nevertheless, if a fellow's experience is of greater value directing others, he shouldn't feel too bad about not being in the thick all the time. Now, if I were Shakespeare, I'd put that line in the mouth of a fond father and not take any responsibility for it myself. After all, you are the greatest pride we have ever had, and whatever you do can't be anything but right.

Letter to Lee, September 11, 1944

Arrived back in India yesterday after a very pleasant and successful little trip. This was trip number two to Anshan for me, and I enjoyed it almost as much as the first time. It's nice to get back to India every time and live amid the comparative comfort of our base here.

Last night, the Group had our regular little victory celebration at the club which is now getting to be a regular ritual after each mission and, luxury of luxuries, we had a limited supply of honest-to-God, Black and White scotch to celebrate with. It went very nicely with soda and ice. Wow! This is sure getting to be a soft war.

Sure did enjoy the last few pictures of you and Ed, My Sweetheart. Ed seems to be growing like a weed, and you look awfully sweet and also awfully tired. Darling, please, please, take it easy and don't do so much running around with your throttle wide open. Rest a lot and take it easy.

Letter to Lee, September 23, 1944

Sweetheart of mine, please don't worry about Christmas. This will make the third Christmas in a row that I haven't been able to send you anything at all. This year will even be worse because I'll be ignoring Ed on his first real Christmas. If you managed to send me a whole lot of things, I'd be so ashamed of myself I probably wouldn't be able to come home and face the music when my tour here is up. You wouldn't want that to happen, would you? No fooling, Darling, just keep your letters coming, and we'll both just skip Christmas once more. Maybe next year this will all be over, and then what a Christmas we will have. Wow!

Sure have been busy this past week. Seems like there's always about twice as much to do as there is time to do it in, and we just never quite get square with the world. Our new boss, General LeMay, had, of course, lots of new ideas, and Ted Faulkner and I are going full steam to try and keep up with the changes.

Letter to Lee, September 29, 1944

Just returned to India from China where we pulled another little mission on Anshan. This time I didn't make the mission. It was Ted's turn, and I ran the show from the ground. It's the first one I've missed except Palembang when I was supposed to go and couldn't quite make it. As far as I'm concerned, I'd much rather fly than sweat them out on the ground. Next time should be my trip again.

There were two letters from you waiting for me when I got back this time, and they were both wonderful letters, My Sweet. It sure sounds as though Ed is growing up. It's hard to realize that he will be walking and even saying a few words before long. I sure am missing out on the fun.

Letter to Dad, October 4, 1944

Dad, I get a big bang out of you and your Shakespeare. He was indeed a pretty smart guy to put anything he wanted to get across in writing and yet keep his own personality in the background in such a manner that you may resent many of the things he says, but you only dislike the characters that say these things, never him. Even if you don't remember his exact quotations, you remember his methods, which are much more effective.

Lee tells me Ed now has six teeth. Golly, he is sure growing. He'll be a year old before too long now. It hardly seems possible.

News from here is pretty slim. We just keep on hitting the ball and doing what we can to finish the war as soon as possible.

Letter to Lee, October 19, 1944

Got back from China yesterday after a kind of protracted sortie. I took writing equipment along with me this time so I could write to you from up yonder, but there just wasn't time. We are sure the busy people these days, as you can well imagine.

The missions this time were rather tame but most successful. Formosa is a very pretty island with green fertile slopes and a mountain backbone 14,000 feet high running up and down its entire length. I only got to make one of the trips and ran the other one from the ground. I went with Gust Askounis, whom you met in Salina. His airplane is The Windy City. As you might guess, Gust is a Chicago boy.

Your mother sent me a swell set of pictures of you and Ed. He just looks as cute as the dickens, and his mother looks like a chorus girl.

Letter to Lee, October 28, 1944

You'll have to excuse the pencil today, Darling. I lost my fountain pen somewhere on the last China trip, and as yet, I haven't been able to get a hold of another one.

Don't believe any of the stories you hear about our being home by Christmas. The quickest way for me to get home is to win the war. We'll just have to go on planning a day at a time and a month at a time, and before we know it, it will be over.

I checked at the P.X. yesterday, and they think they will have a new fountain pen for me in a week or so. Until then, I'll just have to use the pencil and like it.

Letter to Lee, October 31, 1944

This is October 31st, Halloween. Sure would like to be home carving a jack-o'-lantern for you and Ed and helping trim up the house Halloweenish while you were rustling up a pumpkin pie. I used to like Halloween when I was a kid. Fancy costumes and masks and bobbing for apples and all that sort of stuff. Ah me! Over here, it's just one more day. Take it back. Today is a little different than other days. It's payday, and my wallet is so stuffed with Rupees and Chinese CNs and other various and sundry currency it would no longer fold, so I went to our Mail Clerk to have enough of it converted to U.S. dollars so I can send some money orders home. I would rather buy bonds so you wouldn't have to worry about it and keep track of it, but that isn't possible over here, so you'll get $500 worth of money orders in your next letter.

How are we doing on bonds, by the way? You should be buying them hand over fist with all the money you are getting. I don't think, even you, My Sweet, can piddle away $500 a month, or do I underestimate you?

Letter to Dad, November 1, 1944

Here is twenty bucks. Lee's wedding anniversary is November 21. Wish you would use part of it to get her some flowers for me, and Mom has a birthday in November. The other half of the bill should get her some flowers or something else more appropriate.

Thank you, Dad, for standing in for me.

Letter to Lee, November 15, 1944

General LeMay was out to see us yesterday. I'm going to be busier than a cat with a thousand kittens for a while, but it's a nice compliment to our outfit that he will let us go on by ourselves without putting anyone else in over our heads. It will mean much more work, however, because it's a big job, and I have much to learn. I also automatically assume command of the Base, which is also a big job, and one I haven't had much to do with before.

We are having a big ceremony tomorrow afternoon, and the General is coming out to pin a few medals on some of our boys. It will be a fine shot in the arm for them.

As our wedding anniversary draws nearer, I think about it more and more. It has been a wonderful four years being married to you, My Sweet, and the only thing that could have made it more wonderful would have been to be able to be with you all of that time. We'll have the last 40 years together anyway.

Letter to Lee, November 23, 1944

Arrived back in India yesterday after our last little show, and there were letters waiting for me from you as well as the Christmas box. I opened the letters and read them and then finally opened the Christmas box. Somehow since Christmas means so little out here, and we may not even be here in India then—anyway, I thought I might as well open it and enjoy it at once. Do you mind too much, Sweetheart?

It was sure swell. Such nice presents and so prettily tied up. You are a precious wife to take such good care of your husband. The tuna fish is sure going to hit the spot, and the little chess set is quite something. There was also a Christmas box from Bob and Lee Donovan, in the Canyon. They sent some cigars and some pipe tobacco and three little hand-knitted baby caps and socks to match. At first, I thought they were for Ed, but there was a card saying "For Little China," so I suppose they want me to take them up to China next time and distribute them. I'll take a shot at it see how it all turns out.

According to a time-honored ritual, tonight will be party night, being the second night home after a mission. Everyone will meet at the club and drink and sing and toast the boys who didn't get back and tell tall stories to the new replacement crews that have just arrived. One night of relaxation and then back to the grind. So it goes, good-bye to the old, hello to the new, time passes, mission follows mission, and one day we'll wake up, and it will be all over. Not soon, but one of these days. It can't last too many more years.

Letter to Lee, November 28, 1944

Golly, Honey, day after tomorrow, our young son will have his first birthday. It hardly seems possible. You better tell him not to grow up too fast before his dad comes home. It is hard to believe that time can pass so quickly. I hope you have explained it to Ed that his dad wishes he was home and doesn't really like it out here in India and China.

Letter to Ed, November 30, 1944

I've been writing letters to your mother for all these years, and today being your first birthday, it just seemed like a good idea to write to you for a change and let your mother sit this one out. Of course, your mother will probably read this over your shoulder, but then we don't mind that too much, do we? Some day, when you are a little older, I'll explain to you all about women. They are very inquisitive and don't really miss much that goes on around them even though they seem to, sometimes. Your mother is just like other girls except she's very much sweeter and prettier and more understanding than any of the rest. Guess you know that already.

So today was your birthday. What a big day. I don't suppose you have been greatly impressed by all the fuss that was made over you today. If you think there was a big to-do raised about you today, get your mother to tell you about a year ago today. Golly, such excitement. I couldn't even be there myself. I was out in Kansas getting ready to go back to war, and your mother had to carry on all by herself. She's a brave lady. I felt awful bad about not being there, but there isn't much you can do about those things when you're a soldier like your dad is. You and I, Ed, will have to work awfully hard to make up to your mother for all the worry and pain we both caused her that day: you for being there and me for not being there.

Today has been an awful busy day for your daddy, meetings and conferences and things all day long. At 5:30 this evening, just as the sun was setting, we had a ceremony, and your dad pinned Air Medals on 45 of the soldiers in of his Squadrons. There was no band or anything, but the soldiers were all standing up so straight in their cleanest uniforms, and they looked so fine and proud with their new medals hanging on their chests. The American Flag was waving in the breeze with the last light of the sun on it. It's a beautiful flag, Ed, and one that your daddy has followed into some mighty nasty places. You are a little young to understand it now, I think, but someday you'll understand all about things like that.

Today was also Thanksgiving as well as being your birthday. Did your mother ever tell you we were married on Thanksgiving Day, Ed? We were, four years ago, and it was the finest day in my life. It's the only day that's more important to me than the day on which you were born. Anyway, today being Thanksgiving Day, we had a wonderful meal. Wonderful canned turkey, cranberry sauce, mince pie, and ice cream. It was the best meal I've ever had since I left the United States over seven months ago.

Well, Ed, your daddy has to stop writing and go to bed now because he has to get up awfully early tomorrow, and it's going to be a long day. Tell your mother I won't be able to write to her for three or four days but not to worry. Keep her good and busy so she doesn't have time to think too much about things she shouldn't.

So long, Ed, and be a good boy.

Lots of love—Dad

P.S. Tell your mommy how much I love her for me 'cause I haven't time to write to her tonight. Tell her how sweet and beautiful and wonderful I think she is and kiss her goodnight for me.

Letter to Mom and Dad, December 24, 1944

This is the day before Christmas and so a fitting occasion for me to sit down and write you a long, belated letter. Folks, I don't really have much news for you, but I did want you to know how much I'll be thinking about you tonight and tomorrow. Christmas was always such a wonderful occasion in our family. Al and I sure used to have a time of it, and not just the one day, but weeks and weeks in advance. I have so many happy memories of Christmas. Hanging up stockings, and Dad reading The Night Before Christmas, our tree, always the prettiest in the neighborhood, and the big carrot ornament that was always on it, lying in bed on Christmas morning, and listening to you two walking around and waiting for you to come into the room, blowing a horn, the race to be the first one to say "Merry Christmas." Golly—What Fun!! I only hope that my family will have some of the same traditions that you worked up and some of the same wonderful spirit interwoven with thoughts of Christmas. Next year, things will be different.

I sure hope you have a nice day tomorrow. We are going to have one here. The soldiers have a party planned for tonight with a Santa Claus putting in his appearance, and we will have a swell meal tomorrow—canned turkey and canned ham and cranberry sauce with the vegetables to match and ice cream to finish up on. My mouth is watering already.

Letter to Lee, December 24, 1944

It's the afternoon before Christmas. It just doesn't seem possible that tonight is Christmas Eve, and tomorrow will be the big day. We thought for a while we would be spending Christmas in China, but we just managed to get home in time. It will make it much nicer all around.

The Enlisted Men from Group Headquarters are having a big party tonight to which my staff and I have been invited, and they are having a Santa Claus and everything. Also, one of the Squadrons is having a big party in their Mess Hall to which we will go later. All the Squadrons have trimmed up their Mess Halls until they look quite Christmassy. There are even a couple of decorated Christmas trees. Tomorrow, of course, will have to be a day of work, but we are making it as light as possible, and I've declared an unofficial half-holiday for tomorrow afternoon. All the Squadrons are planning their big meal at noon.

Well, Darling, I guess that tells you about our Christmas plans. My plans for next Christmas are definitely different and include, among other things, being with my wife and young son.

We had a long and protracted stay in China again this time. While there, my malaria came back. I don't know whether it was a recurrence of the old stuff or a new dose. The doc wasn't able to tell, but I was a pretty sick cookie for a few days. I'm still on a pretty strong dose of quinine and am not really at my sharpest and best yet, but that will come shortly now.

I'm sending you another medal for our collection. Our Eleventh Group Citation has finally come through, as has my Presidential Citation Badge or Distinguished Unit Badge for being a member of the 11th Group at the time it received a Presidential Citation. It is worn over the right pocket instead of the left as most medals are.

My precious wife, I'll be thinking of you especially much tonight and tomorrow and planning on our next Christmas together with Ed.

Letter to Lee, January 19, 1945

If you have looked at the return address on the outside of this envelope, you will be aware of the fact that your one and only husband is now an eagle colonel. How do you like those apples? Are you surprised? I sure am.

As you know, General LeMay has left us, and although I was in China and didn't get to see him before he left, he left some very complimentary remarks about my Group with the lad who went down to bid him good-bye in my place, and he left a promotion for me. Sure was a compliment to the bunch of fellows we have in this outfit.

Now, My Sweet, I will ask you to send me something. Colonel's insignia is impossible to get out here. I have borrowed two eagles, but I sure would appreciate it if you could send me about four sets of regular-sized eagles and a set of the small ones for my collar. If you give my serial number, you should be able to buy them at most any Military Clothing Store.

Letter to Mom and Dad, January 19, 1945

We have a new pet here you would like, Mom. It's a little fluffy yellow kitten named Tiger who lives in the barracks and makes herself at home in all the quarters. She is visiting me this evening and has been running wild all over the room. We sure have had a lot of fun with her.

It's nice to get back to India this time of year. The weather here since October has been ideal. The most beautiful weather I've seen anyplace. Cool in the evenings and warm all day and never a cloud in the sky. China, this time of year, is colder than the North Pole, and it's a relief to get away from the place. In another couple of months when it begins to get hot down here, however, it will be another story.

Tiger thinks this letter-writing business is really fine. She is sitting on my lap now and purring and rocking back and forth in complete contentment. She sure is a nice little cat.

Tell Bob and Lee Donoran I had quite a lot of fun giving away the baby caps and socks they sent to the little Chinese kids on my last visit. The mothers were very proud of the Migway (American) cloths, and whenever I'd make a presentation, a large crowd would gather to smile and shout "digo hao." Everyone seemed to appreciate the procedure whole-heartedly.

Letter to Lee, January 23, 1945

The war news looks good nearly everyplace again. The Germans' big push in Belgium has been stopped, the landing on Luzon seems to have been a success, the Japs are being squeezed out of Burma, and the Ledo Road will soon be open. The Italian deal is pretty well stagnated, but that is to be expected. Only in China is the news really bad, and I'm afraid it will take landings on the South China Coast before the China situation really begins to improve.

I'm sending you another Oak Leaf Cluster for our DFCs. That will make a total of three apiece for the DFC and the Air Medal.

Letter to Lee, January 30, 1945

Big event today. The P.X. got in some good pens, and I'm writing this letter with a nice new Eversharp pen, which I bought. It sure does work better than that 50-cent job I've been using for the past couple of months. They came in sets, so I have a new Eversharp pencil, too. They are really quite good-looking.

As usual, Tiger is helping me write this letter this evening. She's all over the place and cute as the dickens, but not much help, I can assure you.

Valentines came from you and Ed today. You are a precious wife, and I love you to pieces. I especially enjoyed the one about "Roses are Red, Violets are Blue." That's a heck of a thing to send to a guy way out here who can't do anything about it. I'll get back at you some day.

Authorization came through today awarding our outfit four Battle Citations. One for the Burma Campaign, one for the China Campaign, one for the Malay Air Offensive (as the result of our Palembang, Sumatra missions some months ago), and one for the Japan Air Offensive. Those with the three we already have will give us seven battle clasps on our Asiatic Medal when it comes out and gives us one silver and two bronze stars on the Asiatic Ribbon. Some stuff, huh??

Sure hope we can wind this war up in a hurry so that this coming hot season will be my last in India. At least, the weather here is nicer than it was in the South Pacific. It could never be as miserable here as it was on Guadalcanal.

Darling Wife, this again has been a very poor letter. When things are quiet, I have nothing to write about, and when we are busy, I don't have time to write. It's a heck of a situation.

Letter to Lee, February 9, 1945

Darling, with this letter I'll include a couple or three requests for snacks. We can get candy and sweet stuff here, but most of it doesn't come through the mail in very good shape, and it doesn't last long in this climate. Besides I'm not much of a candy eater anyway, but any kind of snack material is worth its weight in diamonds. Stuff like jars of cheese, cans of olives, canned tuna, peanut butter, sardines, oysters—in fact, anything that can be packed and eaten. Also unsweetened crackers are nice to eat with such stuff. We can get cookies at the P.X., but a ginger cookie doesn't go so well with anchovy paste on it. Any kind of cracker is worth a million dollars. Most of the boys have a pretty good stock of snack material, and I've been sponging off of them.

Letter to Lee, February 20, 1945

Guess I'll have to take bridge lessons from you when I come home because you seem to be winning pretty consistently, and I lost badly in our last session a couple nights ago.

Our raid yesterday was very, very easy and very successful. Actually, none of our missions have been as rough as some of those we used to pull in the South Pacific. I went with Al Bores this time. He's a nice young Captain with a young daughter just about three months younger than Ed whom he has never seen. He has a good crew, and we really did a first rate job on our target, which was at Kuala Lumpur in the Malay states. That made my 14th mission on this tour and ran me over 400 hours of operational time, which is not bad for an old desk pilot like me. I sure am proud of this outfit, Honey. They've done such superior work for me that all kinds of praise falls my way from higher commands that I don't deserve at all. One just couldn't ask for a better bunch of officers and men than I have in my Group.

Today was also a big day for us. This morning Admiral Mountbatten paid us a brief visit, looked the place over, met about thirty of my boys, and chatted with them for a few minutes apiece, and then made about a 20-minute talk to all the Combat Crews. Lord Louie is quite a guy. He made a point of being most informal, and the boys all liked him very much.

Darling, I don't know how much you hear about our individual units here but if you every read about "the Billy Mitchell Group," you will know that is my outfit. Billy Mitchell's widow presented his personal flag, which he used to fly on his yacht, to the 20th Bomber Command, and they had a contest between Groups to see who got the flag. The outfit which did the best job on specific missions gets to retain possession of the flag until the next mission, and the Group winning it three times gets to keep it. We won it once, let another group nose us out once, and then won it twice more in succession to retain it permanently. We incorporated the flag into an insignia and wrote the War Department for permission to adopt it as our official insignia. We received approval and also authorization from Mrs. Mitchell, so we now have our insignia painted on all our airplanes and wear it on our flying jackets. We are quite proud of our title.

Letter to Mom and Dad, February 20, 1945

Dad, I was thinking this evening of one of the arguments you used to use on me when you were trying to convince me that my life wouldn't be complete until I'd mastered the typewriter. You said that Al Cullen became a Sergeant in the last war solely because of his ability to type. Guess I sure have missed the boat. It kind of hurts to know that if I had only followed your advice, I might have been able to work my way all the way up to Sergeant in this war. Sure looks as though my opportunity to get ahead in the Army has passed me by.

If you want to send something out that would bring us all a lot of fun, it would be a collection of 25 cent to $1 musical instruments. Say about four different sizes of sweet potatoes and one of every type of tin whistle or toy flute you can find. There are several of us here who can toot horns by ear, and although real instruments are out of the question over here, we have lots of fun with what few toys we've been able to make or acquire. I've made a saxophone by fastening a little Bakelite flute onto the stem of a bowl of a big calabash pipe, and one of the boys has built kind of a slide trombone out of a homemade bamboo mouthpiece and a bicycle pump. We can even turn out some of the better-known tunes.

Letter from Dad, March 7, 1945

I got a great kick out of what you said about the typewriting business. I can see now that I was slightly off the beam—who ever heard of a big shot using a typewriter—unless it was a very good-looking one. Still, Al Cullen always led me to believe that a Sergeant was quite something to arrive at—of course, we were not personally acquainted with any Colonels in World War I.

I had a strange lady in the office just now who asked me if I was the father of Col. Edmundson, etc. etc.—said she and her family had been following your career and were always looking for news of you.

Just back from the village—got quite an assortment of gadgets for you fellows to blow—we will ship them off tomorrow.

Letter to Lee, March 9, 1945

Sweet, one of the boys here has a book called Blood for the Emperor. I've never seen it before. It's written by a guy named Clausen and is a pretty good account of the early days of the war in the Pacific. There is a little chapter in it about Blondie Saunders and also one about your husband. It would be a nice book for you to acquire for our library.

A few nights ago, it was too hot to sleep, and so about 10:00, I gave up and went out to sit in the dark on the front porch and smoke my pipe until the evening cooled off a little. The moon was shining, and a warm breeze was blowing, and I could almost imagine it was one of those warm evenings in Hawaii when we used to wander down along Pearl Harbor channel to cool off. The illusion was complete even to being able to hear the movie in the distance, down on the other side of camp, just as we used to be able to hear it on the shore of the channel from the boats out in the harbor. It sure did make me homesick for our little house on Hickam Field. We did have a lot of fun there, didn't we, my darling wife. Some day we'll have to go back to Hawaii for a tour of duty, when the war is over.

Letter to Lee, March 13, 1945

We had quite a night last night. About 8 o'clock, we had a local windstorm move through here which really raised Cain. It tore the thatched roofs off of most of our houses and blew the airplanes around considerably. We were lucky in that no serious damage was done to any of our B-29s. They had it much worse at some of the other bases. One base quite near here had big hail with their wind. Our big hope now is that the Indian contractors will get new roofs built on our houses before the rainy season begins. Guess it won't really matter, however, as the roofs leak like sieves, even when new and at their best. These houses are really something. They are straw and tied together with string. They cost us just about 10 times what they are actually worth.

Day before yesterday, I polished off a very successful mission to Kuala Lumpur. That was my 15th since arriving here. There are only four or five pilots in the group with more missions than I have. General Ramey, however, won't let the Group Commanders fly very often, and I'm afraid I'll be dropping by the wayside before long.

It really looks as though the 21st Bomber Command is hitting them a lick. General LeMay is a real soldier and is putting them on the map. I sure would like to be over in that part of the world and socking Japan every other day.

The whole war is looking better these days. I still look to the end of organized resistance in Germany some time around my birthday [June 18]. Then the war against the Japs will really get under way in earnest.

Letter to Lee, March 20, 1945

Do you realize, My Sweet, that of the many, many pictures you have sent me of Ed, not half a dozen of them show you. You look just as sweet and pretty and loving in this new picture as I remember you, and I've been carrying it around in my pocket and taking it out to study when I've had a minute or two ever since it arrived this morning. Why don't you break down and send your husband some pin-up pictures of his beautiful little wife. I would rather have a lot of new pictures of you, My Sweet, than anything else I can think of.

Letter to Lee, March 24, 1945

I'm writing this afternoon with the help of Tiger, our little kitten. She has sure grown and is about a half grown and very nice-looking cat. Since the weather has been so hot, she has acquired the habit of leaving her mouth open and panting like a dog. The boys have felt sorry for her, and two days ago they gave her a clipping. They even did quite an artistic job of scalloping her tail. I can't say it improved her looks at all, but at least she doesn't pant any more.

We had a very nice little mission down to Rangoon day before yesterday. It was highly successful and not so tough either. That brings my total up to 17 for this theater.

Quite a surprise to hear that Ed seems to be turning into a southpaw. It will be a little inconvenient for him but shouldn't cause him too much trouble. His old man has gotten along okay.

It seems to me as it does to you that now the first year is practically out of the way, we are on our last lap. Also, with the war progressing the way it is all over the world, it seems pretty sure that this tour will be the last one. The next time I go on foreign duty, I'll be able to take you and Ed with me. How would you like that?

Letter to Lee, March 30, 1945

Things have been going along as usual except the days are getting progressively hotter all the time. It gets up to 106 or 107 every day now, and in another month, it will be hitting 120 every afternoon around 2 o'clock. What a country!

Darling, it will soon be your birthday. Time sure does fly by. This letter should arrive there before your birthday, but I'll wish you a happy birthday anyhow. I arrived at this Base the day after your birthday last year, so I've nearly rounded out my first year in India. That leaves only one to go if I'm lucky.

The war is sure coming along in fine style these days. The way they are chopping Western Germany apart, it looks as though my prediction of the European War being over in June will work out about right. When that day comes, it should really speed up operations on this side of the world. Those Japs should be able to read the handwriting on the wall.

We made a startling discovery the other day. Tiger, our little kitten, is a tomcat. We have figured from the start that he was a she, but it looks as though we have been wrong.

I'm enclosing another Oak Leaf Cluster for our Air Medal. You can pin it on to the ribbon of the medal. That should make four OLCs for the Air Medal and three for the DFC. Have you received them all?

Darling of mine, I want very much, a picture of you and Ed together. A nice picture. I also want some nice new pictures of you alone. If I don't get some action from you pretty soon on this matter, I'm going to write your mother and have her exert a little pressure.

Letter to Lee, April 2, 1945

Yesterday was Easter Sunday. I was thinking all day about the Easter Sunday we had in Washington two years ago. Remember going to the little church on the corner near our place in Arlington? Also it was on Easter Sunday last year that I took off from Salina on the first leg of the trip over here. It sure does seem a long time ago.

Darling, I'm taking off tomorrow on a three-day pass. It will be my first time off since arriving in the theatre. I want to shop around and see if there is anything to buy and send home to my wife. I have a couple of ideas. I also want to look around and see the sights and eat some good food. It's been a year since I've eaten a steak. I don't have any fancy plans drawn up yet, but Frank Nye, my operations officer, and I are going in together and should have a lot of fun. I'll write you a full report on my return.

Received a letter from George Putnam today saying he had written you telling you about his plans to get married this June. How do you like that old rascal? He sure does believe in trying again if the first few attempts are discouraging.

Letter to Lee, April 8, 1945

Yesterday I returned from my pass in town, and we sure did have a fine time. It is awfully nice to get back to the field and go to work again, but we really did have a wonderful rest and change in town. We got a nice big hotel room on the fourth floor of the biggest hotel, and it was really quite comfortably cool with the breeze blowing in the windows and the ceiling fan on.

We concentrated on our meals, and while we were unable to find any steaks, we did have several mighty fine meals. One hotel had an air-conditioned dining room, which was surely a pleasure to eat in.

One afternoon we spent shopping in one of the big bazaars. There were so few things that were worth buying. Most of the stuff for sale is strictly junk; strictly for the tourist trade, and you wouldn't have it around the house. Most of the things that are worth having, like star sapphires, etc. are now more expensive over here than in the States. Also, the jewelry business here is crooked as the devil, and there is no way of knowing just what you are buying. I looked all over for a silver bracelet for you to replace the one you lost, but the silver is all strictly second-rate. I couldn't find a thing that even approached any of the silver I bought in Fiji.

I finally wound up buying a couple of Gurkha knives. I don't know who we'll give them to or what we'll do with them, but they are nice knives and very interesting. Hope you're not too disappointed in the dismal failure of my shopping tour, but I just couldn't find anything I thought you would like.

We had an interesting time wandering around town and viewing the sights. The temples and burning ghats where the Hindus cremate their dead are worth seeing, but to me, the people in those places are much more interesting than the buildings. There is such a mixture of people on the streets of this town.

The Hindus with their sheets wrapped around them and their caste marks painted or tattooed on their faces and the Hindu women with jewels embedded in the side of their nose. There are Hindu beggars of every description on the streets. Some of them are horribly crippled, diseased or deformed. They have performing monkeys, dancing bears, cobras and mongooses that fight, and all manner of means of begging. There are the Muslims, whose women are never seen. They wear big baggy pants and shave their heads or keep their hair cut short except for a small lock of hair on the top of their head which they let grow long so that Mohamed will be able to grab a hold and pull them up to heaven when they die.

There are the Sikhs from Punjab in northern India who wear tremendous, bright colored turbans. They are all very big, husky men compared with other Indians and frequently get in fights with them. The Sikhs virtually control the taxicab industry in the city. It is against their religion to ever drink, smoke, shave, or have their hair cut. They roll their beards tightly up against their face and stuff all their hair up under their turban. When they get themselves into a fight, the first act of their opponent seems to always be to try and grab his turban so his hair will get down in his way.

There are also Gurkhas, who are mostly British Colonial soldiers around here, and Punjabis who are mostly policemen, and the Bengalis who are tradesmen and shop keepers. It is really a colorful, interesting, dirty, smelly, crowded city.

Letter to Lee, April 9, 1945

Sweet, I got a kick out of your story about the canned fruit cocktail you had managed to get a hold of and were saving for a special occasion, maybe my homecoming. If it is a treat to you, Darling, you'd better eat it before I get there because that is our standard dessert, and we have had it five and six times a week until nobody can eat it any more.

Letter to Lee, April 11, 1945

A very, very swell little letter came from you yesterday. You sounded a little bit lonesome and very anxious to have the war over with. It was a wonderful letter. It is nice to hear that you miss me once in a while. Anyone who says any different is wrong. Of course, I don't want to think that you are too unhappy, but it would be a hell of a state of affairs if you were getting along without me just as well as you would if I was there. It's nice to know you do miss me and need me a little because I miss you so much it hurts. Sometimes it seems as though I won't be able to get through another day without you.

Letter to Mom and Dad, April 11, 1945

I can never get over how lucky I am in having a job that I enjoy, and am interested in. If working for Kress, Goodyear, Douglas, and some of those other places never did another thing for me, they impressed me with the fact that 99% of the people in the world hate their jobs and live for the moments when they aren't working. Their working hours are strictly drudgery. A person is surely fortunate to be able to work at something he is interested in and good at.

The weather here is getting hotter every day. We are in for some pretty miserable weather until the first of July when the rainy season starts, and then it won't really be nice again until around the first of October when it starts to cool off a little.

Sure do hope this will be my last summer in India. The way the war is going now, it looks as though that might be possible. I still think the Germans will fold *around the middle of June, and it will take another 18 months for the Japs. That would wind up the war around Christmas of 1946, and what a great day that will be. It's taken a long time to get this far, but things should move at an ever-increasing pace from here on out.*

Letter from Dad, April 18, 1945

Since I last wrote you, the President* has passed away. I have never seen anything that caused half so much feeling over the country. From the time he died on Thursday, April the 12th, nothing went on the radio until the following Monday except programs paying some sort of a tribute to him—no commercials. Stage, screen and radio stars, radio commentators, opera stars, newspaper men, politicians—all seemed to vie to do him homage.

Well, you seem to enjoy references to my Date Book once in a while—On April 18, 1938—you flew over the Canyon for the first time. On April 16, 1943—we received the first letter from you after you went to Washington.

It seems that the war in Europe is going to naturally peter out. Germany is in the bag, but they go on fighting. Perhaps it is just as well that way—maybe the whole war effort will blend into the Pacific Theatre more smoothly than if there was a big hullabaloo over V-E Day.

We certainly enjoyed meeting Major Putnam and his intended. We had a mighty nice visit. He said one thing out of the clear sky that really stuck in our memories. I have forgotten what we were talking about, but the Major turned to Nora and said, "Your son will be a General one of these days." Anyway, it was a mighty nice thing for him to say.

---

* President Franklin Delano Roosevelt, January 30, 1882–April 12, 1945.

part six

TINIAN, 1945

chapter thirty-four

WINDING DOWN THE WAR

Early in 1945, we got word that a base was ready for us on Tinian (one of the islands in the Marianas) and that we were to move from our bases in India and China to Tinian. This was good news for several reasons. It would put us closer to Japan where we would be able to carry much bigger bomb loads, and we would no longer be faced with the job of ferrying everything over the Hump before we could fly a mission. Also, we would be part of a bigger effort. General LeMay, who had been with us in India and China, now was on Guam commanding the 20th Air Force. There was a wing of four B-29 groups flying out of Saipan and another wing flying out of the other field on Tinian. Two more wings were in training in the States and would be coming out to fly out of Guam. This meant that instead of the raids of a few dozen B-29s that we had been flying out of China, the 20th Air Force would be able to put 1,000 B-29s in the air on a mission. The war in Europe had been won, and the B-17 and B-24 outfits were being brought home, retrained in B-29s that were pouring out of three factories, and sent to the Pacific.

Equally important, we were now being served by a short pipeline that ran directly from the United States, across the Pacific Ocean to us, instead of being on a supply line that ran three-quarters of the way around the world. We were going to be a lot more effective, and that meant that the war would be won that much sooner. We were hitting with power where it hurt, instead of nibbling around the edges. And the capture of Iwo Jima by the Marines meant we now would have fighter escort over Japan from the long-range P-51s being moved into Iwo Jima. And our loss rates went way down. We used to kid that the loss rate of the transport guys flying our B-29s out to us from the States was higher than ours was when flying combat.

And of course, I was now closer to Lee. Our letters got back and forth in a few days instead of a few weeks. Things were surely looking up.

Letter to Lee, May 16, 1945

Golly, Sweetheart, it's been a long time since I've been able to write. Just yesterday, they cleared us to use our new A.P.O. number, and for the present, that is just about all they will okay. We can say we are in the Pacific Ocean Area, which should be pretty obvious since we now have a San Francisco A.P.O. number and, as a great favor to us, they gave us special permission to say we are on an island. You should know that also already, since you are well aware that these airplanes of ours are not very well adapted for Carrier landings and take offs. It's sure a shame that censorship regulations are always so far behind schedule, but that's the Army for you.

It's like old times to have a San Francisco A.P.O. number. Somehow it seems as though I was nearer to home than when you were writing to the New York number. Actually it is closer to home, too, and mail service should be much quicker than it was. Mail is already being diverted to us here from our old address, and I've already received a most wonderful letter from you, my darling wife, and one from the folks.

We are very happy in our new home, Darling. The food is better than it ever was in India or China and is getting better all the time. The climate is perfect, and as it was 120 degrees in the shade on the day I left India, we are sure pleased on that score. Our camp area is still rather rough and is under construction, but already we are having it better than we ever did in India, and in another couple of months, this will be like the Waldorf-Astoria in comparison.

As you can well imagine, we are working like demons, day and night, trying to carry on full scale operations and get established in a new base at the same time while we are short handed and low on equipment. For this reason, I won't be able to write as often as I would like to for a while. Please explain this to our families. I'll write to you as often as I can, and the other letter writing will have to wait for a while.

I made my first mission from here day before yesterday, and as nearly as I can tell, this is going to be the easiest theatre to operate in I've hit yet. The missions are going to be easier and safer than they were in the South Pacific, Europe, India, China, or anywhere else I've been. It sure is a pleasure to be here.

Well, Darling, I have a hundred things I should be doing right now so I'll sign off and go back to work. I just had to knock off for a few minutes and tell my sweetheart hello. I miss you more and more every day, Precious One, and think of you constantly. Now that the European war is over and we now only have Japan to worry about, it seems as though our final and complete reunion is not too far in the distance. The Japs won't be able to stand up to the terrific drubbing they will be exposed to from here on out. Maybe Ed's little sister won't be too much younger than he is after all.

Letter to Lee, May 19, 1945

Yesterday was a big day. I received three wonderful letters from you, two from your mother and one from my folks. Also arrived two swell boxes of snacks and best of all, the proofs of the pictures you had taken. Sweetheart, they are wonderful. I've been carrying them around in my pocket and showing them to everyone I see. I've nearly worn them out just staring at them myself. You get more beautiful as time goes by. How I was ever lucky enough to talk you into marrying me I'll never understand. The best part is that you are about twice as sweet as you are beautiful, and that's really something. Golly, I love you. I just can't get over how wonderful the pictures are. The one of you and Ed together, both all dressed in white, is perfect.

Our camp area is shaping up in fine style, and we will really be well situated in another couple of months. There are so many nice things about this place. The weather is almost ideal. There are almost no bugs of any kind. There are no mosquitoes at all, hence no mosquito nets and no malaria. Even the tap water here is fit to drink without boiling or chlorinating, which sure seems strange. I'm having a hard time getting used to driving on the left hand side of the street, however.

Johnnie East and I live in a nice frame tent with screened sides, board floors raised off the ground, electric lights, and nearly all the comforts of home.

We have a radio set up in the tent so we can hear shortwave broadcasts from the States, and we've built ourselves tables and cupboards out of old bomb boxes, which furnishes the place in fine style. Everyone is sure glad to be here, and the boys are doing a wonderful job so far. If everyone works as hard and as well as this outfit of mine does, we'll polish off the last half of this war in a hurry.

Letter to Lee, May 20, 1945

I'm enclosing a clipping that Major Putnam sent me in his last letter that I think is exceptionally good. It offers as good a picture of the flying truck driver and his job that I have seen. When this war is over, I still plan on transferring back into Pursuit. I still think I'd make a better fighter pilot than a bomber man.

Treasure Chest

ELLIOTT ARNOLD, in "Tomorrow Will Sing" (Duell, Sloan and Pearce)

Men in Bombers

Fighter pilots get emotional because their work is quick and it ends before the emotion has time to end, and the emotion is still with them when they climb out of their planes. A fighter pilot can get drunk, but a heavy bomber just works, an aerial taxi driver, he calls himself ruefully, a freight engineer and he just works and the men who fly with him just work.

Long-range heavy bombardment takes hours, three and four hours going and three and four hours returning, and that is too long for emotion to last. There is brief emotion when the enemy closes in and there is the feeling of combat, vicarious for everyone except the men at the guns at the moment, and the Bombardier gets it briefly when he squeezes and the bombs cascade out, but those moments are lost in the long monotony of the mission, the hours of steady, noisy airplane pounding in the air, the deadly drugging effect of the engines on nerves, the long times, one hour, two hours, three hours, four hours, on oxygen, the careful, precise, no-amusing, can't be done improperly stream of things that the pilot, the engineer, the radio man, the navigator have to do, the sitting and waiting, ears aching, head rocking, mind-alert hours, sometime tilting mentally forward for something that may never come, pitching mentally over when it does not come.

Men who fly bombers and who fly in bombers come out of their airplanes exhausted and bored in a way no one was ever been bored before. Men who fly in bombers are not really older than the men who fly in other kinds of airplanes; they just look that way.

Letter to Lee, May 23, 1945

I sure do enjoy your stories about Ed. I know you only tell me the cute things and keep the others to yourself, but even so, he must be quite a wonderful little guy, and I can hardly wait to get back and make his acquaintance. I would give anything to see him sitting up to his little yellow table in his own little red chair and having a tea party for himself. You tell him not to get too excited about the airplanes he sees. His daddy will take him for an airplane ride some day.

We are going full steam ahead out here. No waits and no delays. That is as it should be, and the harder we work, the sooner the war will be over. That great day is now in the visible future, so have patience for just a little while longer. Sometimes it seems to me that I have been fighting this war all my life. It is going to be a wonderful day when it is all over.

This is my first experience in a real, large-scale operation. We are getting all the things now that we needed so badly in the South Pacific in the early days of the war and were never available to us. After the little token operations we ran from India and China, way out on the end of the supply pipeline, this is like being in a different army and fighting a different war. Only the Japs are the same. They haven't changed, except to become less capable and more feeble since December 7, 1941. They are just beginning to pay through the nose for their poor judgment, and the pasting Germany took is nothing to what the Japanese Islands will look like six months from now.

Letter to Lee, June 13, 1945

Now they have okayed our letting you know that we are based somewhere on Tinian. We aren't allowed to state our position on the island, but a quick look at a map will assure you that it isn't large enough for very many of us to hide away. That will answer your question of where we are and set you mind at rest. It is a very pretty little island, much like Hawaii in many ways. You're liable to see it some day as it undoubtedly will be one of the places we hang onto for a peacetime station. I think you would like it here.

Letter to Lee, June 27, 1945

I've persuaded Gen. Ramey to relax a little bit on my flying, and I got another mission in yesterday. It was a pleasant change from all the groundwork I have now. It's still a great personal satisfaction to get out and drop a bomb or two on Japan.

We are turning loose lots of our boys these days and sending them home. They have decided that 35 missions constitute a tour of duty, and most of my old crews are going home now or in the very near future. Your husband, of course, not being a combat man, is not eligible and will stay here until the war is won. The way things are rolling now, however, it shouldn't take too awfully long. Just a little while longer, My Sweetheart, and we can be together for the rest of our lives.

Letter to Lee, July 6, 1945

Golly, Honey, these are busy days for us over here. It's been several days since I've written, but the pressure is on us, and we are working night and day.

I made another mission the other night. My 27th and that always throws me behind schedule because with missions going out practically every other night, and the planning and preparations takes a day and most of a night, so when I go, I stay up most of the night and all day on the planning, then all night flying it, get a few hours sleep through the next afternoon, and then work a night and a day getting the following mission ready to go. It then takes me a night to catch up on my sleep and another night to catch up on the paper work that has piled up while I was gone. Then, too, around the end of July is the beginning of the Fiscal Year when the Army closes its books, and lots of extra reports are always due around this time of year. It's fun, though, and I'm happy as I can be because we are really hurting the Japs. Also time goes much faster when we are busy.

We had a very bad night here the other night. We lost Ted Watson, who took over my squadron when I went to Group. You and I spent an evening talking to him and his wife at the club in Salina one night. They are the couple that wanted a youngster so badly. Lt. Marsh was with him. It sure hurts to lose boys like that. This is a nasty war.

Letter to Lee, July 13, 1945

I had all my hair cut off again about a week ago. Clipped all over with my bare skull hanging out. I'll admit it doesn't look too sharp, but it sure feels nice and cool. I don't dare come home now for a while, even if I get a chance. I'd have a divorce on my hands for sure. I'll have to wait at least until my hair grows again.

This place is sure busy. It's like living on the inside of a tornado. My only consolation is that it's probably even busier for the Japs these days, and as the old saying goes, "It's better to give than to receive." Anyway, I'm happy not to be on the receiving end of this activity.

Letter to Lee, July 19, 1945

Our scale of operations is increasing all the time. Missions are coming more often and getting bigger and bigger. In addition to our efforts, the fighter sweeps from Iwo and Okinawa are doing a lot of good, and now that the B-24s from Okinawa are getting into the war, the Japs will have no rest. Add to this the constant Naval attacks, both the carrier aircraft sweeps and the shelling by our battle wagons are beginning to bear fruit. And they "ain't seen nothin' yet"!! If they aren't smart enough to quit pretty soon, they won't have anything left to defend by the end of the year. The war is sure going along by leaps and bounds these days.

We are doing our best to improve our living conditions here in our spare time. Our Chapel is now finished, and our Mess Halls are pretty well fixed up. Our next big project is an Enlisted Men's Club.

Letter to Lee, July 31, 1945

Tonight is a big night. The Eddie Bracken Show is scheduled to play at our Bomb Box Bowl at 7:30, and by a strange coincidence, we are in a position to knock off and see the show. Stage shows are few and far between out here, so we are all looking forward to seeing it.

Personal troubles are beginning to take more and more of my time. We are going into our second year away, and lots of things are developing now that weren't happening in such large numbers before—to officers and enlisted men alike. I'm beginning to think that if all the unfaithful wives in the States were stretched end to end, there would be darn few wives left out of the line. There sure have been some heartbreaking cases the past month. I feel so sorry for some of these kids. If it was just a few isolated cases, it wouldn't be so bad, but the situation is so general that I'm afraid the illegitimate babies born to wives of husbands overseas is apt to be a major problem when the boys come home. It's pitiful to talk to them because they are so damn helpless to do anything about it, and it involves more than just infidelity. In one case, his wife had farmed out the officer's young son, and he had a doctor's report that the youngster was suffering from malnutrition and had rickets. The wife was running around with another guy and had admittedly had one abortion, had spent all his money which he had saved to go through Medical School after the war, had sold his car, all their furniture and his clothes, and had run him several thousand dollars in debt. She wouldn't let anyone else have the child and wouldn't take care of him herself. He couldn't take any legal action here. He couldn't even stop her allowance. Other cases are much more sordid. Some of these kids get to wondering just what in the hell they are fighting for, and I'm inclined to see their point. Thank God, that's one thing I don't have to worry about.

Letter to Lee, August 2, 1945

The boys came back today from another very successful mission with no losses in our outfit. Our loss rate has dropped off to the point where we are actually *losing less people per hour flown than they are losing back home in the Training Command.*

We had over 800 ships out last night, which is some sort of a new record, and we are only just beginning. In another six months, we will have more than doubled our effort. It's hard to understand how the Japs can sit there and take it indefinitely.

It sounds as though you have done a fine job in buying up Martini mixings and stuff. I haven't mixed a Martini for so long I'm afraid I wouldn't know how to any more. At least it will take a lot of practice to get back into the groove.

Oh, yes, before I forget it, I had a chat with Mickey Moore up at Iwo Jima the other day. He is a Brig. General now and in command of all fighters on Iwo. He was at Hickam with us. He was C.O. of the Wing Headquarters Squadron before I took it over. He has been in the Pacific for just over six years without leaving it and hasn't seen his wife since she was evacuated on Christmas Day 1941. Some people have it tougher than we do, My Sweet.

chapter thirty-five

A WHISPER AWAY

Paul Tibbets, a flying school classmate of mine, arrived on Tinian with his 509th Group and his atomic bombs. By the time Paul got there, the Japs were already beaten. Paul provided the force to make them admit it.

I was returning to Tinian on 14 August, from a mission bombing the Hikari Naval Arsenal, when we received the news over the radio that the Japanese had unconditionally surrendered. The war was over.

A few days later, I received a phone call in my tent that General Roger Ramey, the 58th Wing Commander, wanted to see me right away. I jeeped over to his headquarters, and when I was ushered into his office, General Ramey told me, "Eddie, I just had a call from General LeMay on Guam. The Surrender Papers are going to be signed on the battleship *USS Missouri* in Tokyo Bay on 2 September. There is going to be a victory formation of 500 B-29s fly over the deck of the *Missouri* at low altitude while the Papers are being signed. General LeMay told me that the 58th Wing was the best wing in the 20th Air Force and that we would have the honor of leading the 500-plane formation. Now I'm telling you, Eddie, that your 468th Group is the best group in my wing. You are going to lead the wing, and I'm going to fly with you."

What a day. I got off a very short note to Lee, "We won the war, Sweetheart, and I'm coming home to you."

Letter to Lee, August 17, 1945

The great day is finally here, My Sweet One. It hardly seems possible, after all this time, that the war ever could have ended, but is sure has. Yesterday was an official holiday, our first since the half-day last Christmas. We had a big party the night before and spent yesterday taking life easy and recovering from the night before.

I saw this old war through from one end to the other. I made the last mission that was flown, and we heard about the Jap reply on our way home. It was a fine mission and highly successful, a fine one to finish up on. That makes 28 for me during this tour and gives me a total of 106 missions for the war. Sure am glad it's over.

Sweetheart, what the future holds for us here now is still a deep and dark mystery. I don't know what we will be doing or how long it will be until we get home. I will get home just as quickly as I can. I've already told the General that the sooner he can replace me and send me home, the better. I do know, Sweet, that it will be rather a slow process. We will have much to do here for a few months, anyway, and I don't really expect to leave here inside of three months. At any rate, we should have next Christmas together. The fighting is all over, and all we have to do now is stand by, and before we know it, we will be together again.

Letter to Lee, August 19, 1945

It's nice not to be grinding out combat missions as we were at one time. I think we'll be kept busy here until such time as we have the Empire completely occupied and disarmed. Just what part we will play in the occupation of Japan is, as yet, unknown to us. It all depends on Gen. MacArthur, and so far he's been too busy to let us know. Guess he doesn't really know himself, yet.

Now that things are relatively quiet, we have started taking Sundays off again, and that is sure a good deal. Today is my first Sunday off since we were in Washington together. I slept in until 7:30 and had a nice leisurely breakfast and came down to the office to clean up what paper work was lying around and to write a letter to my sweet wife. Pretty soft, huh?

Letter to Mom and Dad, August 24, 1945

This is the first letter I've written to you since the cessation of hostilities. (I can't say the end of the war, yet.) Needless to say, these are pretty happy days out here. It will mean a fairly prompt return to the States to many of the boys who have been away a long time. Unfortunately your son, as a professional soldier, has lots of work to do even after the war is won. The citizen soldiers have won the war and now will be released to return to their normal occupations as soon as possible, but as my normal occupation is being an officer in the United States Army, I'm afraid there is still lots to be done out here. Much political pressure is being brought to bear on the early release of draftees, which is fine for them but will mean that the rest of us will have to work just so much harder cleaning up the mess that has been made, reorganizing, regrouping, redeploying, and getting things back to normal.

The worst is over, however. It is going to be wonderful to be able to fly again without being shot at, and my life from here on out will have to be devoted to keeping our Air Corps strong, capable, modern, and tactically sound so that nobody else will ever be able to afford to fight with us again and so others will never have to go through some of the things I've seen and done in the past three years. Some of it has been pretty nasty. I'll never be able to explain to anyone how terrible some of it has been and what an effort it has taken for me to force myself into doing some of the things my conscience has told me were necessary. Anyhow, it's wonderful to have it over, and it shouldn't be too terribly long now before I'm able to come home.

The war came to a very satisfactory conclusion as far as I am personally concerned. I led the entire Wing on the last mission. It was a perfect mission in every respect—tactically perfect. We plastered the target; there was just enough opposition to make things interesting and no losses from my outfit. We received the cease-fire order when we were on our way home. It was a fine finish to the war. It was my 28th B-29 mission and my 106th for the war, including all theaters. As far as I know, I am the only person who saw the bitter end of the war on the final mission that was also present when the war started on Hickam Field.

It's a little hard right now for all of us to get geared back down to normal after the pace we have been working at for so long. We had our first Sunday off last week and everyone had such a guilty feeling to be loafing—it almost took the pleasure out of the holiday. I suppose it will be several months before living a relatively normal life will seem natural to me again, and I guess there are lots of fellows that never will be able to settle down again. Still others who have been working under pressure for so long will fall flat on their face when the pressure is removed and will find they are burned out beyond repair—have been for a long time and were going so hard and so fast that they hadn't noticed it before. Anyhow, anyone who is still alive right now is tremendously lucky.

Letter to Lee, August 23, 1945

We are still more or less marking time until we find out what the plans are for us. It sure sounds as though General MacArthur is going to move in and take over with an iron hand, and I sure hope he has a place for us in his operations. It would sure beat sitting around here not doing anything.

I want to let you know that things appear to be looking up. I think this is the first letter I have ever written to you that was at all hopeful about my coming home, so it is really an event. It kind of looks to me as though I might be home sometime in October if I play my cards right. WOW!! What a wonderful day that will be.

Letter to Lee, September 5, 1945

The biggest news today is that as of right now censorship is being discontinued. It is sure going to be nice to be able to write to just you again and not have lots of other people reading our mail. Censorship has been a necessary evil but also a tremendous nuisance. It is one of the many bothers of wartime living like rationing, shortages, discourtesy, blackouts, and curfews that we will be able to forget about.

They have a new ruling now that when combat soldiers return to the U.S. and are reassigned, they are authorized to wear the shoulder patch of their fighting outfit on their right shoulder even though they joined a new outfit. They wear the patch of their current organization on their left shoulder still as they do now, but in addition, they will be able to identify themselves with the outfit they fought with. I think it's kind of a nice idea, and it will mean that I can always wear the 20th Air Force shoulder patch. I'm glad because it's an outfit I'm proud to have belonged to since it's the outfit that licked Japan.

You will hear claims that MacArthur's Air Force won the war, that the Navy won it, that the Atomic bomb won it, or that the entry of the Russians won the war. This is not the right story. They all contributed, but they were only the additional straws that broke the camel's back. The B-29 boys did the real damage. They were the only ones who could and did hit Japan everyplace, day after day, and a close look at the damage which the Japs suffered was inflicted 99.9999% by B-29s. In my estimation, the submarine blockade was the second-most important factor that contributed. The Navy's help was chiefly in that it brought out our supplies and carried the men who fought for and took the island bases we absolutely had to have to operate from. Their help was of the same order as the help of the aircraft industry in producing and building in larger numbers, a wonderful piece of machinery like the B-29. We couldn't have won the war without any of these things, but the point of the spearhead was the B-29 airplane and the lads that flew them.

Letter to Lee, September 6, 1945

My Sweetheart. This will probably be a very long letter as there is much to tell you. Last Saturday night, we were set up for our last mission. It was a big show formation to be flown Monday morning over the battleship Missouri *during the signing ceremonies. Our 58th Wing, having been in the war the longest, was given the honor of leading the 500-odd B-29's that were to make up the formation. General Ramey flew as Force Commander, and I took an airplane as Deputy Force Commander. I was to fly on his wing in the Lead Element if all went well or take over the lead of the entire show if his airplane had any trouble and couldn't make it. As the evening wore on, it began to appear as though the weather over Tokyo would leave a lot to be desired. Finally, it was decided that the two lead ships would take off three hours ahead of the Main Force in order to scout the weather and make decisions as to whether or not the mission could be run and to decide on the best assembly points and altitude, and radio the information back to the rest of the ships.*

We took off at midnight and arrived over downtown Tokyo at 7 a.m. The weather was much better than we had expected. We sent out radio instructions and then had three hours to just cruise around and look the place over until the main force of B-29s arrived.

From 2,000 feet, we could see everything there was to see, and it sure was a wonderful morning! Of course, I've been there before but always at a higher altitude and always so busy that I hadn't been able to do much looking around. Also, I have studied post-bombing pictures of all the burned out cities, but it is impossible to realize the actual extent of destruction until you can fly over it at low altitude, in broad daylight, and actually take a look. We cruised around admiring out handiwork for three hours and sure enjoyed it. We saw the remaining Jap airplanes lined up on the runways, the burned out cities, the Jap Navy upside down in Yokosuka Navy Base, and our own Navy, several hundred ships strong in Tokyo Bay. There were several hospital ships picking up American prisoners of war. One hospital ship was pulled up alongside the dock at Yokohama taking litter cases aboard. There was a convoy of about fifty (troop ships) transports steaming in through the mouth of Tokyo harbor in single file with their American flags flying and their decks and rigging so crowded with soldiers you could hardly see the ships. I opened the window and tossed out my cigar butts over the Emperor's Palace. Golly, it was a fine sight!!

About 11 a.m., we went to the departure point and picked up our 500-ship formation and led it in a big circle over Tokyo, Yokohama, Yokosuka, and then right over the Missouri *while the signing was taking place. The decks of the* Missouri *were white with sailors in their dress uniforms lined up in review formation for the ceremonies.*

As far as I am concerned, Sweetheart, it was a fitting climax for the war. I wouldn't have missed it for a million dollars, and it was a day I'll remember for the all the rest of my life. It was sure fun to remember back to Pearl Harbor Day while flying around over their place.

We got back to Tinian about 7 o'clock and promptly declared Monday a holiday. Then we had a little party, talked the flight over, and went to bed about midnight, planning to sleep-in the next morning.

At 7:30 the next morning, my phone rang, and the Wing informed me that I was ordered to sit on a Reclassification Board that was to meet at 10 o'clock at Guam and would remain in session for about five days. I sure had to hustle to get up and dressed and packed and fly down to Guam and be ready to go to work at 10. I just made it by the skin of my teeth and discovered that I was the Senior Officer on the Board and presided as its President. It was a lot of work and quite a bit of responsibility.

The Board was still in session about 4 o' clock that afternoon when Butch Blanchard* came charging in and said that I was due at General Spaatz' Quarters at once. We recessed the board until next morning, and I went charging off to General Spaatz' house without a wild idea of what was cooking. There was quite a crowd of people there, and before I knew just what was happening, he had lined a few of us up and pinned the Legion of Merit on us. It sure was a surprise. It is a beautiful medal, Darling, and one I know you will like. It is kind of a rose pink color with a narrow white band on each end of the ribbon. I'm enclosing a copy of my citation for you to keep.

There were several people there that you know and I hadn't seen for a long time. George Shaatzel, Cam Sweeny, Boyd Hubbard, Dick Gussendorf, and many more. It seemed that General Spaatz was leaving for Washington the next morning and had to make his presentations in a sort of hurry. Needless to say, I was in kind of a fog by the time it was all over.

Yesterday afternoon I finished up the work of the Reclassification Board and returned to Tinian rather tired and glad to get back.

This is now Thursday morning, and it's raining to beat the dickens. I have cleaned up the paper work that has accumulated while I was away and now

---

* Col. William H. Blanchard.

can write to my darling wife and let her know why it has been so long since the last letter. That should just about bring you up to date.

Our situation here as to just what we are to do and for how long is still pretty confused. It is clearing up slowly, however, and in another couple weeks I should be able to give you a pretty good idea of when to expect me home. Right now, it is my personal guess that I'll be able to be with you on our fifth anniversary. At any rate, I think we are safe in planning on spending Christmas together. Golly Sweetheart, it all seems too good to be true. Don't make too many plans, Darling, and don't be too unhappy if things do not work out quite as well as you would like; but we can hope anyway, and things do look quite promising.

Well, precious, this letter has been far too long already, and I'll bring it to a close. All my love to you, Darling; get Ed all trained to recognize his daddy. What a sensation that will be!

Letter to Lee, September 12, 1945

I am now working on a project to have our field here on Tinian named after Clink.* I've written several letters to the higher powers telling them why this should be named Clinkscale Field, and I believe I might swing it.

Letter to Lee, October 1, 1945

Golly, My Sweet, as time grows shorter it becomes increasingly difficult to think about anything else but being back with you again. It is sure hard to keep my mind on what is going on around me.

We have moved the first 45 airplanes out now. The 444th Group is completely cleared out, and their first Squadron should be in Mather Field right now. Their last Squadron left here last night. Now we sit tight for three nights while the 73rd Wing on Saipan moves a Group out, and then the 462nd Group (of the 58th Wing) starts rolling again from here. I should be on my way the night of the 16th if the schedule holds, and I should fly home as expected. By the end of this month, I should be home with you. WOW!!

Letter to Lee, October 3, 1945

Monday night, the weather was so bad that the first squadron from the 73rd Wing didn't move out for the States, which threw us all a day behind schedule. Their first outfit moved last night, however, so we are back in motion again. I'm

---

* Lt. Col. Robert Clinkscale was killed in action on August 20, 1944, over Yawata.

now scheduled to leave on the night of the 17th. Sure hope there are no more delays.

Darling, I do nothing else but think about you these days and dream about you these nights. Sometimes it seems hardly possible that the old war is over and we are free to pick up where we left off four years ago. Golly, My Precious Wife, life is going to be a wonderful thing from here on out.

Letter to Lee, October 8, 1945

Here it is Monday morning, and another week is under way. The last squadron of the 462nd Group is scheduled to pullout tonight, which will clean up half of the 58th Wing. Then we have a three-day blank period while the second Group from the 73rd Wing on Saipan moves off, and then the 40th Group here will get under way. I'll be rolling in another 10 days now if everything works out right.

Letter to Lee, October 15, 1945

This, My Sweet, is the last letter I am going to write unless something goes wrong somewhere. It is Monday morning, and this Thursday, three days from today, I'll be on my way. When you receive this letter, you will know that I should be less than a week behind it.

We got five of our airplanes off last night. In the next three nights, another Group will move from Saipan, and then I'll roll with the first full squadron of our Group. It's hard to wait.

I'm going to start packing today. It will be a very simple matter. I have no souvenirs to bring home, and just about everything I own I'm going to throw away rather than bring it along. None of my uniforms are fit to wear in civilized country. I have a few pictures and a few papers, and I'll need just enough clothes to get me home.

Well, My Darling, I'll stop now. I hope this is the last letter I ever have to write to you. I hope I never get so far away from you again that I can't whisper I love you.

EPILOGUE, 2001

Time

The night is soft and beautiful,
Our birds are sleeping tight.
I hear their feathers rustling,
As they settle for the night.

The cats that love the hours of dark,
Have disappeared from view.
The night is filled with many things,
For pussy-cats to do.

I've turned the noisy TV off,
Who needs its raucous blare?
I love the whispering, evening sounds,
The silence in the air.

The sun is gone. The moon is full.
Its silvery gleam is clear.
The mangroves cast their shadows,
And the stars seem very near.

The dolphin snort, the mullet splash,
The horned owls softly hoot.
Peace and quiet cover all
Like a silken parachute.

On such a lovely night as this,
My thoughts drift back in time.
To many things I used to do,
When I was in my prime.

I think about the foolish things,
I did along the way,

To make me be the kind of guy,
That's in this chair, today.

And thoughts turn to the future,
The things that may befall.
If I win next week's lottery,
How will I spend it all?

But scientists now tell us,
That time is something more
Than present, past, and future tense,
As we have thought, before.

Time, they say, is part of space.
It's just a fourth dimension.
And movement back and forth in time
Is possible to mention.

I tend to like old-fashioned time,
That's measured by the clock.
Time that we live, day by day,
As seconds count, tick-tock,

Where we can all enjoy "Right now,"
The only time we know.
The past is gone. We cannot change
What we did long ago.

We must forget the days gone by,
Forget mistakes we made.
Forget the "Might have beens," "What ifs,"
And wishes on parade.

And as the years enfold us,
And as time marches on,
Our future, now, is much too short,
For us to dwell upon.

So, as I sit, alone, tonight,
The time that fills my head,
Is not the "Maybes" of the past
Or futures filled with dread.

So I have made a few mistakes,
My future's hard to measure.
The beauty of this lovely night,
Consumes my heart with pleasure.

So what, if I cheat a bit,
As I sit on my throne,
Savoring of this wondrous night,
In dreams, I'm not alone.

DUKE, 2001

On the last mission, the sky was full of B-29s, but I'm sure they had a better view of it all from down below than we did. There were two things about the mission that struck me at the time. One, of course, was the tremendous, historic event that was taking place beneath us in Tokyo Bay. The other was the amazement at being able to fly around over downtown Tokyo at 1,000 feet altitude and not have anyone shooting at us.

From there on, it was all downhill. A point system was developed to determine who were the most deserving people to go home first. A project called Sunset was announced, in which our airplanes would all be flown back to the States. My group, having spent a year in the China-Burma-India Theater (CBI) and being composed of people, like me, who had flown a previous combat tour, was set to go home almost intact. A fighter group commanded by a friend of mine, Colonel Harrison Thyng, that had been based on Ie Shima (a little island near Okinawa), was scheduled to leave their planes behind and fly home with us in our B-29s. They had been deployed to the Pacific directly from their tour in Europe, and they were a high point outfit. We worked for days painting and polishing our airplanes so that we would look like a real outfit when we got back to the States.

We had been watching the news about the Russians with concern. We knew that they had jumped into the war against Japan in the last couple of days without firing a shot, and grabbed off Sakhalin Island, the Kuriles, hunks of Manchuria, and the northern half of Korea, and it looked as though they were ready to grab for more. We also heard disturbing news about their conduct in Europe, grabbing the Balkans, the Baltics, and most of the rest of central Europe. Many of my guys came to me and asked, "Colonel Jim, why are we going home? The war isn't over until the Russians are under control, and then, we can all relax." I pretty much agreed, but I could only tell them that I was sure our outfit would be kept intact, we'd take some leave, and then we'd be ready to go for the Russians, or do anything else they wanted us to do. I couldn't have been more completely wrong!

The 468th arrived back at Sacramento, California, with all of our wonderful crews and all of our shiny B-29s, and found we were in the middle of a frantic demobilization frenzy. Before we could climb down out of the cockpit, some guy came climbing up through the nose wheel well with a handful of papers. "Sign these," he said, "and turn in all of your equipment, and tomorrow, you'll all be civilians." We were dazed, but we followed this guy into the building where there were three processing lines: those who wanted to get out of the Army in a hurry, those who wanted out even faster, and those who wanted out of the Army "yesterday." What a shock! I had a tough time explaining that I was a regular Army officer and wasn't about to turn in all of my equipment, sign their damn papers, and walk out of there in a pin-striped suit. I shorted-out the circuit. They didn't know what to do with me.

"What happens to my airplanes?" I asked, as they were trying to process me. I was told not to worry about them, that they would be left in a backyard corner of the field, and someone else would figure out what to do with them later. "There's no hurry," I was told, "since nobody wants them anymore."

"What about my outfit?" I asked. I was told that I no longer had an outfit, and to "forget about it."

"Where do I report for duty?" was my last question. I was told, "You have an automatic 60-day leave, and you may go home." Eventually, I was told, "Someone will probably send you some orders that tell you what to do."

In just one lousy morning, back in the States, my group had taken more hits than it had during its many months of combat. My people were scattered to the four winds, my beautiful B-29s were headed for the scrap heap, my proud outfit had ceased to exist, and I had been placed on indefinite hold. It was a glum homecoming for a conquering hero!

So ended my World War II. Of course, this isn't the end of the story. Things slowly began to fall back into place. New units were formed, and most of us were involved in the manning, equipping, and training of these new outfits. I took another fine B-29 group back out to Korea and got in another 32 combat missions in that little affair. Now, it would seem that the Cold War is over. At least, we are fond enough of the Russians to be bailing them out of their difficulties with money provided by American taxpayers, and we are in the bewildering world of today, where places like Bosnia and Haiti and Somalia hold our attention.

I'm sure it will come out alright; America always manages to fumble along and come out on top. But, I can't help wondering if most of my troops weren't a lot smarter than our leaders in Washington, 50 years ago. While America was the proud owner of the finest fighting machine the world had ever known, wouldn't it have been wise to keep it intact for just a little while longer? Sure, the Emperor of Japan had unconditionally surrendered, but weren't there some other players in the game that we should know a bit more about? When you have three aces showing and another one in the hole, it isn't very smart to fold your hand and walk away. Maybe, if we'd played our hand a little better when we had a winner instead of trying to set a new world record in demobilization, we might not have had a Korea and a Vietnam and a Cold War. Who knows?

ABOUT THE AUTHOR

Jimmy, Duke, Jim, Major Jim, Eddie, Colonel Jim, General Jim, and Gentle Jim were all nicknames for my dad, the author of this book. Each nickname was from a different period. When visiting Mother and Dad at their home, if the phone rang and it was for Dad, I could pretty much pinpoint the time when the caller and my dad had known one another. I would say, "It's So and So from the 468th" or "It's So and So from The Canyon." I enjoyed this little impromptu quiz, and my success delighted Dad.

His Sea Scout buddies gave him the name Duke in the mid-'30s because he was such a strong swimmer and his style reminded them of Duke Kahanamoku, who was considered the greatest freestyle swimmer in the world. Ercell Hart was one of those Scouts, and he was the one who introduced Mother and Dad in Hawaii. Ercell naturally introduced Dad as "Duke," and that is what Mother always called him.

During 36 years of military service, he commanded units and bases at every level up to Air Forces. He had over 11,000 hours of flying time in 138 different types of aircraft, and he flew 181 combat missions in three wars. He survived 107 combat missions in World War II, 36 missions in the Korean War, and 42 in the Vietnam War. Dad earned 45 medals and commendations. They include three Distinguished Service Medals, seven Distinguished Flying Crosses, eight Air Medals, three Legion of Merits, a Silver Star, a Bronze Star, a Navy Commendation Medal, and a Purple Heart.

After returning to the United States, he served with the Air Policy Branch in the Office of the Deputy Chief of Staff for Plans and Operations. He completed the Air War College in 1949, and in 1950, he was the commander of the 22nd Bombardment Group stationed at March Air Force Base in California.

On July 1, 1950, Dad's red phone rang. "Edmundson, this is LeMay. Is your outfit ready to go to war?" "Yes, sir!" was Dad's response, and on July 4th, the 22nd group was the first to head to Korea. Near the end of the war, he was commander of the 92nd Bombardment Wing, and General LeMay's plans came into focus again.

As Dad says,

> Operation "Big Stick" was one of the most unusual missions we flew in the 92nd. In August 1953, negotiations were underway for the ending of the Korean War, and nobody trusted the North Koreans. It was decided to send 20 B-36s to the Far East with atomic weapons on board, to be sitting on the alert on Okinawa, in case they were needed. Big Stick was an appropriate name for the operation.
>
> We sat on the alert on Okinawa for about 10 days in all our atomic splendor. The peace treaty got signed successfully up in Korea, Big Stick was declared concluded, and we took off for Fairchild like a flight of ten engined geese. The 92nd was later given the Outstanding Unit Award for Big Stick. It was a one-of-a-kind operation.

Later, he took over command of the 57th Air Division at Fairchild. He was transferred to Davis-Monthan Air Force Base in Arizona to command the 36th Air Division. From there, he and Mother moved to Omaha, Nebraska, where he was the Director of Operations at Strategic Air Command Headquarters for General LeMay.

In 1962, he was finally able to fly jets full-time when he assumed command of the 17th Air Force, U.S. Air Forces in Europe. As he explained:

> Throughout my career as a bomber pilot, I have never quite gotten over my love for the little planes and my desire to fly them. I have always been a fighter pilot at heart, and my greatest pleasure in flying has been in small airplanes. I'm sure I qualify as truly as possible as a square peg who succeeded in spending his life in a round hole.
>
> The 17th Air Force consisted of all the U.S. Air Force fighters in Europe, and had a demanding mission as part of NATO. We provided all of the air support to the American 8th Army, were responsible for the air defense of central Europe, and had an atomic strike mission against targets behind the Iron Curtain in the event of all-out war. Bases under my responsibility stretched from Oslo, Norway through Germany, the Netherlands, England, France, Italy, Greece, and Turkey. Included were the bases in isolated Berlin and Wheelis Field in Libya, North Africa, and the bombing and gunnery range complex at El Uotia, on the Libyan desert. My forces consisted of eight fighter wings, two

tactical reconnaissance wings, a Matador cruise missile wing, and an air defense division consisting of three squadrons of F-102s. The Air Force was equipped with a mixed bag of airplanes, to include F-100s, F-101s, F-102s, F-105s, RB-66s, and even a wing of bent-wing F-84s. I also had an air rescue outfit equipped with HH-43s. My headquarters was in Ramstein, Germany, and I was like a little kid in a candy shop.

I'd had a chance to meet my wing commanders, briefly, at the change of command ceremony, but I got around to all of their bases to meet their people, see their outfits at work, hear about their problems, and to get to know them a little better. Next, I set up a program to check out in every airplane in the 17th Air Force. It didn't take too long, and I remained qualified in every airplane, including the HH-43 "eggbeaters" for the entire three years that I was there. Two or three times a week, I'd climb into an F-100 and dash off to one of my bases to fly a mission with one of the squadrons. What a life!

Mother and Dad enjoyed a return to the United States aboard the SS *United States* before he assumed his new role as Director of Inspection under the Office of the Assistant Secretary of Defense. In 1967, they went back to Hawaii for the first time since WWII. Dad served as Vice Commander of Pacific Air Forces, and they moved into 601 Bouquet on Hickam Air Force Base. This was same house that Gen. and Mrs. Rudolph lived in when Dad was the general's aide-de-camp in 1941.

In 1970, he and Mother moved to Florida, where he became the Deputy Commander in Chief, U.S. Strike Command at MacDill Air Force Base. This command included the Middle East, southern Asia, and Africa south of the Sahara. It was on one of his trips to Iran that he met with Mohammad Reza Shah Pahlavi, the Shah of Iran. As he recalled these experiences:

> I was in every corner of this lovely country, roamed the ruins of Persepolis, the ancient capital of Darius and Xerxes, and flew with most of the units of the Iranian Air Force. I still have a set of the Iranian Air Force wings awarded by the Shah. He was an accomplished pilot in his own right. I once flew a KC-135 tanker on a refueling demonstration flight with the Shah as my copilot.

Before retiring in 1972, Dad and Mother discovered Longboat Key, a barrier island across from Sarasota, Florida. It was there that they built their retirement home although they never did actually retire. Dad served on the Town Commission twice, and also served as vice mayor and as mayor during a period of dramatic growth on the island. He frequently contributed to both local and national publications. He wrote for our town's newspaper, the *Longboat Observer*, for 12 years; during the Gulf War, he wrote a day-by-day analysis for the *Sarasota Herald-Tribune*. He also wrote for national military magazines, such as *Klaxon*, *The Old Breed News*, and *Officer Review*. He contributed to The History Channel production of *Unsung Heroes of the B-29s* and to the PBS feature *Race for the Superbomb*. He wrote chapters for historians' books and was always ready to help with any author's research in the areas of military aviation, United States and world history. He gave hundreds of talks to local and national civic and military groups.

He was honored several times by the town, but it was after his death in 2001 that a Congressional bill was passed to name our local post office after him. He would have been proud of that—and I think he would be particularly pleased as a stamp collector most of his life.

In January of 1999, Mother died at home, with Dad by her side and holding her hand. That night he wrote:

Nothing, no matter how perfect it may be, lasts forever. This is the nature of the world in which we live. But things of charm and beauty live on, long after they are gone, in the memories of those who were fortunate enough to have experienced them. And so, now that my wife, Lee, is no longer here, she leaves the world of ours a better place for having lived in it, and she will live on in the hearts of her family and her friends, and her goodness touched the lives of many who may never have known her in person.

She was a gutsy little lady. In her early twenties, she wanted to see the world, and her first step was to sail to Hawaii, when Hawaii was a mystical and far away place. She took with her enough money to live in Honolulu for a week and to charter a return passage on next week's boat if she was unable to find a job in that week. Needless to say, she found a job.

She was a true patriot and as brave as any soldier who ever wore a uniform. She devoted her life to her country and to the people who served with her. She was a lovely flower that bloomed in grace and beauty for 85 years. I am blessed to have been permitted to share 58 of those years with her as her adoring husband.

Rank	Date	Insignia	Age
Second Lieutenant	February 1938	Gold bar	23
First Lieutenant	October 1940	Silver bar	25
Captain	April 1942	Silver double bar	27
Major	June 1942	Gold oak leaf	27
Lt. Colonel	April 1943	Silver oak leaf	28
Colonel	January 1945	Eagle	30
Brig. General	December 1953	One star	38
Maj. General	March 1958	Two stars	43
Lt. General	April 1965	Three stars	50

PLANES CRASHED

PT-13	B-29
B-18	B-47
A-17	F-84F
B-17	T-33

KINDS OF AIRCRAFT FLOWN

Trainers, 14	Fighters, 24
Transport, 22	Helicopters, 8
Attack, 22	Bombers, 20
Utility, 15	

PLANES FLOWN AT MACH 1

F-100	F-84F
F-105	Lightning
F-101	T-38
F-106	Mirage
RF-101	F-104
F-111	B-58

PLANES FLOWN AT MACH 2

F-104	F-106
Lightning	B-58
F-105	F-111
Mirage	

World War II: The Global, Human, and Ethical Dimension

G. KURT PIEHLER, *series editor*

1. Lawrence Cane, David E. Cane, Judy Barrett Litoff, and David C. Smith, eds., *Fighting Fascism in Europe: The World War II Letters of an American Veteran of the Spanish Civil War*

2. Angelo M. Spinelli and Lewis H. Carlson, *Life behind Barbed Wire: The Secret World War II Photographs of Prisoner of War Angelo M. Spinelli*

3. Don Whitehead and John B. Romeiser, *"Beachhead Don": Reporting the War from the European Theater, 1942–1945*

4. Scott H. Bennett, ed., *Army GI, Pacifist CO: The World War II Letters of Frank and Albert Dietrich*

5. Alexander Jefferson with Lewis H. Carlson, *Red Tail Captured, Red Tail Free: Memoirs of a Tuskegee Airman and POW*

6. Jonathan G. Utley, *Going to War with Japan, 1937–1941*

7. Grant K. Goodman, *America's Japan: The First Year, 1945–1946*

8. Patricia Kollander with John O'Sullivan, *"I Must Be a Part of This War": One Man's Fight against Hitler and Nazism*

9. Judy Barrett Litoff, *An American Heroine in the French Resistance: The Diary and Memoir of Virginia d'Albert-Lake*

10. Thomas R. Christofferson and Michael S. Christofferson, *France during World War II: From Defeat to Liberation*

11. Don Whitehead, *Combat Reporter: Don Whitehead's World War II Diary and Memoirs*, edited by John B. Romeiser

12. James M. Gavin, *The General and His Daughter: The Wartime Letters of General James M. Gavin to His Daughter Barbara*, edited by Barbara Gavin Fauntleroy et al.

13. John J. Toffey IV, *Jack Toffey's War: A Son's Memoir*